Tapping The
MIGHTY MIND

Simple Solutions to
Stress, Conflict, and Pain

Rose,

Wishing
you a wonderful
EFT journey,
Robin

ROBIN W. BILAZARIAN

Robin Bilazarian's book, *Tapping the Mighty Mind* is full of her "smarts" and wit. She has painstakingly and generously given us a valuable primer for living. With her practical wisdom and sense of humor, as well as her humanity, she offers us many ways to gain mastery over life's challenges. It's a must have and a must read - over and over. A wonderful collection of self-help skills for all of us struggling with stresses of the human condition. - Paula Susan, LCSW, Trauma and Relationship Specialist

Tapping the Mighty Mind is a heart-warming, wonderful guide. Robin somehow blended science, theory, and practice so it makes sense. - Victoria McFadden-Novak, Clinical Coordinator, Psychiatric Emergency Services, Gloucester County

Robin brings a wealth of practical information to an easy to use format.....it is a clinical tool I will use often." - Karen Ann Brook, LCSW

ISBN-13:9781542546706

Library of Congress Control Number: 2014908864

CreateSpace Independent Publishing Platform

North Charleston, South Carolina

DEDICATION AND APPRECIATIONS

"Write me as one that loves his fellow men."

– James Henry Leigh Hunt

This book is dedicated to my parents, Bernice and Harry Waldman - two exceptional people who embodied the word "resilience." They survived difficult childhoods somehow intact. They persisted, succeeded, and practiced the opposite of how they were raised. They instilled a love of mankind – believing that it is how you treat people that matters in the world. My parent's wisdom included:

1. You have to give before you get, and everything you give (good or bad) comes back to you.

2. The best revenge is success. (It channels your energy in a positive way)

3. Church/Synagogue is how you behave in your life and not necessarily within the walls of a building.

4. Love your fellow man (and stand by your spouse no matter what sickness may come).

5. Before you get married, keep your eyes WIDE open. After you get married, SHUT your eyes a little!

6. Sometimes all you can do is laugh!

I find nothing more interesting than people, and thus, I am my parents' child. Our house was full of people from various ethnic and cultural groups before it was fashionable.

This book has 60 varied techniques but it is the bonus ones that keep me balanced. This book is dedicated to the brilliant family I created: husband Pete, one of my editors and life companion; daughter Laura, who sees endless possibilities in the world; and my son Greg, who also embraces extraordinary opportunities and who graciously allowed photographs within this book. Also, this book is dedicated to my brother, Mark Waldman as well as to his delightful family. Loving family – *Stress Management Bonus Technique 61.*

I need to mention Pippi Doggery, aka Sniffery, Barkery or Woofery! Pippi is a rescued chocolate Labrador Retriever and Husky mixed All-American mutt. I am not sure who saved who? She got dropped off to my home, supposedly for a 2-month stay and that was 6 years ago! She stole my heart and makes me laugh with her exuberant "wiggle-bum" tail greeting - every time I walk back into the house. She consoles me with her attentive empathy and guaranteed confidentiality! A dog is a *woman's* best friend, and thus, I am never alone. Pets – *Bonus Technique 62.*

I want to acknowledge many others who support me. This includes my clients, who bravely open up their wounds so they may heal. I thank my clients for the honor of being allowed to work in such sensitive areas and to learn from them.

My other acknowledgments include many friends, who share my life. We really do extend mutually caring. Through conversation, we chronicle our lives and make it rich and real. My college dorm-mate, Maria C. Brown, who is my lifetime confidante and unofficial therapist who keeps me grounded. Her brilliant husband, Paul C. Brown, PhD, Software Architect rescued this book technically. I also acknowledge my very active social director, Angela Nocera, and my former neighbor, Cindy Jilling, who keeps me forever bound to breath-taking, coastal Newport, RI. I acknowledge Reed Hofmann, a mature teenage neighbor that is always ready to help, and Tanya Paretchan, Louise Huttner, Liz Barone, & Berj Murray who just always stay in touch. Friends – *Bonus Technique 63.*

Many of my colleagues have crossed the line into friendships that sustain me. These colleagues include my peer supervision group, consisting of: Paula Susan, Ed Silver, Camille Palumbo, Karen Brash McGreer, Karen Brook, Dr. Amy G. Love, Dr. Jing Yang, Emily Harker-Sauler, Rhona Case, Dr. Greg McGreer, Kathleen Shelmire, and others. They also include my Rhode Island colleague Brenda Bachman and my book club, which is comprised of another 13 therapists. There are too many exceptional colleagues to mention. However, I want to specially note and thank my work colleagues/friends. These include Risa Swell, Liz Staib, Paula Watson and Ronna Stedman. They support me in many ways including promoting my professional use of the Emotional Freedom Techniques (EFT), or Tapping, and provide assistance to various workshops. They also lift me up and center me. Stimulating colleagues – *Bonus Technique 64.*

I always remain grateful to those who are expert developers in this field of EFT, Tapping, and Energy Psychology. These expert developers include the following masters: Gary Craig, Dr. Roger Callahan, Dr. John Diepold, Jr; Dr. Dawson Church, John Freeman and Dr. Fred Gallo. They also include: Sandy Radomski of www.allergyantidotes.com, who saved my career by lessening my debilitating allergic asthma; Dr. David Feinstein, Donna Eden, CJ Puotinen, Helena Fone, Jondi Whitis, Nick Ortner and Dr. Ang Puig. (See Bibliography.) Gracious, exciting, and sharing experts – *Bonus Technique 65.*

I also thank *Toastmasters*, which is a public speech club; and the Haddonfield, NJ group for believing in me. I am grateful to Dr. Maeda Galinsky, my wonderful professor/mentor/friend from University of North Carolina-Chapel Hill, who delights in the hilarity that I married into the Duke and UNC basketball rivalry. I extend my deepest appreciation to Carole Kinsey, my Oxford University Workshop colleague/friend, who crossed the ocean twice to co-lead EFT workshops with a nervous me. I thank Karen Lacey, who with grace did the first edit of this then very-rough manuscript. In so doing, she taught me many things about writing. I am forever grateful to Dr. Amy G. Love who added exceptional final editing to a flawed manuscript! Teachers and mentors – *Bonus Technique 66.*

Important Note

A book cannot do everything. Please take care of yourself and get professional help if you are struggling.

Get medical clearance to try any of the pain methods.

If you are in crisis and are not safe on any level, remember that hospital emergency rooms are open 24/7 and will help you get the right level of care you need. Go there or call 911 if you need emergency help.

Nothing in this book is meant to substitute for qualified medical advice. This is a self-help book for the difficult frustrations of life, to manage chronic pain, and to improve communication patterns. The author and publisher do not assume responsibility for you and your use of this book. For most people, this book will be a wonderful addition in their life. For others, please find a qualified therapist to guide you, perhaps bringing this book to that therapist to work together. You can find a therapist by calling the local mental health center in your area. If you do not know how to find that, call the local hospital and ask to be connected to the social work department. They may guide you to some therapists that specialize in your issues.

Stay in close contact with your medical doctor regarding any problems and pain which you suffer. It is important to follow his/her medical advice.

I wish you well on your self-improvement journey, as you evolve to be the person you want to be - free of old emotional clutter, and emotionally smart!

Robin Bilazarian, LCSW, DCSW, DCEP

CONTENTS

INTRODUCTION

Stop stressing! Release the way chronic pain is stored. And do it now. Do it quickly. Do it before more damage is done. If you struggle with stress, anxiety, pain, conflict difficulties or emotional upsets, read on!

Stress is anything that takes us outside our comfort zone. We like comfort, we like predictability, and we like familiarity. Changes in our world spark disequilibrium, discomfort, and instability. Pain changes who we are.

Stress is at epidemic levels. According to many doctors and psychotherapists, there is growing appreciation that stress affects the mind, the cells and all the receptors within the mind and the physical body too. Stress contributes to illness.

When stressed, the mind is a jumbled puzzle and the body is on high alert. Neuroscientists explain that under stress your reptilian brain dominates, making you attack like a rattle snake. That reptilian part of the brain reacts with four "Fs: -- Fight, Flight, Freeze and Foggy brain! You may respond with silence or verbal or physical violence, which are poor coping tools. When stressed, you are not emotionally smart. That foggy brain clouds your ability to think intelligently. And that is not good for anyone or any relationship!

Stress also kicks up adrenaline, which in dangerous situations can be lifesaving. It heightens the strength to lift a car off a child, to fly upstairs to revive a coding patient, or to scan efficiently for an intruder. Thus, not all stress or anxiety is malevolent. This built-in alarm system is beneficial when we are in danger. Unfortunately, the fast-paced, modern world-loaded with deadlines and other non-life-threatening pressures trick our brain into releasing the same danger-fighting adrenaline.

Running late, a difficult assignment, a broken date, a check that did not clear, an upcoming test, a social requirement, or an argument may even show up physically - such as a queasy stomach tightening up like a vise.

Stress causes physical symptoms. Under stress, the mind fights to focus, while the body is trying to overcome a churning stomach, pressure in the chest, aching shoulders, tightening throat or other physical discomfort.

Many concerned people will suggest to "just calm down." This is good advice, but not easy to achieve. No one chooses to stay stressed; they just do not know HOW to calm down, how to let go and how to interact with others tactfully. They lack the skills explained in this book. Learn these, bring them home and teach them to others.

These techniques are fast. Most take about 5 minutes, some are even shorter. There is no need to linger uncomfortably with stress, pain or stay tongue-tied.

Many of these techniques are now taught in prestigious business schools, including Harvard and Yale. These include Active Listening – *Super Technique # 1* on page 15. Bumbling, ineffective communication also increases stress by creating problems and difficulties.

This book could have been two books except that the reduction of stress and effective communication are entwined for comfortable, successful living. Pain written about last, but not least, is another focus. You can choose to read this book straight through or skip around according to your interest. Some may want to only increase their communication prowess, while others may want to manage anxiety, grief, anger, pain or stress.

When stress reactions go *down,* intelligence, problem solving skills, diplomacy, effective communication, personality and reasoning power come *up!* This increases healthy self-confidence and feeling of empowerment.

Take a moment and think about whether any of these questions apply.

Do you need to let go of stress?

Do you wonder how others release stress so easily?

Do you have issues that haunt you?

INTRODUCTION

Have you been criticized about your communication skills?

Do you want to negotiate conflict better?

Are you able to articulate your needs to the people in your life?

Do you long for more meaningful and empathic connections?

Would you like help with social situation?

Do you have issues with co-workers?

Do you struggle with stress, anxiety or physical pain?

Have grief or anger ever overwhelmed you?

If you answered yes to any of these questions, the 60 techniques that follow will guide you to improved responses.

Half of the mighty mind is logical and intelligent and the other half is emotional. Some emotions provide instinctive protective warnings. Some bring excitement to savor the world's wonders. Sometimes they inhibit or cloud our thinking. This book is about being strong enough to try simple solutions that balance emotional and physical pain and cultivate verbal savvy to ultimately feel confident and strong about dealing with life's tribulations.

Several authors, me included, believe these techniques should be explained to everyone; as it is just good communication. These techniques are drawn from years of trainings and taught in a communication and conflict workshop called *It's How to Say It*. This workshop teaches simple techniques for everyday use, for all types of personal interactions and even enhanced customer service.

Here is a frequent comment from that workshop.

> "This workshop should be mandatory; everyone needs to know these simple formulas on how to communicate" Another slightly humorous comment: "If I had taken Robin's workshop earlier, I probably would still be married!"

These communication techniques were "life-changing."

Communication often misses the mark. This is often the reason that many individuals and couples go into psychotherapy.

The early chapters of this book lay the groundwork by discussing standard "tried-and-true" techniques for managing stress and simple tips for everyday effective communication. Vital life and communication skills that are covered include:

- Active listening (should be required of everyone)

- Writing and venting

- Problem solving

- Benefit to *us* of forgiving others

- Graciously setting limits and boundaries

- Essential communication tools

- Sandwiching criticism

- Worry time

- Metaphors to quickly capture our point

- Networking

- How thinking affects feeling and physical reactions

- Reframes - finding the rainbow

- Agree to disagree

- How to start a conversation

- Distraction and imagery

- Tone of voice

- Conflict management tools

Specific topics, such as grief and anger are explored in greater detail in Chapter 9 and 10. Chapter 13 takes an in-depth look at anxiety.

Chapter 3 begins the "tried-and-new" mind-body techniques. They are considered evidence-based practice, because they are supported by 80 peer-reviewed, published research articles. Thus, this book combines standard techniques with mind-body interventions such as the Emotional Freedom Techniques aka Tapping.

The Emotional Freedom Techniques (EFT), Tapping, Meridian Therapies, and Energy Psychology are many names for similar desensitizing systems. They emanate from 2000 – 5000 year-old acupuncture theory. For convenience, I call them all EFT which includes Tapping. The founder Gary Craig had the wisdom to put on "S" on the word "technique_s", which implies some differences.

EFT is a surprisingly easy relaxation technique of self-applied light touch (or tapping) on "acupoints" on your face, hand, and upper torso. Focusing on your upset while touching (or tapping) these acupoints; releases, collapses, and desensitizes the upset quickly. My workshop at the hospital on this is entitled: *Stress and Pain Management using Acupressure: The Emotional Freedom Techniques.*

Odd? You may think that EFT is weird. But you can look at Chapter 7 and recognize our body language mimics these acupoints every day, everywhere, and all the time. EFT is a desensitizing stress management technique that is literally right at your fingertips

The Emotional Freedom Techniques provide very rapid relief in all 3 areas affected by stress. These 3 areas of stress are intertwined, but the connection is often missed. They are:

- Thoughts

- Emotions

- Corresponding physical discomfort.

Most people know that stress evolves from reacting to upsetting events with thoughts and emotions. Did you know that it is also felt physically? Yes, stress is felt physically - a lump in the throat, pressure on your chest, jiggling legs, butterflies in your stomach, tightness in your shoulders, and other body sensations. Chapter 6, the Mind-Body Sweep, is a way to calm the body first before tackling the big issue. Pain is discussed in Chapter 15.

Throughout this book are many case examples which you may similar to our own battles. Due to confidentially, details of the cases have been changed, but never is the intent of the main issue lost. The process is the same; the demographic identifying information has been changed.

Cases drawn from work situations include: job loss, work horror, working parents, burn-out, upsetting colleagues and supervisors, and technostress. Other cases come from grief, anger mismanagement, unwelcome sexual advance, car accidents, and medical difficulties. Anxiety spectrum cases include: panic attacks, social anxiety, anxious brides and grooms, flying, test- taking, rodent phobia, and the number 1 dreaded phobia - public speaking! (Look in the index to find the case that relates to your issue.)

You can use the book as a workbook, or you can read straight through. Stop and pause long enough to practice these techniques. Each time you read this book, you will discover more stress management and effective communication solutions. There are questions and worksheets to reinforce concepts and for easy reference later. I think you will enjoy learning both the standard techniques and the newer stress management tools, such as EFT aka Tapping, which are gaining mainstream acceptance.

The Author

Let me introduce myself, the author, your guide through this book.

If you ask a psychotherapist what his or her specialty is, sometimes you will learn about the personal struggles of the therapist. Stress and anxiety are my clinical specialties. They are also my life-long personal struggles. I have always been aware of stress and its overwhelming capacity to overpower ability, intelligence, actions and even my physical comfort. In Chapter 13 you can read about Generalized Anxiety, a clinical name for stress that I lived with all the time. My expertise in stress management grew from personal desperation. I am both a therapist and a client.

Approximately one in every six people suffers from some form of anxiety. As the world has grown more dangerous since 9/11, stress has heightened and follows most of us, surprising even previously laid-back folks. My brother once said he had no need to worry, since I did enough worrying for the entire family. Sadly, he was correct. I was able to leap to catastrophic conclusions in a single bound. I worried about worrying!

Many of my clients share how crippling it is to feel too inhibited to interact freely with the world. It is a jail sentence to be locked within oneself; it is made worse by knowing that we are our own jailer. This is often called Social Anxiety, which is also discussed in Chapter 13. Whether one is called "anxious," "highly sensitive," or "stressed-out", it is important to learn ways to cope and to communicate effectively. Technique 57 *Layers of Communication* in Chapter 13, discusses ways to initiate and carry on conversation once EFT has settled down the Social Anxiety. It is included, because everyone struggles a bit to open interactions. People symptomatic with social anxiety NEVER know how to start a conversation!

I spent twenty years exploring the confines of the best practices of psychotherapy and looking for the key to deal with stress and anxiety. Every workshop described stress and anxiety, but effective solutions were less forthcoming. Several of the techniques described in the first few chapters emerged through these years. Within my little office kingdom, I was a competent therapist. I accumulated legitimate credentials at esteemed colleges (University of Pennsylvania, and University of North Carolina.) I was offered challenging field placements (Duke Medical Center Psychiatric Outpatient Clinic). My employment was in every level of inpatient and outpatient mental health and Employee Assistance Program (EAP). And I learned abundant counseling and communication skills. But I was still anxious about everything.

I know the exact moment that I experienced my astonishing liberation. Ironically, the key became visible through my most handicapping anxiety—public speaking.

Public speaking and public performance phobias are the number one phobia in this country. In a meridian-based Thought Field Therapy (TFT)[1] workshop, the leader asked if anyone in the room had a public speaking phobia. I certainly did not volunteer, knowing I would have a panic attack in front of this class!

---

[1] TFT is one of the first meridian therapy techniques brought to the United States. It was designed by psychologist Roger Callahan, PhD, and is a sister technique to EFT.

After the demonstration we divided into pairs to practice on any phobia. I requested to work on public speaking to the surprise of my partner. I explained I could work on it quietly with one person, but was too paralyzed to be in front of the class.

Surprisingly, my inexperienced workshop partner and I copied the meridian technique demonstrated and *cured* me of the extreme symptoms of my phobia of public speaking. Within those few minutes, the jail door opened. I was liberated from forty years of withholding any of my ideas that required public speaking. The fear is one of being scrutinized and judged. In this workshop my fear of panic, visible shaking and blushing were gone. I was liberated and free. And…I could not shut-up!

I then fully participated in this workshop by asking questions throughout and using examples from my own caseload. I spoke in front of the class AND lead the group exercise!

Since that liberating day, I lecture everywhere on these meridian techniques to churches, schools, universities, local and national conferences, and psychiatric grand rounds. I have provided continuing education credits to psychiatrists, medical residents, social workers, nurses, licensed professional counselors, marriage and family therapists, drug and alcohol counselors, and employee assistance counselors on using EFT. I lecture about twenty times a year locally, nationally, and recently internationally on EFT/Tapping and Communication Techniques.

My transforming experience with meridian techniques, including EFT, opened up a new world of potential ways to help clients. This is a world that I threw myself into. It was in this world that I learned about the far simpler Emotional Freedom Techniques (EFT) for the first time. EFT is a sister meridian treatment to TFT. However, EFT – with one protocol fits all, is easier to learn than TFT, as you will see in Chapters 3 and beyond.

I am not "in the closet" with EFT. For the past 22 years, I have used EFT while employed in mainstream mental health facilities (a Community Mental Health Center) and in an Employee Assistance Program (within a regional trauma hospital). I often quell Acute Stress Reactions (which are those early reactions to horrific disasters) with First Responders in just a few sessions. I suggest using the "Mind-Body Sweep" of Chapter 6 first to help quell Acute Stress Reactions and as demonstrated in Example 6.1.

INTRODUCTION

The United Kingdom has a large following of meridian practitioners who use Emotional Freedom Techniques (EFT). I was fortunate to meet many of them at an international training workshop at Oxford University. I am a Certified Master EFT Trainer through a primarily British international organization, the Association for Advancement of Meridian Therapies (AAMETInternational.org). I am a Diplomate in Clinical Energy Psychology from an American based group called ACEP –Association of Energy Psychology (Energypsych.org). I highly recommend both for exceptional training and professional conferences.

Several of my seasoned colleagues complain that their psychotherapy practice has emotionally exhausted them and is now impacting their personal lives. They suffer from "Compassion Fatigue" or "Burn-out (discussed in Chapter 12). As an Energy Psychology, EFT clinician, I never burn out. I cannot burn out, when I am witnessing instant improvements in people. AND I am applying EFT simultaneously to myself to quell my own compassion fatigue reactions to their horrific events.

I watch my clients' distress dissolve in front of my eyes. I see the perplexed wonder in their faces as they no longer feel the agonizing frustration they reported ten minutes prior. They look at me with a wrinkled forehead in wonderment with the question, "How did you do that?" (Remember to look at Chapter 7 if you are still thinking this is way too impossible.) Dissolving pain too, seems like magic.

I feel like Merlin! These wonderful shared and humorous moments with my clients are my reward. The clients feel total liberation, indifference and calm regarding a former intensely disturbing event. I marvel with them that a stressful occurrence or situation is often transformed to calm in five or ten minutes. Unencumbered, therapy can then progress to incorporate better communication styles, problem solving and goal setting.

In summary, more than 60 clever, comprehensive and quick stressbusting solutions and essential communication skills are presented within this book. This book will describe "tried-and- true" methods of managing stress and essential communication skills. It will also present modern, cutting-edge methods that are used internationally. These modern methods are growing in mainstream America. There are also plenty of common-sense solutions and simple counseling tools for enhanced communication results.

Pain as an interesting aside, often lessens in intensity with tapping and EFT. Is it the acupressure effect or the lessening of the upset? I do not know, but have watched it for 20 years. Discuss in Chapter 15, indirect and direct approaches to pain management, page 293, are explained.

I am delighted to be part of a large movement of humanitarians willing and able to risk time, circumstances, and reputation to bring an expedited psychotherapy (i.e., EFT, Tapping, Energy Psychology and "meridian therapies") into mainstream practice. I use these techniques every day with private clients, with staff as an Employee Assistance Counselor in a remarkable regional trauma hospital, and with first responders and educators.

I am genuinely fascinated by people. I have been a people-watcher since childhood. I do not think there is anything more interesting or exciting than people. I am awestruck by the life path that each person has followed, including what the person has experienced, endured, or overcome. Many people have developed unfathomable resilience under horrific circumstances and I am humbled by their willingness to open these wounds in counseling.

I am not by nature an author. Therefore, I ask your indulgences for any literary bumbles made in this book. I am humbled by all I do not know about writing. However, these important, emerging techniques on how to treat stress need to be disseminated. I am a seasoned clinician and lecturer, who have a career-filled story to tell and techniques to share.

Enjoy your journey, desensitize the roadblocks put in your path, and actualize your purpose and dreams. Enhance your communication skills. Free yourself of old nonsense, in order to become the amazing person you were meant to be!

Best to you and peace,

Robin

Robin Bilazarian, LCSW, DCSW, DCEP

INTRODUCTION

ACEP Diplomat in Clinical Energy Psychology (DCEP)

AAMET International Certified Master EFT Trainer

Web. RobinEFT.net

YouTube.Com *EFT-AAA Instructional*

YouTube.Com *Heart Assisted 2 Minute Stress Relief*

YouTube.com *Pain, Tapping & EFT*

Pesi National Training DVD. Bilazarian, R. (2017). *Emotional Freedom Techniques & Tapping: Evidence-Based, Mind-Body Treatment Approach to the Anxiety Spectrum Disorders* 6-hour training DVD with CEU's. https://www.pesi.com/store/detail/21530/emotional-freedom-techniques-eft-and-tapping (pain included in video)

Online Audio Relief Workshop: Social Work Online CE Institute with CEU's. Bilazarian, R. *Clinical Application of the Emotional Freedom Techniques: Desensitizing Undesirable Emotional and Mind-Body* *Reactions*

CHAPTER 1

STRESS

"The first thing a child should learn is how to endure. It is what he will have most need to know. "

— Jean-Jacques Rousseau

Stress in Our Lives – a Story from When the World Went Crazy

Life happens, stuff happens and therefore, stress happens.

Much of this book is a guide to effective and surprisingly easy 5-minute stress and pain management techniques. Some of these stress solutions have been with us for a while and are well-known and some are new. Additionally there are many effective communication techniques included too. It is good to lower stress; it is even better to combine calm with the sophisticated expressive skills discussed throughout this book.

When did stress explode in America? Indulge me for a few pages for a true story - upfront and personal - that occurred when a major calamity in

America increased stress in all of us. America and the world went crazy and terrified us and changed us forever!

Here is the story. I have no conscious recall of the moment I volunteered, but it was sometime a week after 9/11 occurred. I felt compelled to go. As a brief therapy expert, I excel at treating new traumatic stress reactions rapidly and gently – a crucial requirement in the mayhem that followed 9/11. I expected to work with traumatized survivors and worried families from the worst invading attack on America soil. That mission called me in the same way as did writing this book about overcoming stress and how to become an effective communicator.

I traveled that breezy September day to the New Jersey edge of the shimmering and alluring Hudson River. There, I stared at a tormented New York City just ten days after the September 11, 2001 terrorist attacks, and the loss of over 3,000 innocent lives.

My journey to Liberty Park began sitting in the last row of the Gloucester County Mental Health Center van, my mind and body on high alert. My insides pounded like a jackhammer. We were heading north on the New Jersey Turnpike to volunteer at the New Jersey Crisis Response Site in Liberty State Park, ten miles from Ground Zero - just a river away from massive destruction.

Our route carried us parallel to Newark International Airport. On any day, low flying airport traffic that crisscrossed the highway was spooky enough, but that day it was terrifying. The descending planes closed in on us, reminiscent of the sinister planes that toppled the Twin Towers. We all ducked a bit and laughed that nervous giggle of school kids pretending to be brave.

Our van appeared to move in slow motion - the slow motion of fear where every instant feels like hundreds of tortuous hours wondering if our time on earth was about to end. Stress elongates time and confuses perception. Were terrorists piloting these overhead commercial planes too? Hovering endlessly above, the planes felt like bloodcurdling hungry buzzards circling their prey. Never was I so tormented being near an airport and never again would planes be seen simply as transportation to luxurious vacations. Life changed for all of us.

As we journeyed on, our fright abated enough for renewed eye contact. I calmed myself by lightly touching acupoints on my face and hands, otherwise known as the Emotional Freedom Techniques (EFT) or tapping - a fast, easy technique explained in Chapter 3. Others copied me. Maybe it was the acupoints or maybe it was the camaraderie, but we sighed deeply and let ourselves slump back in our van seats. Onward we headed to a dread-filled, uncharted course -- psychotherapists helping Ground Zero survivors and families hopefully waiting what became a futile search.

Liberty State Park—a historic train station and the current passageway to Ellis Island and the Statue of Liberty—bustled with activity. Police checked everyone's credentials. National Guardsman rested from working at Ground Zero. FEMA volunteers issued financial vouchers. And at every turn, the Red Cross tried to nurture by endlessly feeding everyone - dinner, crackers, water, more crackers, cakes …. Lawyers working pro-bono, expedited death certificates. These enabled dependents to access benefits immediately and not have to suffer through the normal three-year wait for missing persons. Therapy dogs encouraged vacant-eyed humans to reconnect via petting these gentle, compassionate animals. It was to this environment that we office-trained psychotherapists arrived, without a clue how to work in this field situation.

Improvisation occurred one day among a contingent of psychotherapists and clergy tending to grieving families. We were escorted across the river to a large, wooden dignitary platform—similar to a well-constructed deck—at the 9/11 site. This front row view exposed the magnitude of the physical destruction of the Twin Towers. Even behind us and across from the skeleton of the Twin Towers, destroyed high-rise office buildings looked like doll houses with their front walls totally missing. Looking in, you could see twisted desks, destroyed furniture, and everywhere white debris blowing in the wind.

The viewing platform allowed heartbroken families time for private moments and grief. In route the police stopped traffic throughout Jersey City, providing the honor to our massive motorcade of plush buses, of uninterrupted passages to the waterfront. There, ferries stocked with food and teddy bears for each family member took us to the NYC pier, and then a short walk to the 9/11 site.

Police directed the therapists to walk on the outside of our procession as a shield against photographers. The police fiercely postured toward tourists that tried to photograph our unusual collection. We walked past hundreds of teddy bears on the side of the 9/11 site. Both in NYC and at New Jersey Liberty State Park, mourners' candles and posted photos besieged us, begging for any information on these missing people.

As I looked around at the overpowering destruction, I wondered about why I was here. It was only because I know rapid Emotional Freedom Techniques (EFT) - a stress relief tool that combines Eastern acupressure and emotion words – introduced in Chapter 3 in this book. EFT or tapping can offer a single session relief, sometimes in as little as 5 minutes. Fast, simple and efficient. EFT/tapping belongs at these tragedies – not only for the victims, but also for the first responders. How true it was that day. After working with a 9/11 first responder on his incapacitating frustration, we finished, to his amazement, by curtailing his lifetime fear of heights as well. Note, that since I used EFT or tapping simultaneously, I quieted my jitters resulted from listening to the chaos he expressed about the scary, frantic 9/11 evacuation.

From the New Jersey side of the glimmering Hudson River, at sundown the glow of the burning and smoking destruction illuminated the night, a new truth added to the forever-changed American tapestry. None of us had ever counseled families in a futile vigil. We did not understand that we, too, as Americans, were traumatized. This experience is known as secondary trauma; we stood witness to these devastated families, traumatized survivors, and the loss of the America we knew. Traumatic reactions linger when a devastating event is coupled with helplessness.

We often debriefed using the techniques in this book, – both at the 9/11 scene and months later as we continued to work with Americans whose lives were life changed by that event. Everyone reacted to 9/11 by reevaluating their priorities. People got married sooner, and conversely, unhappy spouses decided not to wait any longer to get divorced. Veterans and others with past traumas were emotionally reactivated, as one trauma reminds you of another. People often worried about the whereabouts of their families and colleagues, even without reason. Generalized anxiety, discussed in Chapter 13, was everywhere.

Everything changed in those days for America, for the world, and for all of us. Safety and personal freedom slowly evaporated and stress took hold. Stress in this country - in our economy, in the wars we fight, in our jobs, with our children, our families, in our airlines, public assemblies and within ourselves - intensified dramatically. Terrorism terrified us! And did not go away! What horrific event would be on the news today?

My first publication exploded from my frenetic fingers to the local newspaper during September 2001. Written about *ways* to cope with the trauma of 9/11, it was written from a consciousness outside of me, as if the keyboard typed without me. It was my first "how to" publication.

It is with the same sense of purpose and obligation that I write this book to manage stress, pain and review effective communication. 9/11 was the start of national generalized anxiety, stress and worry. Our bubble of safety was shattered by a foreign invader successfully staging a massive attack on American soil.

Another ingredient is the explosion of technology that is taking us into uncharted human territory. Technology is continually changing, faster than we can grasp. According to Jean Houston, Ph.D., information is doubling every four years. Worldwide addictive use of electronics and the expectation of instant responses are changing the way we live. Face-to-face social skills are dwindling as texting becomes the preferred level of contact. More is written about technostress in Chapter 12.

In the rest of this chapter we will look briefly at the definition of stress. In Chapter 2, we will jump in to typical methods of addressing stress and communication difficulties. These include both things that happen in a psychotherapist's office and in honest discussions with others. They include active listening, problem solving, simple relaxation techniques and more. For some of you, this will be new.

There may be a family member, friend or colleague with whom you want to share these techniques, so they too can grasp better ways to deal with stress and effective communication. Active listening, *Technique 1* on page 15, should be mandatory in school, work and life!

So, hold onto your hats and here we go. First, let's take a brief and closer look at stress, this prolific, new American epidemic.

What is Stress?

Stress is *anything* that takes you outside your comfort zone - a death, a promotion, a new baby, or acts of violence - any misfortune or even anything new to you. Stress is damaging our well-being through lowering our resistance to disease, disrupting our sleep, creating mood problems, scaring us, and disrupting our relationships, all of which reduces our ability to perform well in our lives.

Stress has an effect on your body too. According to Dr. Mark Hyman writing on stress reactions in the Huffington Post of 9/7/2014; stress is "a cascade of adrenaline, cortisol, and other stress hormones floods your system, raising your heart rate, increasing your blood pressure, making your blood more likely to clot, damaging your brain's memory center, increasing belly fat storage, and generally wreaking havoc on your body."

A normal adjustment period to any major life event is three months. If you are still freaking out three months after the event, get some help. Certainly you can go sooner, but if you are not back to normal functioning by then, never let it go longer.

Stress can affect us in two ways: transitory or chronic. It can feel like a momentary punch, which is transitory, or it can chronically clutter up your system, leaving little energy for anything productive. Economic, familial, educational, relational, all types of life turmoil threaten our sense of personal safety and leave a scar. Here are categories where stress thrives:

Grief and loss - death, relationships ending, relocation, job loss, economic losses.

Mishaps, misfortune or trauma – accidents, attacks, fires, crime. In other words, "Bad things that happen to good people"; (book title from Rabbi Kushner.)

Work-place stress (includes school and organizations) turmoil caused by a mixed group of people with different ideas and values. We often find ourselves in clashes over these differences. This is a form of organizational *politics*. Where does work place stress occur? Everywhere including: office politics, school politics, church politics, temple politics, hospital politics, police politics, military politics, sports politics, volunteer politics....

Relationships – miscommunication, anger, differing values, disagreements, bullying, insensitivity, oversensitivity, parent-child issues, marital issues, in-laws/outlaws, friendships, coworkers, colleagues.

Intrapsychic distress – anxiety, depression, confusion, irritability, low-self-esteem, inept behavior, struggling with reactions, "old baggage".

Most stress subsides within three months adjustment period, but stress may get worse over time. Stress can also become ingrained in someone most of the time as in an anxiety disorder. It becomes a habitual and predictable style to overreact. These ongoing anxiety spectrum traits are discussed later in chapter 13.

Poverty and the crime it cultivates are havens for stress, including traumatic stress. Trauma develops when people feel helpless in the face of horrific events. I am always amazed when I interview people who live in poverty how quickly they mention a murdered relative. Their outrage battles with resignation, helplessness, and despair. It clouds their view of life.

Stress is experienced in our thoughts; our emotions; and as physical discomfort. These three are interrelated. They react to stress and also to its opposite, calm. Too often, the point of treatment focuses only on one of these reactions rather than all three.

For example, psychotherapy typically focuses on thoughts and emotions, seeing physical calm as a byproduct. Medication, on the other hand, focuses on physical symptoms and views the calming of thoughts and emotions as the byproduct. However, the newer meridian therapies discussed beginning in Chapter 3 address all three - even without medication. Long lasting treatment belongs in all three arenas—thought, emotions, and physical comfort!

An Experiment

Here are a few scenarios to highlight the connection thoughts, emotions and physical comfort. Try this experiment and note how interrelated they are.

Imagine a sunny day at the beach. The temperature is perfect and your body melds into the sand. What are your thoughts, emotions and physical state?

Probably your thoughts of the sunny beach are enjoying nature's paintbrush, your emotions are serene, and your body is relaxed and mellow.

Now, imagine you're in the middle of a fierce storm and tornado watch. The electricity in the air is raising the hairs on the back of your neck. Your mind is busily scanning for danger signs of the tornado, your emotions are worry and fear, and the knots in your stomach are competing with the tightness in your shoulders.

How different are your thoughts, emotions and physical sensation in the storm experience compared to the beach scene?

Here is an example that may surprise you. Picture winning the lottery. Your thoughts are of all that money flowing, your emotions are exuberant, and your body is strong, probably jumping for joy right off the floor! Although happily excited, you may also notice some confusion and too much physical energy (such as you can't even sit down) and clouded thinking! Extreme excitement can be stressful too. A therapy tip is to consider telling yourself you are "excited" about an event (positive thinking) even if you are anxious as your body feels similar.

These 3 examples demonstrate the interface of thoughts, emotions, and physical state. These reactions are inextricably connected. This is the mind-body connection, and you experience it every day, in both positive and negative ways.

Let's add one more component as we think about stress. Alcoholics Anonymous has an expression often seen as a bumper sticker: "Shit Happens." It does. Stuff Happens and Stress Happens too. That is the truth. You can be completing a mundane errand, when an energetic child chasing a ball darts in front of your car. Even with successful braking, thoughts and feelings about the close call flood your body with stress hormones. Your body reacts as the stress response builds; your blood pressure rises, your heart races. You notice a churning stomach, tightness in your chest and a knot in your neck. Thought, emotion, and physical reactions are entwined.

Because of this brief but intense experience, you struggle through the day, out of sync with your body and your emotions. You try to be mentally present, but you're not thinking clearly and you're emotionally drained. Your back-to-business-self wants to push forward but your body wants to collapse in a heap. You are mentally, emotionally and physically out of sync but you fake your way through the day. Stressed-out!

Is All Stress Evil?

Not all stress or anxiety is bad. Emotions teach us valuable life lessons. We learn to drive more carefully, do our homework, not swear in front of our parents, pay attention crossing streets, and to not impulsively walk out of stressful jobs.

A loud car horn for that oblivious child playing in the street may increase his protective anxiety becoming a benevolent scolding that creates a lesson for his self-preservation. Yes, I did say to increase the anxiety of the child. Stress and anxiety are also beneficial warning signals. So, sometimes stress-induced awareness is very useful, while sometimes it is excessive.

We do many things to avoid these negative emotions and consequences. To get a feel for this, complete the questions below. You will begin to see that there is value to certain uncomfortable emotions that they help us behave better and create better choices.

You are too guilty to _____.

You are too scared to _____.

You are too sad to_____.

You are too angry to _____.

For example, I am too guilty to steal your wallet, too scared to walk alone at night, too sad to work in a funeral home (but admire those who can), and too angry to work with sexual perpetrators (and admire those clinicians who can). These emotions are usually accompanied by physical discomfort, which in itself may help to restrain behavior.

Emotions are great teachers. They keep us socialized and well-behaved in accordance to societal standards.

A problem may arise after the learning solidifies; the emotional disequilibrium may linger needlessly, excessively and interfere with our day to day functioning.

Physical discomfort such as muscle or chest tightness, may linger too, even without the mental remembrance of the cause.

Significant emotional reactions may paralyze our maturation and growth. Untreated triggers from our past cause us to react badly, sometimes even dangerously.

Let me repeat. It is excessive, lingering stress that is the enemy, particularly if it inhibits you from doing everyday things. Lingering negative emotions fuel stress and need to be released.

Treating Stress, Where Stress Develops

For decades the approach to anxiety and stress has been to attempt to acquire a relaxed state - the antithesis of frazzled apprehension. Relaxation and stress/anxiety cannot co-exist. An anxious person wants tranquility and never says, "No, thanks, I prefer freaking out at the moment." So, it is almost comical to tell a stressed person to relax. He has no idea how to attain relaxation. It is like telling an insomniac to just get some sleep. The advice is absolutely correct, but it is an unfathomable mystery wishing for a solution.

Here are some illuminating questions that show us where stress can develop.

Questions to Identify your Stress. Write your answers for future reference. Come back to these questions to address your answers as you read the techniques in Chapter 2 and 3.

- Do you have old emotional clutter that weighs on you, shows up in disguise, and inhibits the path you want to travel?

- Is there someone in our life that you cannot address effectively and you do not know why?

- Do you wonder if current upsets are activating an older event?

- Are issues that have haunted you for years still controlling you?

- Have you been to traditional psychotherapy with mixed results?

- Maybe psychotherapy was pleasant, but are you not better, or just slightly better?

- How did you cope after the announcement that layoffs are about to occur?

- How do you react to a work-related accident?

- How do you calm yourself if your position makes you the bearer of bad news?

- What if you have to do the same work with smaller work forces?

- What if you cannot tolerate your supervisor, supervisee, or co-worker?

- How do you handle an overload at work?

- How about if you returned home from vacation to find burglars had had a party at your house and took your family heirlooms?

- Maybe your child is frustrated and struggling and what effect does this have on you?

- What if he was bullied emotionally or physically and was unwilling to return to school?

What is keeping you stressed this week?

_____

_____

Stress is invited into our homes every night at 6PM.

How about unsuspecting victims we see or read about in the news? They were just living their normal lives until a fire, plane crash, or other outrageous event deeply challenged their sense of security. You, too, react to their sorry plight.

Onward to "Tried-and-True" Techniques

In the next chapter mainstay approaches currently used by psychotherapists are explained. Consider learning them, too. These include:

-Venting/Ranting: A 5-step technique, page 20, for effectively getting upsets off your chest by venting to an empathetic person paving the way to a cathartic release. This should be required reading.

-Problem Solving: A 5-step technique of problem solving, page 39, to create a strategic plan to conquer a dilemma.

-27 of the 60 techniques are covered in Chapter 2. They are essential for stress management and effective communication.

Pain management is explained later in Technique 60, page 293. It is last, but not the least.

All of these techniques refine and enhance your Mighty Mind. Technique 1, page 15, and Techniques 3, page 20 should be mandatory of all and requirements to graduate school! These teach listening skills, empathy and the way upsets are typically processed and released. Important to know.

CHAPTER 2

STRESS & COMMUNICATION

What Any Good Therapist Should Teach You about Stress Management and Effective Communication

> " Life is what happens to you while you're busy
> making other plans."

-John Lennon

Stress Happens Every Day - Simple Stress Management Tools

As hard as we try to make our lives work out perfectly, events still occur that we would be happy to miss. But they find us anyway. Faucets leak, employers downsize, cars malfunction and the flu is contagious. Stressful happenings (and stress) can be defined as anything that takes us outside of our comfort zone.

Tremendous relief is possible if you pause from your busy life for 5 minutes (or sometimes even less time) and use one technique from this chapter. That brief pause, far from a waste of time, actually enhances your productivity and thinking ability.

This chapter covers several mainstream techniques. It covers traditional everyday, personal growth techniques that any good therapist should teach you. The first two techniques - that of effective venting (cathartic release) and of problem solving - are broken into 5 steps for easy understanding. The remainder of this chapter lists additional 5-minute coping strategies. Use one or all of them to assist in managing your own stress. Chapter 3 and the following chapters address gentle yet powerful cutting-edge ways to combat stress. You can even combine techniques for maximum benefit.

The first conventional way to defeat stress is to talk it out, vent it, and not suppress it. Therapists know (and studies demonstrate) that when people put words to their dilemmas, they feel better. Thus, "whining" or "unloading" actually has a beneficial effect, providing the person listening has some empathy.

> In graduate school, I remember dreading anything the professors said that would be a "learning experience." It meant I was about to be taken far outside my comfort zone. One such example of these "learning experiences" entailed accompanying an elderly and institutionalized, chronic schizophrenic woman as she was being reintegrated into a poor community in North Philadelphia. Over stimulated and beyond calming, she screamed loudly as we walked down the street together. I wanted to hide under a rock. I worried about the perception of the watching community.

> This was stressful for both of us. It was unexpected and it happens! Venting later to a classmate helped to calm me, and repeating the same woes to my supervisor later added more benefit. A few weeks later, I could even laugh about it and it became one of those interesting stories worth repeating due to its comic value!

Therefore, venting (or ranting) is one useful tool to clear thinking and build resiliency. If stress levels are high, thinking capacity is low. Venting lowers stress. Sometimes those that need to vent, like first responders, stoically suppress feelings. Venting happens when you have a safe person to listen. Here is what to do to be that safe person. *Actively listen*. The formula is the same; the content varies with each situation. This technique could also be the missing ingredient in how to be a good spouse, friend, co-worker and supervisor. It is just that important to learn and thus is presented first!

Super Technique 1 - **Active Listening**   Essential Interpersonal Skill

Have you ever been verbally attacked after you offered good advice to someone who did not want it? Active listening is what they may have wanted from you, and this technique will help you through many difficult situations.

Active listening is a way to demonstrate caring and empathy towards another who is upset. It can also be used to calm the other person. It includes: listening while nodding your head affirmatively; asking clarifying questions; and whenever possible summarizing thoughts and emotions. Active listening does NOT include fixing the problem, which may be the reason you were verbally attacked! Active listening should be required training in all schools and workplaces. Examples of summarizing or paraphrasing looks like this:

> "That stinks and is annoying" (rather than laying out a plan to fix it)

> "So you are very upset that ...your boss doesn't understand when you have to leave because your child is sick" (rather than discussing how to address the boss)

> "So you miss me when I am working so much and you understand we need the overtime pay." (Rather than focus only on the work explanation.)

TIP: A quick word about summarizing or paraphrasing. Never use their exact words, as it feels like mockery. Suppose that a person says, "I am so upset with my diagnosis." If you repeat, "So you are upset with your diagnosis," the person will say or feel –"Hey! I just said that!"

Use your own words to paraphrase, such as "so you did not expect to be sick." Re--state their sentiment in your own words.

Expect them to nod appreciatively, because finally someone *understand*s them.

Again for emphasis, you are *not to try to fix the problem* by offering possible solutions. Nor are you to minimize feelings by saying "don't be so upset, don't worry or cheer up."

As people rub each other the wrong way from time to time, do not hold a grudge toward the person being complained about. Tomorrow these people will love each other or resume a wonderful friendship while you remain annoyed and confused. Try to remember, much of venting releases pressure so those people can intelligently work out their problems.

Venting or complaining is meant to be a cathartic release--a dramatic emotional expression of every single upset about this issue! It is even acceptable if the person cries telling you the story as those tears will release a bunch of beneficial soothing hormone. Try to remember that crying and even anger build-up and releasing those feeling safely is helpful. Unload your upsets to a caring listener.

Active listening creates a safe situation to let go of negative emotions. This reflection of thought and feelings honors the struggle and helps to let go of the negativity - so moving on is possible.

Active listening includes asking relevant questions on topic of what the other is discussing. *How, Who, When, Where, and What* are good places to start your questions. Some examples:

- How did you find out?

- Who was involved?

- Where did this happen?

- When will you know the outcome?

- What do you want to do?

Notice, none of these questions has "I" in them. It is not wrong to relate similar experiences, but do it very sparingly so the focus is on the other. The reward is the appreciation from the other of how you made him feel supported.

TIP: "Why?" questions often make a person feel defensive and uncomfortable. Try to turn a" why question" into a "what: question. For instance: Instead of -why did you think that? Ask: What about that made you think that way?

Active listening is how to be a compassionate best friend as well as a basic counseling technique. As a 22 year-old counselor working in a psychiatric unit, I was taught to summarize the expressed thoughts and emotions of patients all day long. Thus my inexperience did not get in the way of the patient's healing. This technique is still taught to counselors of all levels and should be taught to everyone!

Advanced Active Listening: The word "*And* "

This is more advanced and often unnecessary and it is how many counselors make suggestions. First and foremost, active listen is explained above. Paraphrase or summarize what they said "*AND*" only then offer your ideas. Try to use the word "*and*" instead of "*but*" to link ideas when doing active listening *and* offering suggestions. Here is why you want to use the word "*and*".

A group of trainers and authors (Bandler, R & Grindler, J 1975) who call their work, *Neuro-linguistic Programming* (NLP), figured out that using the word *"and"* between thoughts was better, because it meant everything on both sides of *"and"* were equally important. "And" is a connecter while "but" is a disconnector. (Using the word *"but"* can sometimes feel patronizing or insincere.) Thus, you can add in your thoughts AFTER you summarize their upset; meaning your thought is just as important as my thought.

Use the word *"and"* as often as you need. In the art of delivering the message, pause a second before you add the next *"and"* phrase so they absorb your previous empathetic comment. Here are some of the advanced ways to do that using the word *"and"* from the examples above. I use upper case *AND* to emphasize that on one side is the summary of their issue. On the other side of *AND* is your suggestion and thoughts. You can also use as many *"ands"* as a way to soothe the other as I show in the italicized *and*.

> "That stinks *and* is annoying *AND* can I help you with any of it?"

> "So you are very upset that your boss doesn't understand when you have to leave because your child is sick *AND* I wonder if you might meet with the boss to explain your situation."

> "So you miss me when I am working so much *and* you do not like being alone with the children all night AND I want you to know I miss you too."

One more example from parenting, using a student that is unhappy with math, who perhaps just had a melt-down talking about this.

That mother could say:

> "I know you don't like math this year *and* you are unhappy that the teacher is going so fast *and* you do not think the teacher is fair *AND* (your suggestion) if you just put your mind

to it, and get your homework done quickly, you will have the rest of the evening to play."

You can learn more by doing a computer search on "active listening", a popular and effective counseling and communication tool that began with psychologist Carl Rogers in the 1950s. (Rogers, Carl. 1951. *Client Centered Therapy)*. The spectrum of this technique extends from counseling and couple communication, to customer service - and even into prominent business schools as a way to close deals! Thus, in business, the drug representative says to the doctor:

> "I can see your waiting room is full *and* you are so busy *AND* if you will just sign this form, I will leave medication samples with your staff."

Psychologist Harville Hendrix took active listening into couples work, calling it "Mirroring." Essentially, you ask your partner to "mirror" your comments about your upsets without making any defensive responses, at the time. Your partner is only allowed to discuss their reactions about the issue after the next day. It is the gift of listening. His best sellers include a series of books on *Getting the Love You Want,* (1988, 2008).

Try to practice active listening every day and integrate this super tool into your life. Techniques 50 to 53, p. 215 are key ways to successfully address conflict and are located in the section on dealing with anger, Chapter 10.

Here are examples of possible stressful issues that venting may help. Some may even be considered traumatic. Stressful areas we may bemoan are serious, even traumatic such as accidents, illness, physical attacks, conflict, death, bullying, divorce, breakup of a romance, or a fire. But stress more commonly arrives in smaller packages that also have negative effects - a missed appointment, an unrealistic deadline, a complicated project, work or school problems, parenting, miscommunication, an electric outage, driving errors, and more. A build-up of any level of stress is not good for you.

What events from your life still resonate and have a negative hold on you? Pick one of them that still makes you squirm, makes your stomach churn, or ruminates in your thoughts. Venting is a great way to release some stress particularly if the person you are venting to knows active listening and gets comfortable with the steps from Technique 3, p. 20.

Technique 2: **Write or Vent**   **A Therapist Tool**

Write out your feelings on paper, but *never* mail them. Write out your feelings with full abandon and without concern for punctuation or spelling. Write until you are tired and can say no more.

I recommend you destroy these writings immediately, as they were how you felt at that moment. You don't want someone to find what you've written and believe that's how you always felt about him permanently. I have written some scathing letters to some of my friends. It is how I felt at the moment. Once calm, I decide if I want to rationally discuss the issue with them.

If you vent on your computer, remember that a computer whiz can reproduce anything you delete. I recommend writing on paper so you know you can permanently destroy.

Vent out loud to someone you trust about the project, the issue, or whatever, but be discrete when venting about people, which might best be done on paper. Once you have tried out venting, go to the next part of this chapter to super Technique #3.

Now let's get more organized in the way we process our upsets. Look at the 5 steps to healing below to understand how to eradicate the harmful effects of stress from your current life. Follow these 5 progressive steps for maximum benefit using the issue you picked above.

Super Technique 3: **Five Steps to Healing, aka Simple Psychotherapy**

If you wonder what happens in a psychotherapy office, these 5 steps are a typical view. Add in there a compassionate and non-judgmental counselor with knowledge about human development and psychology.

Feel free to try this on your own, even if you say it aloud or write it out. If you are fortunate enough to have a kind, concerned friend or family member, ask them to read the rest of this chapter as a mutual guide. Their job is to LISTEN actively, so remind them to read and maybe even re-read Technique 1 above for smoother sailing.

Don't skip any of the 5 steps, particularly in major upsets. We humans are multi-faceted and, thus, simple desensitization explained later in this book is wonderful but often just not enough. Some individuals will need a professional psychotherapist with whom to work through these steps. For others, a very good friend will do the job just fine.

Step 1) Name It Because It Happened

Describe the stressful event out-loud to yourself or someone else. If you prefer, write about it. Something happened to cause stress and this step makes it real. It is real. "I got fired, attacked, yelled at, picked on, discriminated against, or left by my loved one. My family member died." Whatever the event was, verbalize it, preferably out-loud.

This step breaks through your denial defense. Denial keeps symptoms circulating in your system forever. Unfortunately, these symptoms often come out in camouflage. It takes energy to keep denial contained by holding it in.

An example of being stuck in denial is pathological grief. You appear to cheerfully carry on in life yet never fully recovered from the stressful event of losing a loved one, perhaps a spouse. Years later, you may be hospitalized for a myriad of phantom complaints all stemming from the unresolved and denied stress.

Acknowledging the event happened starts the healing process. Venting is a cathartic release. It starts the process of the painful bubble bursting. Admitting it out-loud sometimes relieves much of the energy it took to subdue it. Something awful occurred. You wish it had not occurred, and it aches, makes you furious, or both. You may need to discuss the stressful event more than once.

> I sent a suicidal client for a second opinion to a busy emergency room crisis evaluation team. She repeated her

story so many times to so many people, (intake staff, nurse, crisis worker, second crisis worker at change of shift, ER doctor, and psychiatrist) that she let go of the deadly sentiment somewhere in the middle of all the interviews. Her intent lost its power over her. She said it grew into a ridiculous and remote idea.

You many need to say it over and over again to break through denial. Vent, moan, whine, complain and lock your mind around it. Tears, a loud voice, and animated body movements are encouraged and become the mechanisms that release the toxicity of what happened. Don't stifle these expressions of outrage if you are in a safe place, as they are temporary expressions on the way to personal recuperation. It is similar to lancing a boil to release the toxic puss so it can heal.

Your events are your stories, and your stories are your life. You need to state them and be heard and respected for the effect they have on you. Jumping too fast into a technique, even those defined later in this book, is premature. Your stories must be heard, validated and respected!

Step 2) Grieve It

Acknowledge it was awful, terrible, frightening, disgusting, painful, stinky, hurtful, overwhelming, haunting, infuriating, sucks the breath out of you, and more. Really admit just how bad the event was. Let the anguish out. Grieve it, discuss the awful outcomes from it, let your emotions surface, explore them and the horrible effect this has had on you, your family, and all involved. Have tissues for the expected tears!

> "The house fire was awful. All my photos and life history are gone. I have trouble sleeping at night now. My children cry quickly about small things since then. I am so angry over everything!"

Deeply explore the losses, the upsets, and the fallout from the event. Identify all the emotions. Honor the pain, don't deny it, and certainly don't sugarcoat it. Honor just how terrible it was or is. Confide in an empathetic person, write it out on paper, or even tell a compassionate animal. Really! Dogs are empathetic, loving, loyal, and provide wonderful therapeutic moments with guaranteed confidentiality! A droopy eyed Saint Bernard mix, named Ziggy, licked my tears through my tumultuous teen years. Currently, a Chocolate Lab mix Pippi Doggery aka Wiggle Bum, makes me laugh even when the world is not that funny!

It's not just grief that you must acknowledge, but also any other strong feeling that comes up. Consider anger, indignation, fury, outrage, guilt, worry, or feeling discounted, insignificant, condescended, slighted or even just unimportant. These are all emotions that need to be recognized. It may seem petty to you based on what is going on with the world, but it happened to you, and for you it is painful. And if it's not painful, it may just be downright irritating.

> *"I'm furious that my office mate ruffles through my desk and intrudes on my space."*

> *"It is so unfair they just walked him out the door without any notice."*

> *"I am still in shock that I was not invited to that party."*

Furthermore, negative and stressful emotions are often manifested physically within the body as you will see in Chapter 6. For example, an upset stomach is a classic symptom of anxiety, as are a lump in the throat, tight shoulders and a stiff neck.

When a young child states they have an upset stomach, two questions will usually resolve it. First, question to see if the child needs to have a bowel movement, as they often forget this cue. Second, ask what is wrong in their life. Are they upset with school, mommy, a sibling, a project, etc.? As they tell you their woes, they might cry, and their stomach ache will dissipate. The stomach ache was real, not imagined, but letting out the emotional upset released the corresponding physical pain. Their miseries may have been one of the following:

> *"School was terrible. I got yelled at when it was the girl next to me that was talking."*

> *"I got scared because they fist fought in the gym."*

"My stomach had butterflies while I waited to perform."

Tip: Really young children will confide in a puppet, even if it is your squeaky voice asking the questions.

Physical manifestations of stress in the stomach area alone can include aches, pain, churning, butterflies, jumpiness, a loss of appetite or excessive hunger, tension, heaviness, and nausea.

The throat area, another favorite involved in noting stress, could show signs through a choking sensation, difficulty in swallowing, tension, an inability to talk, a lump in the throat, or excessive or minimal salivating. It is amazing how the mind can provoke physical symptoms.

The chest area with tension is often described as a pressure, tension, heaviness, stabbing, twisting, burning, etc. Shoulders manifest stress through pressure, heaviness, tension, tightness, and stabbing pain.

The neck's manifestation of pain is tension, a crick, an inability to turn the head, limited mobility, etc. Limbs manifest stress through arms and leg weakness or muscle tension and tremor or shaking in the arms, legs, and hands.

Acknowledge these physical manifestations as part of the adverse outcome from the stressful event. In Chapter 6 you will see a way to use these physiological manifestations as the point of treatment to lessen both the symptoms and the emotional upset as well.

TIP: Sometimes you are stuck because your problem or illness is not abating. Grieve it and be upset, *AND* also balance it with some positive news. For instance, "I am frightened of this cancer *AND* the tumor is shrinking, new science is emerging daily, my employer is being quite empathetic or my family is sticking with me. Thus, it becomes a balancing act, to loudly be upset *AND* to loudly be grateful for any rays of sunshine!

Step 3) What Can You Learn?

All of life is learning. You can learn as much from a bad role model as a good one, because you can learn what not to do. Once the emotional turmoil is alleviated, valuable lessons can be learned from unfortunate events. You can avoid alcohol if that was a family problem. You can finish college after watching your parents struggle. You can decide to curtail edgy, rude behavior and take classes on better conflict management techniques. A few lessons learned the hard way include:

"I sure will never do that again!"

"I will never do that to my children."

"I will be a fairer boss than my last employer."

"Cape Diem." –Seize the Day.

Can the stressful event be changed?

Can you go back and apologize, renegotiate, or correct it?

If so, do so. If not, what can you learn for the future?

Can you approach the person diplomatically and address the conflict?

Can you find solutions for the future, if the event re-occurs?

Is mediation (with a third person) a possibility?

"I'm sorry about what happened. I didn't see all the components. Can we take another look at it and see if we can do it differently?"

Step 4) Heal from It

You need to mend and recover from bad stuff. Many times going through Steps 1-3 above and Step 5 below are all you need to heal and fulfill step 4. Sometimes you need more. Teaching you how to heal from stressful situations is the main purpose of this book. This step is address over and over in later chapters too. It's important to place this vital step within the context of the four others, in order to fully recover from whatever disaster happened.

There are several more techniques, mentioned below in this chapter that may help with healing. Problem solving gives some insights on how to untangle dilemmas. A list of stress busters at the end of this chapter adds to your coping skills. After reading additional desensitizing skills in Chapter 3, you may want to circle back here later to plug those skills in this step.

Step 5) Move On, Get Back into Life

In the words of Winston Churchill, "If you're going through hell, keep going." Step 5 is critical. Your mishap is not the end of your life. Pick yourself up, brush the dirt off your backside, and get on with your life. Slide back in slowly if necessary, baby step by baby step, and relearn how to walk tall. Hoist yourself back up on the horse that threw you off, or get a new ride. For you, this might mean find a different venue, a new house, new job, new car, new friends, and that's all fine. You may need to push through defeatist moods to get going again. Your new mantra is resiliency –the ability to bounce back!

When my mother, who had suffered many strokes, went to a nursing home I was devastated. This dynamic, intellectual person was now debilitated and surrounded by "old" people. However, a clever activity director eventually had my wheelchair-bound mother screaming in laughter as they played competitive balloon volleyball. This wasn't the expectation I had for this monumental, dynamic person in my life, yet it became another enjoyable chapter of living.

Do not let your awful event be the end. You can ease back into life with the help of a friend, support group member, neighbor, therapist or family member. Close the chapter on whatever happened. By using the healing techniques set out in this book, this will be a much easier process. Accept you can find and also thrive within a "new normal."

A special issue worth discussing in the context of networking and the "Five Steps to Healing" involves "re-entry worries".

RE-ENTRY INTO WORK, SCHOOL OR LIFE

If you've had a terrible event or a prolonged absence, re-entry into your former life can be tricky. Prepare yourself that out of concern, most of your friends, acquaintances, and colleagues will ask about you and the event. If you wish to talk, do so. If it is overwhelming and you're not ready yet, rehearse a statement that you can repeat to each person that is factual, but vague. "I am on the mend, thanks for your concern." A response to a person's next inquiry about your situation might be, "Doing better, thanks for your concern." And if they prod more, vaguely blame it on a private family problem! People will eventually back off.

Let's not forgot humor. If you work in an environment where humor and joking is the norm, you may need to break the ice. Upon your return, your colleagues are not sure how to handle you. Here is an example.

> "Good thing I am back so people will finally do some work around here."

You are the elephant in the room. You have reappeared into their world. It is common courtesy for them to inquire of your return after an extended absence. You, however, probably don't want to spend your entire first week back rehashing the horror of the reason for your absence. So a polite, "Thanks for your concern, I'm doing better now," will work well. By the way, some of them are as nervous as you about asking you this. Your casual answer works for both of you!

A Review of the 5 Steps to Heal.   (Coping with being fired)

Using an example of someone who got fired from his job -summary of the Five Steps to Healing from most difficulties

---

Step 1) Name it—"I got fired."

Step 2) Grieve it – "I am sad, mad and scared."

Step 3) Learn from it.—"I can cut several bills, update my resume, & keep a nest egg."

Step 4) Heal.

"I am resilient." I will read on in this book to locate any technique that works for me.

> Step 5) Move on from it and return to a "new normal." I will volunteer to network and be social.

The five steps take you through the pain and back into life, which is critical.

Once you are desensitized from an upsetting issue, step 5 above gets you back into life.

Read on for another therapeutic tool is called the reframe.

Technique 4: **Reframe - Finding the Rainbow**

This is a way to look at turmoil and see possible beneficial growths. It is finding the rainbow after a heap of garbage came your way. Furthermore, in Chinese the word "crisis" is often times closely connected to the word "opportunity." In other words, a crisis isn't just a disaster of some sort. It's also an opportunity, where things can change, and sometimes for the better. A crisis might be an opportunity to change your path, to grow, to learn, or to re-think an old idea or set of beliefs. A reframe can be a spontaneous insight that emerges about the other ramifications of the problem.

My own lesson from my devastating parents' deaths was to make every day count. Today is all you know, all you really have. Cape Diem, seize the day. In the spirit of this lesson, I treated myself to a long overdue and wonderful Caribbean vacation.

- Here are some helpful reframes:

   "Perhaps it was a good thing he broke off your relationship so early. This way you won't get attached to a person who isn't interested in a commitment."

   "Maybe she's in peace now that she's died. Her painful, debilitating illness lingered for so many years and caused her such extreme suffering. And it took a toll on you to watch her suffering too!"

"Possibly this illness has given me a break from the corporate treadmill, so I can evaluate my priorities in life."

"Have you considered that not getting that promotion is a gift in disguise? You did dread all the overtime involved.

TIP: Please note the tentative wording such as: "perhaps; maybe; or possibly." These reframes need to be relayed gently as possibilities and not as absolute truths! Tentative wording leads to less resistance to the idea. Similarly ask questions like: what do you think about this? Do you mind...? Would you consider...? These tentatively worded questions elicit more progress than demands such as: do it my way; and any other "my way or the highway" statements.

Through life's interminable ups and downs, I've had the opportunity to learn many more lessons. The tougher it's been, the more I've been able to learn, provided I kept my head on straight and continued to ask, "What can I learn from this?"

I bet you can guess the crises I had from which these lessons were born!

Many of these lessons will ring true for you too.

I have learned to:

have more than one good friend

always have a plan B in case plan A nosedives

have money in the bank

not burn bridges when I leave a job

break fears into smaller parts and treat them individually

be more courteous than I want to be

not trust everyone with my innermost thoughts

not dwell on the negative, but to intentionally think of something pretty or pleasant

fake a smile until I actually feel better

use a microscope to enlarge the positives in life

keep my thoughts to myself about difficult relationships that others value

try not to cross boundaries

set realistic limits on myself and others

not ask people for more than I would do myself

make my own judgments about people even if there is damaging gossip about them

find the humor in the mundane

make my point clearer using metaphors or analogies

calm down by taking a walk before I react

forgive quickly to eradicate carrying anger

sleep on a problem and be less reactive at the moment it occurs

remember to apologize quickly

and

use EFT/tapping meridian therapies (coming in Chapter 3) whenever I get overwhelmed.

And…. A plethora of life's lessons come observing clients.

> Lessons from my clients include:
>
> cheating on your spouse is exciting briefly and then horrendous for everyone
>
> child abuse messes up your view of the world for an extremely long time
>
> addiction is a life changing, painful illness that no one is immune to
>
> change is worth fighting for
>
> be realistic with promises and keep every one of them
>
> learn to say "no" graciously
>
> don't take everyone's opinion to heart
>
> understand everyone has "stuff" and weak areas
>
> trust yourself more
>
> pay your bills on time
>
> divorce is difficult for everyone
>
> gambling and alcohol work only in moderation
>
> cheating messes with your head
>
> be careful about what you agree to
>
> keep appropriate boundaries with others
>
> practice "professional", public and formal behavior at work
>
> you will lose a friend if you sleep with his former girlfriend
>
> value yourself and value others too
>
> find time to listen to another's woes or joys
>
> celebrate every chance you can as I promise the problems will find you

quiet the "critic within", which at the time taught you important lessons, but now just beats you up follow directives, but do not take everyone's opinions to heart

set and hold boundaries as you cannot do it all without having a nervous breakdown

And if your life was filled with difficult people, remember you can value the lessons from a bad role model on what not to do!

TIP: Think of this amazing question in life next time you are debating a small point with a loved one.

Do you want to be right or do you want to be happy?

Remember when you allow your partner to have his/her way; you win too by basking in their gratitude! It is the antithesis of what you learned growing up in a competitive society. Graciousness is a virtue and is hugely appreciated in personal relationships!

Life's Painful Lessons.

What life lessons have you learned? What difficult situations brought these insights? Write out your list:

_____

_____

People Resources.

Make a list of those people with whom you can discuss your difficulties and get advice on how to not make the same mistakes in the future.

Is this a good friend, medical doctor, therapist, spouse, sibling?

Keep these people close to you!

Develop more friendships, if needed. Look for someone who has empathy and a wise head on her/his shoulders. Make sure you evaluate all advice to see if it fits in your lifestyle.

_____

_____

_____

We now discuss 4 additional stress management and effective communication techniques: persistence, networking, metaphors, and humor to the absurd; as well as the relevance of these 4 techniques to the "Five Steps to Healing".

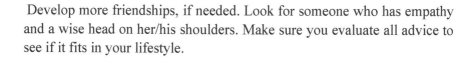

Technique 5: **Persistence**

Try, try and try again - 3 magic repetitions! Don't give up too early. My clients often have wonderful ideas but give up if not successful on the first attempt. Actually, it often takes 3 tries to get comfortable with an idea or new behavior. The first time is so novel that it is hard to absorb. The second time is more familiar and the third time feels like it is "old hat" and relaxed. This is true in learning new material and also when meeting new people. Strangers become familiar acquaintances who become companions. (Sometimes it even takes 5 tries, if the new idea is so novel.)

If you decide to impose a rule on children's behavior, just remember they will "forget" and test it 3 to 5 times. Remember to attach a consequence for misbehavior too, which they will also test 3-5 times.

A teacher reinforced for me that 3 is a magic number. He said the first is instruction, the second try is practice and the third is mastery. Try things 3 times with yourself and others before you dismiss the idea.

Hang in there, it is worth it.

Technique 6: **Network Everywhere for Everything**

If you need something new, remember to network by asking others if they know of the availability of what you need. If you lost your partner or moved, then you need to find a new network of available people and activities. This new world will fill much of the empty hole left by his or her absence. It's a new chapter with a different story line, but enticing in its own way. It may develop more slowly than you desire, but persistence has its rewards. Try this resource in your area, www.meetup.com, which provides a listing of activities in your community. My clients have found or formed groups for movies, art appreciation, business networking, plays, games, writing, wine tasting, kayaking and outdoors activities, just to name a few.

The internet is quite a tool to find new resources. Do a search with any word that describes your situation. Add a geographical location and you will often find a social group or information equipped to help, e.g., "Widowed, Cherry Hill, NJ."

If you lost your job, ask others if they know of an opening. You may need to take additional training or find a temporary job through a temporary job agency. Maybe the temporary job will open the possibility for ongoing employment. Maybe even find volunteer work. You will be around people and create the potential to network and socialize.

Don't limit where you look to build your new life; network by asking everyone, everywhere.

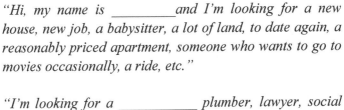

"Hi, my name is _____ and I'm looking for a new house, new job, a babysitter, a lot of land, to date again, a reasonably priced apartment, someone who wants to go to movies occasionally, a ride, etc."

"I'm looking for a _____ plumber, lawyer, social dance club, singles group, newcomers group, senior activity center, scrabble group, psychotherapist, AA group, financial planner, training program, girl scout troop, barber, etc."

When I say network everywhere, I mean everywhere. This includes the hairdresser, the doctor, a neighbor, a colleague, at church, at temple, your barber, a waitress, the fireman, the store clerk, your cousins, the bartender (bartenders and hairdressers do more counseling than any other profession), etc. Name what you need and put it out to everyone and the universe. You never know how or when it will get back to you.

In the book *The Secret* (Rhonda Byre, Atria Books 2006), the author describes manifesting desires through the law of attraction. The idea is you attract to yourself that which you focus on.

The people she interviews often use vision boards to fine tune their focus. A vision board might be a pin-up collage of what they want posted in an area they frequent. Before long they see things they missed that are associated with the goal. For example, if you decide to travel to Paris you will begin to notice anything French. You will hear a French accent, see a French bakery, and notice an advertisement photo of the Eiffel Tower. French travel deals will jump out at you!

You attract certain things because you are focused, and this focus makes you more aware. You are now attuned. That bakery has been unnoticed for years, but it's been there all along. If you are looking for friends, you start to see people who are available, who are into activities you like, etc.

Add networking to this idea of focusing on what you want. Share out loud what you're looking for in your life.

Most people feel rewarded by being helpful. This probably is true for you too. In fact, this is even a category in the new psychology of happiness and positivity. You receive more than you give when you are helpful. Helpful people feel productive and positive. Allow people to feel good about them by being helpful to you! Do not deny people the joy of being helpful to you!

> Years ago, my husband and I were forced out of the housing market in Rhode Island unless we built a house. The bank would not qualify us for a loan. While commiserating to my husband's cousin about this terrible state of affairs, he up and offered to build our house for us at an economical rate. All we needed now was the piece of land.
>
> We told everyone we knew that we were looking for land, everyone. Hi, my name is Robin, and my husband and I are looking for land to build on. Eventually it manifested through my babysitter's husband, a fireman who worked

with another fireman who was building a house on one of five available lots!

There are ways to say things and there are ways to be more effective. Metaphors and analogies are great tools for making our point.

Technique 7: **Metaphors and Analogies to Nail Your Point**

Metaphors and analogies are communication methods that make a point by pairing dissimilar ideas. The relationship between the two is vague enough not to give direct information, but universal enough that others can figure out the connection and attach their own meaning. They capture a deep meaning quickly.

A metaphor is a figure of speech in which a comparison is made between two unlike things that actually have characteristics in common. Metaphors are somewhere between conscious and unconscious and go to both sides of your brain, creating an encompassing picture. (We will use them later - Technique 60-to disrupt the way pain is remembered.)

> Aristotle said: "It (use of metaphors) is a sign of genius; for a good metaphor implies an intuitive perception of similarity between dissimilar."

> It is the ability to see similarities between dissimilar things.

They can even be used to ease your transition on your first day back in school or the job. Their vagueness protects your privacy while offering a respectful response.

> *"Thanks, I am on the mend."*

> *"I am bouncing back, thanks for your interest."*

> *"It was stormy for a while, but the sun finally came out."*

> *And of course, "I learned how to make lemonade out of lemons."*

Metaphors can be used in almost every situation. They are even called therapeutic metaphors, because they override psychological resistance and people grasp a deeper level of empathy and understanding.

- That was a nightmare!

- Trying to do that new thing, I felt like a fish out of water.

- Your pain must feel like a grizzly bear; let's try to turn it into a Teddy Bear with some treatment.

- You exhaust your battery at work all day, and then you discharge your battery again at home caring for your family. Find a fun activity you enjoy to recharge your battery or you are going to end up with a dead battery. So do something for you to recharge.

Metaphors can also be used in more light-hearted ways. Here is an example. An elevator I was in stopped unexpectedly at a floor and the door opened. The other person looked at me inquisitively. Realizing he was waiting for me to get out, I pointed my finger up and said, "I am on the penthouse". He laughed.

Technique 8: Taking Humor to the Absurd -- A Gentle Brush Off

Boundaries refer to what people will and will not say or do. Sometimes people cross your boundaries and ask you information that is too personal. I am not going to talk about my sex life, even if you ask. I am not going to help you move heavy furniture, even if you ask.

Taking humor to the absurd is a stress management tool to gently push people back who cross your boundaries. It can be used in a variety of situation including re-entry worries. You will want to generate way out, crazy, impossible answers. The art of delivery needs to be a matter-of-fact tone of voice, possibly playful, but not sarcastic. When returning from a medical leave, here are some possible responses when others inquire how you are doing now.

"I was traveling around the world, but got bored and decided to come back to work"

"Hollywood wanted me for a talk show, but I missed you guys."

Taking humor to the absurd can be used in other awkward situations as well. It is a tool for neutralizing conflict. When asked about how much money you make, you can respond:

"I am not sure. The little men in my counting house keep giving me different figures, but somewhere between one to two billion dollars."

"Taking Humor to the absurd" lets the other know you are not going to answer an intrusive question, but you are not going to attack them for asking the question. It is a comical, gracious win-win for both people!

Super Technique 9: Learn to say "NO" Graciously. More on Limits and Boundaries

It is imperative you set boundaries and limits in your life. Boundaries are what you will and won't do. People with good boundaries and limits feel well, are productive, and value their own needs. I will see a client at 5:00PM, but not at 5:00 AM as it will not work for me. It will disrupt my bio-rhythms, making me drag myself through life for days.

I will visit a sick neighbor and help them find help to hire, but will not move in to care for them. Be as helpful as you can to others, but know yourself and what you can do without overextending yourself and becoming overwhelmed. That is good boundaries. People with good boundaries understand their own emotional and physical limits. People-pleasing people who say "yes" to every request become exhausted. They find themselves in impossible situations. Learn to say "no" graciously.

We now go back to the first technique in this book - to advanced active listening. Let us experiment with a gracious way to say "no." Everyone wants to be validated, and to do so is the definition of empathy!

Remember the recipe?

(Summarize their issue first *AND* then add your explanation.)

In order to set boundaries in the context of using advanced active listening, summarize someone's issue *first AND* then *politely decline* while offering another possible solution. Here are some examples.

Situation: Trying to arrange an appointment.

> "Gee, that is a shame that you only have time to come in at 7:00AM *AND* I regret that I do not function at that time, so let's look at some other times we can agree upon. When do you get off work?"

Situation: A plea from a sick relative for help.

> "Man oh man, it does not look like fun that you feel so bad! *AND* I am too busy at work to be much help. Maybe I can get you the name of a visiting homemaker to help you several days a week."

Situation: A friend asks you to help him move.

> "I see that you need help moving *and* I would like to help *AND* I have a bad back (or I am working too much to help). Maybe you can locate a short haul, inexpensive moving company."

Super Technique 10: **Problem Solving**

Here another 5 steps, this time for solving a stressful problem.

All of life is solving problems. And conflict is everywhere. The earlier you accept this, the easier your existence will be. Instead of saying bad things always happen to me; understand bad things happen to everyone. Determining how to solve a problem is more realistic and productive. Furthermore, the sense of mastery and competence experienced through problem solving is a reward in itself. Conquering problems is the cornerstone of self-esteem.

Do you want a child that can solve his own problems? If so, step out of the way and to let him develop those skills. You and he can follow these steps even though your issues vary.

Here is a simple 5 step problem-solving model illustrated by a typical example. Little Johnnie is upset about an issue at school.

Step 1) Identify the problem:

> After a few tears, mom and Johnny figure out his upset occurs because he never gets picked by the teacher to be her helper.

Step 2) Brainstorm some ideas:

> Mom can call the teacher to inquire if there is a reason;
>
> Little Johnnie can try to always be well behaved in class;
>
> He can talk to the teacher; or
>
> He can ask a classmate if she did anything special to get picked as her helper.

Step 3) Pick One:

> Little Johnnie decides he will talk to the teacher at recess, BUT he is still a bit upset and nervous about doing this. He may need to feel calm and secure doing this. He can rehearse what he is going to say and get some coaching tips. Also, the next chapters address a major desensitizing technique to release his worry about talking to his teacher.

Step 4) Try it.

> He talks to his teacher at recess.

Step 5) Evaluate the selected solutions and outcome.

> Mom and Little Johnnie will discuss how he made out talking to the teacher and if he got what he needed. Perhaps he will now have his turn as helper, and, if so, this intervention is over and worked well.

But what if the teacher shared that Little Johnnie is so silly with his classmates that she thinks he would be disruptive as her helper? Then, Johnnie and Mom are back to Step 1, trying to identify how, when, and why he does this, and if he is willing to change.

Problems are an inherent part of daily living, and finding and applying their solutions build character. The first valid post college job in a mental health hospital in-patient unit wasn't given to me because of my academic accomplishments, but rather because I had driven my father's dry cleaning route for six months since his car accident. The interviewer saw this as an act of resiliency and tenacity. It also was awful. (There's nothing quite like driving a broken-down car during a gas rationing crisis as a delivery person.)

Problem solving is one of many keys to conscious living and optimal self-esteem. It builds a personal sense of competency and maturation. The more it is practiced, the more strength one feels to handle whatever comes one's way!

Technique 11: Tone of Voice Changes Everything

Studies say the tone of voice is 85% of the message. I think it is 100%. You can say difficult things - if you can keep your tone neutral or even upbeat. Play with several variations of your tone of voice on the difficult statements below. Say them straight, sing-song whiney, sarcastic, quiet or screaming. Engage another to do this with you for some critical and humorous awareness.

> I need you to pay back the loan I gave you.

> There is a $50.00 charge for missed appointments.

We had a complaint about your body odor in the waiting room and know depressed people often stop taking care of their hygiene. We need you to agree to have a shower within 24 hours of your appointment.

I am unable to be a bridesmaid in your wedding because of the money and time commitment involved.

Did you notice a different emotional reaction based on what tone of voice used? These statements are not easy to say at all. Saying them with a matter-of-fact tone is just compassionately direct. Hopefully, throughout this book you will find several stress management tools to calm yourself first to then say what you have to with dignity, compassion, tact and as inoffensive as possible.

Technique 12: Sandwiching Criticism to Say the Strong Stuff

Here is a great way to motivate someone to correct their ways. It's also another way to say "no" graciously.

All the techniques in this book are formulas, protocols, or recipes for how to be more effective (which is also stress reducing). Here is one called *Sandwiching Criticism*. It is a way to deliver criticism in a way that increases motivation to change.

The criticism (the difficult part) goes in the middle. The other two parts of the sandwich are honest compliments, kind words, acknowledgements of positive attributes and behaviors. To illustrate, I will break this into 3 parts, where 1 and 3 are the sandwich ends and 2 is the criticism.
It looks like this.

Sandwiching Criticism

1. "You are a great, hard-working employee and a pleasure to work with.

2. There are some times that your disorganization affects us all, such as the need to get your statistics in on time. Please work on that.

3. And be aware we appreciate all your creative input and extra time spent on our complex projects."

<u>Saying "NO" Graciously, a Necessary Life Skill</u>

1. "I appreciate how much you have done for me and that you are always there to listen.

2. I regret I am unable to get to your party due to some other earlier commitment.

3. However, I will be there in spirit. I know your party will be wonderful, and you will enjoy your other guests."

Sandwiching criticism is an excellent way to address chronic issues as it lets the person know they are valuable too. Their motivation to work on these issues is increased.

Next is a way to curb obsessing and worrying.

Technique 13: Worry Time – Stop Obsessing!

Need to stop obsessing? Pick a convenient 15 minute block of time, same time every day. This is now your "worry time". Thus, if you start to worry during the day, you remind yourself that this is not the time to worry and you will do it later. This is a wonderful tool, when you are overwhelmed and obsessed with the issue all day long. It gives you back your life. This has even saved marriages after an affair!

If you are angry about something your spouse did, or an issue from work; agree that you will worry, even obsess about it every night from 7:00 PM to 7:15 PM. If you start to obsess and worry at noon, you remind yourself now is not the time, but you will do that at 7:00PM. Thus you get the rest of the day to engage in more life enhancing activities.

Also note *if you missed your worry time and it is now 8:00 PM, you cannot worry until tomorrow.* Of course you realize the goal here is to get you to worry and obsess less, especially on issues that you cannot change. There is a huge difference between thinking (and solving) a problem and obsessing and worrying about something that is upsetting but not fixable.

Next let's consider some important lifestyle changes to integrate into your life, described below in Techniques 14-16. Any improvement in these three will help immensely.

Eating and Drinking Troublemakers

Super Technique 14: Food and Nutrition   Wellness

Eat 3 regular balanced meals and make sure you consume fresh vegetables and fruit every day. Watch out for trigger foods that drive you to overindulge, such as cake. Frequently, overweight people have a problem with sugar, white flour and grains. Interestingly, white flour is processed grain, while most hard alcohol such as vodka and whiskey, are fermented grain. Chemically they are very similar. Given this, it's not surprising that some people can't handle white processed flour, similar to how some people can't handle alcohol. Some people struggle with all grain carbohydrates, perhaps are carbohydrate intolerance. Some people successfully plan for healthy snacks too.

Remember to eat. I probed during an entire session with a client who decided she needs to try anti-depressants only to later learn that she does not eat every day. Be sure to consume nutritious fuel everyday for the body to run on.

Stay hydrated with lots of water. Consider carrying a water bottle. Muscles get weak and rubbery without hydration thus effecting strength and vitality.

Keep athletes hydrated for better muscle strength and performance. People often feel hungry rather than thirsty when they could use more hydration.

Technique 15: **Caffeine**

Sleep problems, stress and anxiety are fired up with caffeine; it's an inexpensive, legal stimulant. If you run anxious, have panic attacks, or have sleep problems, then consider decreasing or eliminating caffeine. Anything you eat or drink remains in your system for 20 hours. If you drink several 8-ounces units of caffeine a day, you have a stimulant in your system at all times. No wonder you are anxious or can't sleep!

Many people notice significant relaxation and lessened vigilance when they get off caffeine. If you think this is you, cut one unit (8 ounces) every three to four days to avoid withdrawal. Common symptoms of caffeine withdrawal include headache, irritability and difficulty concentrating. Substitute your caffeinated drinks with good decaffeinated products, so you don't feel deprived.

Technique 16: **Alcohol Issues**

In moderation alcohol can be fine, but if you drink excessively there are multiple issues. Do not drive with any alcohol in your system! If an accident occurs everyone will be sympathetic; unless alcohol is involved and it then becomes criminal. Many major crime and abuse victims will testify that alcohol was involved.

Alcohol can be called both - *liquid courage,* and *liquid stupidity.* It gives us the courage to do very stupid and criminal things. Alcohol lowers inhibitions – the restraint that keeps us dressed modestly and sitting on chairs with our behavior in control. Excessively lowering our inhibitions allows us to dance on the bar with scanty clothes, looking like fools. This is a comical example of how alcohol can cause poor judgment. Bar fights, promiscuousness, auto fatalities, stealing, sexual abuse and aggressive behavior are less humorous products of excessive drinking.

Do you have an alcohol problem?

Consider these questions.

> Do you drive after drinking?

> Do you fight or act aggressively when drinking?

Do you remember everything that occurred or do you have blackouts?

Do you act irresponsibly?

Do family members hide when you are drinking?

Do you behave in ways you regret when drinking?

What do people tell you about your behavior when drinking?

If any of these apply, you have problems while drinking and that makes you a problem drinker!

Begin with some rules of drinking, such as no driving, no arguing, and what you can drink and how much. If you can follow this advice, great! If not, you have a problem and can eliminate the cause - alcohol. Alcoholics can still drink -- just not alcohol. They can drink soda, water, juice, tea, coffee, and all sorts of other satisfying beverages. There is lots of help out there, including groups like Alcoholics Anonymous, and for family members, Alinon. Serious addiction may need a higher level of interventions ranging from outpatient therapy, to a day or evening program to inpatient rehab centers.

Let's conclude this chapter with a presentation of 7 additional general "stress-busting techniques" (or "good advice"), described below in Techniques 17-23. They are simple, 5-minute stress management techniques. Like medicine, they only work if you use them. Pick one to use today and practice it. Pick another in a few days and practice that too. Soon you will have your own tool chest of coping techniques.

SuperTechnique 17: "What's Right?" Positive Thinking

Sometimes you need to intentionally make your brain get off an upsetting subject by focusing on positive thoughts. Positive thoughts calm you; they tell the body to turn off your adrenaline. *Change Your Thoughts, Change Your Life,* writes inspirational, motivational speaker Dr. Wayne Dwyer (drwaynedyer.com.) He is right. You can even yell at yourself to STOP in a technique called *Thought Stopping* when you are thinking negatively. Make yourself think of positives! It will calm you. You cannot stop your thoughts for long, but you can focus them intentionally onto pleasant ideas. The newest psychology degree on the block is coming from the University of Pennsylvania, a master degree in Positive Psychology. It is the pursuit of: *What makes you happy.*

Examples of "positive ideas" might include:

- What's right in this room?

- What do you like about the weather?

- What do you like about your house?

- What parts of your relationships are good?

- What do you enjoy in your job?

- What benefits are there living in the US compared to Third World countries?

- What success you are feeling in the project you are currently working on?

- What small, sweet, nice thing someone did for you recently?

- What small sweet thing can you do for another?

Nothing about these issues kicks on any adrenaline-the hormone that revs up heart rate, blood pressure and the autonomic nerve action in readiness for danger. Look at gratitude, Technique 48 on page 213.

If you are afraid or phobic of anything, such as elevators, think of a positive event from your past, present or future. Focus on it in great detail to keep that scared mind of yours busy during the elevator ride. You may even end up smiling and that will make the others in the elevator wonder. Smiling is wonderfully contagious. (You can also read an entire chapter on dealing with phobias, Chapter 14.)

Technique 18: Agree to Disagree – Conflict Management 101

What about when you just do not agree with someone and it is getting hot? Democrats and Republicans. Yankee and Red Sox baseball. Cooking recipes. Organization projects.

Conflict is everywhere and those who learn ways to navigate in conflict feel comfortable in the game of life. A good strategy is to "agree to disagree." It can save long-term friendships and partnerships. It is okay that we do not agree and that others are entitled to different opinions.

Shrugged shoulders say this too. Take a look at Technique 50 on page 215, for a way to avoid engaging in an argument. I call it the "surrender position" and initially it looks like shrugged shoulders, possibly hands turned outward. With use, the shrug often becomes so tiny; it looks like a slight raise in one shoulder. Its meaning is: *I do not agree with you and do not want to fight with you.* It is useful in conflict and disagreements. It allows you to hold a different opinion without engaging in nonsense.

Technique 19: Intentional Breathing to Relax   Stress-less

There are lots of breathing tools that calm. Some people like Donna Eden in Energy Medicine even trace meridians that go throughout your body while doing breathing exercises. Here is one popular one that I learned at a Harvard/Mass General Hospital presentation quite a long time ago.

Diaphragmatic Breathing

Inhale into the lower abdomen, hold for three seconds and then slowly release your breath. Repeat it 3-20 times. This relaxation technique is taught to anxious people. It is also taught to singers, preachers, news reporters and cheerleaders, in order to open up their lungs to increase their volume. We automatically belly breathe when laying on our stomachs.

I also wonder if this is the outcome that cigarette smokers are seeking. Deep diaphragmatic breathing, all the way to the lower abdomen, below the belly button, brings air into the area where cigarettes smokers inhale. It is a cigarette break without the cigarette. Cigarette smokers crave cigarettes to relax or to get a nicotine fix. It is the deep breathing that relaxes the smoker, as nicotine is actually a stimulant. Substitute inhaling with a pen at your next cigarette break.

Breath and breathing are the main instruments of many techniques, including yoga, Mindfulness and other meditative practices. Breathe air in through the nose and slowly let it out through your mouth. It rebalances your system in a relaxed manner.

There is one meditative state where as you breathe, you mentally focus only on that very breath. Breathe in, breathe out and mentally focus on your breath. Note where the breath comes into your chest and then just breathe. Do it for several minutes or longer. It is very relaxing. Focus only on the breaths.

Breathe in shorter and breathe out longer (again like a cigarette) shifts you into a relaxation response. So breathe in through your nose as if sniffing the flowers and breathe out slowly like you are blowing out candles. Said another way, inhale for a count of 4, exhale for a count of 7. Try 5 to 20 of these to relax.

In the next section let's look at a physical way to burn off stress. Stress can turn on too much adrenaline, cortisol and other stress hormone that needs a release.

Super Technique 20: **Movement, Walking, and Exercise**

Move! You can literally burn off stress. Do heavy cleaning, exercise, walk, jog, dance, or take up yoga.

Walk outside, stretch, or alternate tighten and loosen your muscles. Tension is released through movement and exercise. Try to walk for 30 minutes or more as endorphins kick in after 20 minutes of activity and you want to get at least 10 minutes of naturally mood-elevating and pain relieving endorphins. Like any well-functioning machine, idling makes us sluggish and inefficient.

Take a walk to clear your head, work your body, and release all kinds of stress-reducing hormones including endorphins. Walking creates the natural alternating, bi-lateral stimulation promoted by some newer brain-based psychotherapies. When a stressful event happens, you may have processed it through your creative and emotional right brain but your resourceful and logical left brain will put it into perspective. The right brain is saying "Oh my gosh! How awful" while the left brain comments "it will be okay, you can cope." Walk to get your engine running, think and process your dilemmas and ideas. Many people say they take walks to "clear their head" and actually, they are correct.

If you're stuck in an awkward or conflict-laden situation that is overwhelming, excuse yourself and walk to the bathroom. This is not rude; it's a socially acceptable way to get away from a stressful situation in order to regain your composure. Plus, as discussed above, the movement helps clear your thoughts and feelings.

Technique 21: **Music, Dance, Theater, Literature, and Art**

Culture elevates us: music changes our mood; a good book occupies our mind; dance changes our physiology; a drawing, coloring or a play shifts our dimension. All are excellent tools for reducing stress. The key is to allow you the time and space to partake in these activities. Often, we feel guilty looking after ourselves. Remember if you can't look after yourself, you can't help anybody else either. Maybe the airlines have it right. In a crash, put the oxygen mask on first *and then* help others!

Technique 22: **Imagery – Let the Mind Meander**

Imagery is mentally leaving your stressful situation behind for fifteen seconds or more while thinking of a favorite place such as a vacation spot; the mountains, the ocean, or a theme park (e.g., Disney, Six Flags, etc.). Buy postcards; keep them taped to the bottom of a drawer you can peek into or post them on your bulletin board. Take mental pictures (an aquarium, spring's flowers, the boardwalk, and your cute children) that you can access when stressed.

Where do you feel the most peaceful?

Note it and remember it so you can access it when needed.

_____

_____

Imagine 5 to 10 things you would do if you won the lottery. What are they?

_____

_____

Next is an entirely different but delightful way to manage stress.

Super Technique 23: **Humor and Laughter – Comic Relief**

Don't take yourself too seriously; learn to laugh at yourself and the human condition. As a psychotherapist, am I more psycho or therapist? Anything you laugh at does not have a hold on you. It is comic relief.

Ironically, whenever I ask people if they want to go hunting with former Vice President Cheney, they laugh. Comic relief can easily come from something just plain awful, such as when the vice president of our country shot his hunting partner. During a recent gas crisis I saw a cartoon of a bride showing her engagement ring and the caption said, "We are registered at Exxon, Getty, and Mobil." Comic relief! Late night talk show hosts soothe us with comedic stabs at the days' politics.

Possibly humor goes to a different part of our brains. Think about bringing humor into your relationships. You can nag an annoyed husband about putting his dish in the dishwasher or you can humanize the dish by saying: "Please, sir, I am lonely in the sink and want to be in the dishwasher with all my friends." He will probably laugh, but the bigger payoff is that he will probably remember next time! Consider taking a second to figure out a humorous way to get others to do their chores or change annoying behavior. It beats belittling or nagging him.

Here is another physical and mental way to release stress.

Technique 24: **The Autogenic Relaxation Technique**

This is a mental technique to relax the body. You cannot be anxious and relaxed at the same time. You will not hurt yourself with this technique even if you do have a physical problem. This comes from a 1987 Harvard/MIT workshop on treating anxiety.

Slowly repeat each sentence below two to three times, imagining the sensation described.

Practice this two to three times a day for two weeks to fully memorize the relaxing *sensation*. The objective is that you will be able to obtain this state of relaxation recalling only one sentence, usually the first or last sentence. Remember to read each line *SLOWLY* 2-3 times while imagining the sensation.

> My forehead and scalp feel heavy, limp, loose, and relaxed.
>
> My eyes, nose, and mouth feel heavy, limp, loose, and relaxed.
>
> My neck and shoulders feel heavy, limp, loose, and relaxed.
>
> My arms, hands, and the central part of my body feel heavy, limp, loose, and relaxed.
>
> My stomach, pelvis and buttocks feel heavy, limp, loose, and relaxed.
>
> My thighs, calves, and legs feel heavy, limp, loose, and relaxed.
>
> My feet, ankles, and toes feel quiet, calm, comfortable, and relaxed.
>
> My entire body feels heavy, limp, loose, and relaxed.

Most people memorize the first or the last sentence, in order to reproduce the relaxation response.

Super Technique 25: The Way You Think Affects You (Cognitive-Behavioral Therapy)

Much has been taken from Cognitive-Behavioral Therapy (CBT) and incorporated into other therapies. CBT is a focused way to examine how you think and to debunk myths in your thinking. The goal is to add more conscious decisions about helpful ways to process your thoughts. If you dwell on negative, scary or upsetting thoughts, you are going to feel bad. Thus you correct faulty thinking.

If you overgeneralized that everything is bad, it will lessen the quality of your life. Find the polar opposite good news to focus on, even a reframe discussed in Technique 4, page 28. There are lots of ways to do this. Feel free to read more on the internet or through the www.BeckInstitute.org for this highly beneficial therapy technique that is a cornerstone of many types of therapies.

Technique 26: Pause – Get Off the Treadmill

Crucial down time. Pause, take a moment. Multi-tasking is expected and now the norm. There is an expectation you will answer emails and text messages immediately. Take a moment here and there to recharge your battery. Prioritize some downtime. Hear yourself think.

Ponder life; get off the treadmill of all you are trying to do. Look at nature, enjoy an aimless walk. Be realistic about your schedule and to-do list. Maybe turn off all electronics, even if it is only 30 minutes, an hour, or maybe half a day. Sleep in occasionally, without an irritating alarm to arouse you. Program some time for doing nothing.

Let yourself feel emotions. Maybe even let yourself cry over something that you pushed away. Crying is a powerful cathartic discharge releasing stress hormones. It may stimulate the production of soothing endorphins.

Time is an interesting life factor. Some people live in the past, some in the present and some in the future. Anxiety clients tend to hold onto the morose past and project doom onto the future. Living in the present is recommended and of course the present includes this week or month. It does not include worrying about college choices for a toddler!

After pausing, consider other ways to nurture yourself. Plan and take a vacation. The planning, the actual trip and the memories are three different enjoyable and therapeutic experiences. Walk in nature and really focus on the trees or the ocean. Call an old friend for no reason than to just connect. By doing so, it lets them know of their importance to you. Use the nice things you own as you deserve the elegance they provide. Clean out some clutter by donating them to a good cause which is a double win for you and them.

Technique 27: "Trapped," Let Go and the Serenity Prayer:

When working with anxiety a key concept to address is feeling trapped. "Trapped" in our ancestors' world was probably equated with death, as they were about to become someone's meal. Anxiety is heightened even if people *feel* trapped in a room, a relationship, a deadline, a job, a movie, etc. To counter this, people need to always have an optional plan B. Plan B may be to take a walk outside, to give the couples counseling 6 months, to get an extension on the deadline, start looking for another job, or simply slip away to the bathroom if you do not feel well. Paradoxically, the Plan B option is rarely needed, because the person no longer feels trapped. Having a Plan B calms the trap-induced anxiety so the person can think rationally.

Sometimes, you just need to let go. Sometimes you need to jump in. Always you need to know which is better! Here is a poem adopted and endorsed by Alcoholics Anonymous -*The Serenity Prayer*, authored by the American theologian Reinhold Niebuhr [(1892–1971).

> God, grant me the serenity to accept the things I cannot change,
>
> The courage to change the things I can,
>
> And the wisdom to know the difference.

There are so many benefits inherent in this poem. People often attempt to control others and situations. You have influence, but others maintain free will. People have *different* values, not better or worse. For example, some people are Democratic, some are Republican. Some spend money freely, some are frugal. To connect to others, accommodate their views and value the difference. That is what makes it interesting! (yes, frustrating at times, but you will gain more through honoring differences than trying to stomp it out!)

In summary, the 27 stress management techniques, described above in this chapter, involve "how to care for oneself" and "how to have effective interactions with others"—all critical in your life. These quick (often only 5-minute) stress management techniques are useful if you practice them. Make a commitment to learn a new one every few days.

REVIEW

How many of the 27 techniques did you know? _____

How many do you already use? _____

Which one really caught your attention?_____

Consider picking one that you are willing to practice every day this week?

Which one? _____

What nice reward will you give yourself if you practice it every day this week? _____

Once you feel good about using one technique, please add another technique next week to practice. Keep adding another each week.

(This may seem obvious, but like any medicine, these techniques only work if you use them and the more practice, the better!)

For more Conflict Management Techniques skip to Chapter 10; dealing with anger. Anger and Conflict behave like twins, where one is the other is sure to follow. Look at Technique 51, page 215, to use I-Statements in disagreements; Technique 52, page 216, for a formula on how to approach conflict; and Technique 53, page 217, for the Business Letter approach on how to specifically ask that your needs be met.

The next chapter introduces the powerhouse stress management-methodology of them all! This methodology involves the *Emotional Freedom Techniques*, a meridian-based technique also known as *Energy Psychology, Tapping,* or *Meridian Energy Techniques*. Once learned, it is a double winner in being the most effective and the simplest technique to implement.

CHAPTER 3:

EFT AKA TAPPING – THE BASICS

Let Go, Desensitize, and Release Old Garbage

> "A person who never made a mistake never tried anything new."
>
> --Albert Einstein

Here is the introduction to the nuts and bolts of the meridian based Emotional Freedom Techniques (EFT). Hold on for something too simple to be true. It may even be body language you already use, as illustrated in Chapter 7. It may even lower pain without even being the focus.

Super Techniques 28: **Emotional Freedom Techniques (EFT), Energy Psychology, Tapping and the Meridian Therapies**

- What if the key to calmer functioning is literately at your fingertips?

- What if you have the capacity to rebalance your own rocky emotions back to comfort and composure?

- What if you can quickly release years of turmoil that interfere with current living?

- What if you could release negative emotions, thoughts and/or physical discomfort?

Do you wonder if this is too good to be true? My experience has shown me and more than 500,000 people/practitioners that it possible. This is how many people followed Gary Craig on his web site and also were registered to listen to a Tapping Summit. Multiply that by how many people of those registered have told or treated others using the meridian based techniques. One estimate is that there are 6 million people worldwide practicing these meridian techniques. These techniques have appeared on Oprah, Larry King Live, and Dr. Oz as well as reached number 5 on the NY Times Best Seller list and number 1 on Amazon's best seller list, the *Tapping Solution*.

Let's take a peek at ways stressful situations have been calmed using meridian-based Emotional Freedom Techniques (EFT), sometimes called the "Tapping" technique. Consider where it can take you too. Think of EFT/tapping as a powerful desensitizer; one that pacifies, releases and soothes thoughts, emotions and physical reactions. In other words, EFT/Tapping is a way to release all those things that your friends and family have told you to let go of.

There is even peer-reviewed, evidence-based published research in clinical practice. In 2012, in a randomized controlled trial, Church, Yount and Brooks showed a 24% reduction in cortisol (stress hormone) levels, one half hour after treatment with EFT. Their study, *"The Effects of Emotional Freedom Techniques (EFT) on Stress Biochemistry"* was published in the Journal of Nervous and Mental Disease 200(10), 891-896. There are eighty published research too and you can access them at www.innersource.net or www.energypsych.org.

Let's first look at an explanation, and then we will jump to learn these techniques later in this chapter. Some people want to understand the origin of a technique and some just want to see the technique. You can read this section now to understand the history or just jump ahead a few pages to the section entitled Nuts and Bolts of EFT. Either way you are in for a wonderful surprise to see how easily EFT can be incorporated into your life and expand the possibilities of the mighty mind.

How Does This Work? Explanation and History

EFT is a form of *needle-less* acupuncture or acupressure using only two fingers application. (To repeat-no needles at all!)

What happens is this. By applying light touch or tapping to 11 acupoints on your face and hands while stating the negative issue; the negative emotions, thoughts and physical discomfort associated with the issue is released. Memory is not impaired, so you can always access the thought, but it just doesn't bother you the way it used to. It is desensitized, rapidly processed and released. Often this release is as rapid as 5 minutes or less. Even for very difficult issues, it is usually no longer than 20 minutes. Imagine shifting terrible events from your past in 20 minutes or so. It seems activating the acupoints with our fingers is very relaxing. Applied while talking about upsetting issue, EFT quiets and collapses the impact of the issue.

So here is the theory. Acupressure is a sister of acupuncture. Acupressure and acupuncture are foreign to those of us raised in the Western medicine atmosphere of medication, bandages, and surgeries. Here in the West, if we have pain in our throat area, we visit our primary doctor, who may refer us to an Ears Nose & Throat (ENT) specialist. This ENT specialist, if unable to decipher the etiology, may refer us to a gastroenterologist. We would pass from one specialist to another.

In China and Asia for the past 2000 to perhaps 5000 years, we would see one clinician, an acupuncturist, who is trained to treat the body as a whole. Remember the song, Dem Bones "The knee bone is connected to the thigh bone; the thigh bone is connected to the foot bone, etc.?" An acupuncturist conceptualizes the whole body as connected and that body system components are interdependent. In our country doctors specialize on specific organs and body parts.

Chinese and many Asian medicine orientations are also much more mind-body. Chinese medicine knows unequivocally that if you bang your toe (the lowest extremity of your body), intelligent thought (the highest level of your body) will be jumbled until the pain subsides. Acupuncturists conceptualize that we are like an interconnected electrical system, where any disruption may cause weaknesses, illness or discontent. EFT usually re-sets that disruption through balancing the system (and re-balancing when the goal is good health.) Here is a simple example.

> I once worked with a colleague who was terribly stressed out over an upcoming speech. She had only a few minutes before a worrisome presentation. EFT requires applying light pressure or tapping to specific acupressure points on the body. She agreed to copy me on herself as I lightly touched the acupoints on my body demonstrating the location of the acupoints. After this 5-minute impromptu treatment concluded, she gave a relaxed and clear speech on her topic. The next week she came back for an explanation. A few years later, she took my workshop and now uses these techniques in her practice.

Here are a few more pages about the history and governing bodies of EFT, before we jump in to describe the details and mechanics of EFT.

Meridian-based therapies, including EFT aka tapping in one form or another have been in the United States for thirty years. Psychologist Roger Callahan, PhD, was the first person to introduce a meridian-based therapy here with his creation, Thought Field Therapy (TFT) aka The Callahan Techniques. His famous first-case was of failed treatment of a water phobia until he added meridian-based treatment.

In Eastern medicine, meridians, which are used in acupressure and acupuncture, are mapped out bioelectrical pathways circulating throughout our body. The existence of these pathways has been proven by isotopic studies. (See EFTUniverse.com – Dr. Fred Gallo reports that French researcher Pierre De Vernejoul injected radioactive isotope into humans and tracked meridians using a special gamma imaging camera.)

Acupuncture meridians are so named by the major organs they support. Therefore, there exist the heart, gall bladder, stomach, small intestine, large intestine, thyroid, lung, circulation-sex, bladder, kidney, and spleen meridians. Additionally, there are two more meridians: one goes through the front of your body, the Central Meridian, and the other through the back of your body, the Governing Meridian.

Chi is the life energy source flowing through the meridians and is the foundation of these therapies. It is often translated to "energy" or "life force." The Chinese see us humans as having an energy flow through and around our body, and in various ways this energy influences our health and well-being. If our energy gets stuck, issues and emotions loop repeatedly through our system.

These techniques have many names (too many in my opinion). Following are some of the different terms and names that are used for these techniques. I also mention my teachers, colleagues and supporting organizations. Refer back to these next two paragraphs when you want to learn about resources or are looking for some more hands-on training or talented colleagues to connect. These organizations are welcoming to both licensed clinicians and those who are not licensed.

The Sources and Resources

These are my mentors whose footpaths I follow. You can see my video demonstration of EFT at www.YouTube.com and then type in "EFT-AAA Instructional." You can see my other demo of Heart Assisted 3 Times 3 (Technique 30) at www.YouTube.com and then type in: Heart Assisted 2 Minute Stress Relief." They can also be accessed via my name.

Energy Psychology and Meridian Therapy are general terms for all the techniques in this area. The Comprehensive Energy Psychology organization, (ACEP), www.energypsych.org, an American based organization, and the Association for the Advancement of Meridian Energy Therapies (AAMET), www.aametinternational.org, an international organization based in England, rigorously credential therapists in these modalities. I am credentialed by both organizations. They also have a separate credentialing track for those who are not licensed clinicians. I recommend their conferences highly.

These modalities and their founders include:

Emotional Freedom Techniques (Gary Craig) www.emofree.com;

Thought Field Therapy (Dr. Roger Callahan) www.tfttapping.com)

Heart Assisted Therapy (John Diepold, Jr. Ph.D.)
www.heartassistedtherapy.net;

Dr. David Feinstein's work in Energy Psychology and his wife, national lecturer Donna Eden's Energy Medicine www.Innersource.net.

Dr. Fred Gallo's book Energy *Tapping for Trauma*;

Tappas Acupressure Techniques (Tappas Fleming) www.tatlife.com;

Dr. Dawson Church's research and work with veterans www.EFTUniverse. com and www.Stressproject.org;

Nick Ortner *The Tapping Solution (and for Pain)*
www.thetappingsolutions.com

my website RobinEFT.net.

In Gary Craig's early wisdom, he put an "s" on his techniques to include many variations and viewpoints. I viewed all of his videos including guests like Sandy Radomski, who treated my asthma, and uses meridian therapies for allergy treatments (see: allergyantidotes. com.) Thus the Emotional Freedom Techniques encompassed many additions and evolutions. My particular view on EFT has evolved from many of these masters, but like a good cook, I have put my spin on it. I take responsibility for my evolution of EFT and all that is written within this book. I have streamlined and added my development from seeing thousands of clients, participating in thousands of discussions and attending many workshops with colleagues including Gary Craig in the EFT world.

Gary Craig, a Stanford University trained engineer, personal coach, and minister, simplified Callahan's techniques and called his result Emotional Freedom Techniques (EFT). EFT, a meridian-based therapy with the same theory base as acupuncture, is estimated to be 85% effective by those who extensively use it. It may be higher in efficiency depending on the skill of the user. It can be reproduced easily with or without a therapist. EFT is successfully used on individuals, families, children, small groups, and large groups. It is practiced internationally and has a wide following in England. Stress knows no geographic boundaries.

The Emotional Freedom Techniques, Thought Field Therapy, Energy Psychology, Tapping and the meridian-based therapies are rapidly developing. You have my apologies for too many names for very similar techniques. I only hope I honor Gary Craig in this book. Gary is a huge humanitarian whose techniques have been explored by more than half a million people worldwide. He truly is my guru.

Are you ready? Here we move ahead to help you to live life to the fullest. EFT will help you to do this by helping you to be in charge of stress and to gain emotional freedom.

The Nuts and Bolts of EFT/Tapping and Meridian Therapies

Let's tap that mighty mind to reach unimaginable benefits. There are five quick and easy steps to get meridian therapy like EFT/tapping working for you. It's much simpler than you might expect, and you start enjoying the benefits right away. Examples of what has worked for other people are included with the hope that will enhance your learning.

In Chapter 4, you will build on the bare bones explanation found in this chapter. First the basics - how to rate how upset you are and where the acupoints are located.

<u>SUDS</u> You will rate how upsetting issues and emotions are by using a commonly used scale called SUDS, which stands for *Subjective Unit of Distress Scale*. Pain patients are familiar with this scale. In this scale, 0 is no upset or intensity at all and 10 is the worst possible. Here is a simple diagram of a SUDS scale.

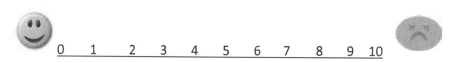

SUDS – rating the intensity of your upset

Figure 3.1. Subjective Unit of Distress Scale (SUDS)

Some stress, like a lost wallet, is clearly a SUDS rating of 8 or more, while waiting in a short line may be more like a SUDS rating of 2. Rating the upset is important, because the results are so dramatic that people actually forget the prior level of misery. The SUDS reminds them it was worst.

Acupoint Locations Let's do some exploration about exactly where those acupoints are. Slowly and lightly touch each acupoint for one breath, or a count of 5-7. You can tap 5-7 times, if you prefer. You can watch a visual of me on www.YouTube.com. Type in: *EFT-AAA instructional*. That way you can see exactly where they are and can copy me. You can change the words used there to highlight your issue. You can also find the acupoints on the next chart or in photos of each acupoint after that.

Here is a chart in Figure 3-2 below of where the acupoints are located.

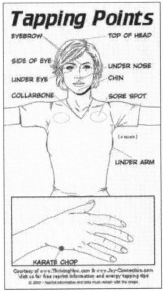

Figure 3.2. Body Locations of Acupoints (courtesy of www.thrivingnow.com). Although called tapping points here, you can also use light-touch to activate the meridian's healing power.

Acupoints and a Breathing Demonstration

Try this one minute experiment using the pictures in Figure 3.3 below to locate the 11 acupoints.

Take a normal breath and note how much of your lungs fill. Rate it on a scale using 0 to 100%. Perhaps this normal breath is 20%, 40%, 60% or so. Note the rating of your normal breath.

Now go through these acupoints for two rounds, meaning you _lightly_ touch each of the 11 acupoints, hold each point for one normal breath. Then go through the cycle a second time. Remember to go slowly, so each acupoint meridian has time to respond. They can be touched on either side or even both sides if you wish. The touch is _exquisitely light_, just enough so your nerve endings know you are there. No bruising with this very gentle touch!

Hold each acupoint for one breath (or the count of 5-7 seconds) before you move to the next pictured acupoint. This light touch is an adaptation of Dr. John Diepold's "Touch and Breathe." You can also tap 5-7 times if you prefer.

1) Side of hand, often called the karate chop. (Actual acupoint. Make a fist first. It is the fat crease next to the little finger on the palm of the hand)

2) Top of head, will even work through hats or wigs

3) Inner eyebrow

4) Side of outer eye-very close to the eye

5) Under the eye – (on the bone below the eye) – remember very lightly

6) Under the nose

7) Under the lip

8) Collar bone, either side-not the middle

9) Under the arm – 4 inches below the armpit

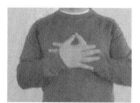

10) Gamut point –located in the indention or gully on the back of the hand between the bones connected to the little finger and the ring finger.

The next acupoint, the heart hold, is not part of the Gary Craig protocol, but I often include it.

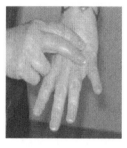

11) Heart hold – one hand over the other. This point comes from another Meridian Therapy - Heart Assisted Therapy created by Dr. John Diepold (see: www.heartassistedtherapy.net) discussed as Technique 30, later in this chapter.)

Figure 3.3. Acupoints 1-11

Each round of activating all 11 acupoints takes about 30 seconds. Let's see what your breathing is like now after two rounds, which took only one minute to accomplish. Take another normal breath and note the new rating as it fills your lungs. What is your rating based on 0 to 100%?

What difference did you notice between your first breath you measured and the breath after applying the acupoints?

Most people experience a 20% improvement and feel like they are breathing deeper. In addition to this demonstration, it may help you if you struggle to breathe when anxious. If we did this together, you would copy me as I sit a few feet away. That way, we would both get the benefit of being rebalanced and calming.

Do one more demonstration. This is particularly important if you are about to help another. It allows the person to overcome the weirdness of this technique before working on something seriously upsetting. Pick something in your life that is annoying you, something with a SUDS rating of 3 or 4 (based on 0 to10 per the graph in Figure 3.1). Don't pick anything bigger for this first demonstration. Some examples might be a bill that is wrong, a car repair, one rude remark, getting stuck in traffic, a dinner that was late, etc. Just make sure you can feel that upset *now* and the SUDS rating of intensity is below 5. Write your SUDS number down so you can compare it before and after you do this. _____

Go back to the photos of Figure 3.3 of the 11 acupoints. As you copy each acupoint, state and repeat out loud the upset about your issue. This repetitive utterance is called the *Reminder Phrase*. Repeat this for 3 rounds or for a mere 1 ½ minutes. Remember, if you need a video example, you can go to my YouTube video at www.YouTube.com and type in "EFT-AAA Instructional." Change the *Reminder Phrase* words to suit your issue and add the heart hold too.

How calm are you NOW about this issue? _____

Typically a 2 - 4 point drop occurs with every three rounds of EFT. If you are still uncomfortable about the issue, just repeat 3 more rounds. Like exercise, the more rounds of the 11 acupoints you complete, the better are your results.

If you did not notice any change, refer to Technique 42, page 181, for directions concerning how to do a simple one-minute rebalance using the "Pretzel" or the even faster 10 second Brief Energy Correction, Technique 43, page 183. Like rebooting your computer, both of these rebalance methods are quick and easy and will reset your system. Then repeat the EFT acupoints while saying your Reminder phrase.

So now that you know where the acupoints are, let's get into the 5-minute stress management capabilities of these techniques. Let's see what the fully charged EFT approach can do on real issues. The goal is to:

Bring Stress Down **to Bring Intelligence Up**

When calmer about any issue, your ability to address the issue intelligently and diplomatically is enhanced a hundred fold!

Here is a summary of the 5 steps associated with an EFT session. As an easy reminder, the first letter of each step spells CARES. CARES is a mnemonic to help us remember the steps. Thus, EFT CARES for us and our stress.

C 1) **C**hief Complaint (the issue at hand) and SUDS of the level of upset thinking about it for 5 seconds. SUDS = _____

A 2) **A**spects –what parts of this bothers me?

R 3) **R**eminder Phrase (RP) is drawn from the emotion about the issue (i.e. *mad he cheated*)

E 4) **E**FT - eleven acupoints are touched or tapped while repeating the RP until the initial SUDS decreases to a significantly lower number, indicative of being desensitized.
--Repeat on any other aspects identified in step 2.

S 5) **S**pontaneous, liberating, and intelligent insights emerge!

Here is an explanation of each step so your practice of EFT becomes more comprehensive.

Using the Five Steps to Emotional Freedom and Releasing the Stress That Binds You

Here are the steps and some recommended question.

Step 1) Chief Complaint -

What are you upset, worried, angry, or agitated about?

_____

_____

TIP: Try saying what is bothering you out loud, as if you were talking to a friend.

Ex. "I am mad about others cheating at work."

- Tune in to the issue that's bothering you. Clearly bring it up from your memory and let the emotions flow. Don't hold back. Think about it for 5 seconds. You have to feel it to treat it.

- Rate how upsetting it is NOW, in this moment, because some desensitization and processing have occurred since the event happened. Rate using the SUDS rating 0 to 10 where 10 is the worst possible. You are trying to clear the _remaining emotions_; the uncomfortable residual from stressful events from the past. SUDS = _____.

Go gently into the night...

For many issues you can go directly to the distressing event, that is, what specifically upset you. However, sometimes the issue is just too full of painful emotion to deal with directly. It's too strong, too fresh or powerful. In this case, bring up a side issue that is related, but not the core issue, one that you comfortably can begin with first.

> <u>Example</u>: I had a client who was in a terrible car accident. In our first session she couldn't discuss the accident; it

was too emotionally distressing for her. Instead, we began with how she felt when she hears ambulance sirens. This was more than enough stress for her. By the time we de-stressed that issue, she was able to continue into the core event, which was the traffic accident itself.

> **STEP 2) A**spects/Defining Moments. EFT is more effective when an issue or event is broken down into small parts, or aspects. An issue frequently has several aspects. which you can identify and list. Later you will desensitize each one by using the acupoints. As explained by EFT founder Gary Craig, think of this as a table with various legs. On the top of the table is the issue. The legs of the table are the aspects. Keep desensitizing the aspects - the legs of the table until the issue placed on the top of the table desensitizes and crumbles.

So once you think you are done, go back to the original chief complaint on the top of the table to see if it has resolved. If not, go find more legs of the table or legs to desensitize.

Examples of Several Aspects of the Same Problem

Note their slight differences and remember it is about how you feel about the *emotion* and *the issue*. Here are some examples of various aspects about the same problem.

Mad that others cheat; mad that they get away with it; mad that I have to struggle when they don't; or sad that I am not appreciated because they present better, etc.

Answer the questions below to help find the aspects of the issue that upset you. Listing your answers on paper is useful way to capture your ideas.

- What part of this issue is upsetting for you?

- What part of this are you comfortable working on?

- What was the defining moment, i.e., what was the first or worst time you experienced this issue?

71

Pick an issue you are upset about. Now list all the aspects or parts of that issue.

_____

_____

Clarification:

Meridian Therapies including EFT or Tapping are strong, but like anything they have weaknesses. If you bite off too big a chunk of a problem, it may not work. Thus, you have to work on each bite (aspect), and let EFT chew small manageable pieces. For instance, if working to desensitize a flying phobia, some contributing aspects may include: fear of turbulence; fear of heights; claustrophobia; remembering scenes from 9/11; or dislike of the new ground security.

Remember to think about the main upsetting issue sitting on top of a table. Then the legs of the table are various upsetting aspects. Keep desensitizing aspects until the main issue, fear of flying, collapses and loses its negative influence. Fear of flying is the issue on top of the table. Keep desensitizing and knocking out the "legs of the table", as the negative influence falls away and the issue (and table) collapses.

In Summary: To effectively desensitize your upsets, you have to experience the *current* effect on you in this very moment - NOW. This means that you think about the experience: the thought, the emotion, and frequently, the physical sensation for only about 5 seconds and then rate the SUDS = 0 to 10.

Reminder Phrase: Forming the *reminder phrase* is the hardest part of the technique so be gentle with yourself if you need to review it a few times to get it.

Step 3) Reminder Phrase(RP) is drawn from the aspect selected in step 2 above. It is the upsetting emotion you feel about the issue. Use this reminder phrase to focus on what you are desensitizing. Here are two examples of the RP. The reminder phrase has the following two parts:

*Emotion about the **Issue**.*

*(**worried** about **turbulence during the plane ride**)*

*(**mad** that **others get away with cheating**)*

This *RP* is the part of the technique that people struggle with. I always get asked, what should I say? It is individualized and is the hardest part. Further, *reminder phrases are italicized* in this book to help you recognize them. There are several more examples to follow.

Clarification:

The *reminder phrase* is that which accurately describes the *emotion* about the *specific issue*. The *reminder phrase* is said at each acupoint. It keeps you focused on the issue at hand, so you do not mentally wander off into the myriad distractions of everyday life.

To create the reminder phrase, remember to be honest and specific. First, what specifically, is the issue that's bothering you? Here are three different examples

- My boss yelled at me during a meeting.
- I suspect my wife of cheating on me.
- All highway drivers are reckless idiots.

Second, what specifically is the dominant emotion related to the issue? (Go ahead and name all emotions associated with the issue, but then isolate the strongest one to use in your *reminder phrase.*)

- Embarrassment.
- Heartbreak.

- Rage.

Next, by using the specific event and corresponding emotion, create your reminder phrase. Here are some different examples where the *reminder phrase* is italicized.

- I am *so embarrassed* about *my boss yelling at me in front of my colleagues.*

- I am *so heartbroken* about *the possibility my wife might be cheating on me.*

- I am *so flipping mad* about *highway drivers who are all reckless idiots.*

And there you have your reminder phrases. There are examples later are in this chapter. Remember to try to isolate the issue and corresponding emotion, and then combine them into one phrase.

Now let's look at the Set-up Statement. This is an optional soothing phrase you can add to the beginning of your reminder phrase. It's used in the very beginning of EFT.

Optional Set-up Statement.

The set-up phrase is optional. Some of my clients really enjoy an affirmation like:

"I am okay even though…"

It resonates with them. They like the self-acceptance the set-up statement instills. Others find it silly. I think its best use is to increase focus on the problem. To include the set-up statement, hold the acupoint on the side of the hand, the karate chop (Figure 3.3, picture 1), and state the set-up statement 1-3 times at the beginning of your EFT session by adding:

"I am okay even though… (I am *worried about the turbulence)*

Many EFT people intensify the Set-up statement and use self-loving words. Here is an example.

I deeply and completely love and accept myself even though…..(I am *worried about the turbulence*)

You decide which type of set-up statement you want to use, if any. Below the reminder phrase is *italicized*. Examples of two types of the set-up statement wording ("I'm okay even though...") look like the following:

- I am okay even though I am *so embarrassed about my boss yelling at me in front of my colleagues.*

  or

  I deeply and completely love and accept myself even though I am *so embarrassed about my boss yelling at me in front of my colleagues.*

- I am okay even though I'm *heartbroken about the possibility my wife might be cheating on me.*

  or

  I deeply and completely love and accept myself even though *I am heartbroken about the possibility my wife might be cheating on me.*

- I'm okay even though I'm *so flipping mad about highway drivers who are all reckless idiots.*

  or

  I deeply and completely love and accept myself even *though I'm so flipping mad about highway drivers who are all reckless idiots.*

When the issue is currently active—for example, you just got cut off in traffic—there is little need for a set-up statement; the reminder phrase alone will do. Just state the reminder phrase:

"upset I got cut off in traffic."

This simple *reminder phrase* captures it all, grammar is not the issue.

Step 4 puts EFT all together. After a few tries, the steps will become second nature to you!

STEP 4) EFT: Use the diagram in Figure 3.2 or the pictures in Figure 3.3 above to remind you where the acupoints are.

*Remember to state the reminder phrase (emotion about the issue), while lightly touching each acupoint so you stay focused and desensitize this emotion and issue.

*Repeat the 11 acupoints round at least three times or more until you feel the upset collapsing. This is evidenced by more and more relaxation and calm as you think of the issue. After each three rounds of the acupoints, check in to what your SUDS rating (0 to 10) is on the issue.

*Repeat this process until you can bring the SUDS rating as low as possible; close to zero is ideal.

*Reassess: Once this aspect is very calm, cycle again through the process described above at the beginning of the explanation of step 2, looking for new aspects (if any) of this very same problem. You want to clean out the entire upset to be rid of its negative influence.

Emotion Worksheet example: your boss yelling at you.

Touch and hold for one breath or tap about 7 times:

Acupoints and say the Reminder Phrase

(the emotion about issue)

Karate chop	*embarrassed about my boss yelling at me publicly.*
Top of head	*embarrassed about my boss yelling at me publicly.*
Inner Eyebrow	*embarrassed about my boss yelling at me publicly.*
Outer eye	*embarrassed about my boss yelling at me publicly.*
Under the eye	*embarrassed about my boss yelling at me publicly.*
Under the nose	*embarrassed about my boss yelling at me publicly.*
Under the lip	*embarrassed about my boss yelling at me publicly.*
Collarbone	*embarrassed about my boss yelling at me publicly.*
Under the arm	*embarrassed about my boss yelling at me publicly.*
Gamut Point	*embarrassed about my boss yelling at me publicly.*
Heart hold	*embarrassed about my boss yelling at me publicly.*

Figure 3.4. Example of putting it all together - Acupoints and Reminder Phrase.

After *embarrassment over your boss yelling at you publicly* has calmed down, let's say your dominant emotion has now shifted from embarrassment to anger. Go ahead and switch the reminder phrase to:

"so angry at my boss for yelling at me publicly"

The goal or "top of the table" is to calm down about being yelled at publicly by knocking down the aspects holding the "table" up. *Embarrassment* was one aspect or "leg of the table" while *anger* was another aspect "leg of the table." The key is to be as specific as possible and to be persistent in locating as many aspects of the stressful issue as possible. Remember we tend to repeat the whole process in series of three rounds; and it depends on how may rounds it takes to diminish the SUDS intensity. It may take 3, 6, 9 or even 12 rounds to desensitize.

More Aspects

Are you done with your upset with your boss? Maybe and maybe not. If you are still upset, there may be more aspects to this issue. Like peeling an onion, there may be different layers to the problem. Keep your mind open to the idea that there may be more to work on.

 and Ask Yourself

- What else is bothering me about this issue?

- What other angles are upsetting me?

At some point, the entire chief complaint, the feelings about the issue you identified at step 1, become inconsequential and without any upset. After collapsing each aspect, review the issue to see if it too is totally desensitized. If not, go find another aspect and treat that. When all is calm, step 5, Spontaneous Insight emerges.

Step 5) Spontaneous insight is a liberating idea, a plan of action, or total emotional freedom from the previous upset. EFT calms excessive negative emotions, - thus liberating your problem solving skills, and ability to be diplomatic when approaching this issue with your boss. Once calm, most people have a spontaneous insight, an "aha" experience where the issue and a possible solution are clear.

It is what you feel or think after the issue is desensitized. The disturbing thought and feeling from the past no longer push you into unhealthy reactions. Your thinking is no longer clouded by emotions. It is more resourceful. My clients often signal this shift has arrived by a new smile.

In this example, the spontaneous insight may be considering talking to him privately about his behavior, the effect it has on you and hopefully coming to some better agreement. If that does not work, a conversation with someone from your Human Resources Department may help.

Incorporating EFT: Remember you read about five steps for healing in Technique 3 on page 20. Add EFT to step 4 as a way to heal. EFT is the way to desensitize many emotions including your fear, allowing your courage and confidence to merge.

Here is a piece of wisdom from the master himself!

Technique 29 : Personal Peace Procedure

Personal Peace Procedure

Gary Craig created an EFT Personal Peace Procedure. Write down anything that bothers you. Anyone who is honest will have 20-50 things very quickly. Now imagine eliminating one a day, and at the end of the year there will be 365 things that just do not bother you anymore. What a way to de-clutter our emotion driven, mighty brains! I did this for about 3 years and now there are 1000 things that I am grateful that do not bother me! Please do this too.

Sometimes a person begins to have EFT shortcuts where you can use one acupoint to obtain benefit. Some people begin to note 1 or 2 acupoints that just does it for them. Have you noticed any acupoint that releases a lot of your tension?

Next is another powerful Energy Psychology technique.

Heart Assisted Therapy

Heart Assisted Therapy (HAT), created by psychologist Dr. John Diepold, Jr., is demonstrating some spectacular promise for obtaining profound results. This is a comprehensive mind-body approach that incorporates many theories of psychology. I strongly recommend Dr. Diepold's workshops to gain advanced usage of this promising technique. My admiration to Dr. Diepold on his inventiveness and contributions to Energy Psychology. (See: www.heartassistedtherapy.net). My adaptation follows.

Technique 30 : **3 Times 3**

I borrowed several components of HAT for a simple, soothing stress management technique, calling it "3 Times 3," to easily remember what to do with your hands. This "user-friendly" technique is applied by 3 hand shifts and 3 breaths on each hand shift. Basically, hands are placed one on top of the other, in the center of the chest over the heart, as the person verbalizes his issue. This feels like a gentle, self-hug, but the calming capability is more powerful than you would think. I have used this technique in noisy health fairs to calm stress. Besides stress management, I have taught this to several very angry clients as a quick anger-management tool too. See Figure 3.3, picture 11 for the placement of your hands over the middle of your body at the level of the heart.

You can see my demonstration of this on www.YouTube.com and then search for - Heart Assisted 2 Minute Stress Relief. (You can also find my YouTube.com demonstrations by searching for my name –"Robin Bilazarian").

Pick something that is bothering you.

Here is an example.   *Furious that I did not get picked for that position*

Here are the steps:

- **First Hand Shift:**

To begin, place your hands over the middle of your body at the level of your heart. Here is an example of the verbalization that is repeated on all 3 hand shifts:

> "I am okay even though... (*I am furious I did not get picked for that position*)"

Sit quietly for 3 breaths.

- **Second Hand Shift:**

Then, shift the hands, so the top hand is now the bottom hand. Repeat the same statement.

> "I am okay even though... *(I am furious I did not get picked for that position)*"

Sit quietly for 3 breaths.

- **Third Hand Shift: (actually is the same as the first hand shift)**

Lastly, shift the hands again so the current bottom hand is on top again. Repeat the same statement.

> "I am okay even though... (*I am furious I did not get picked for that position*)"

Sit quietly for 3 breaths.

Useful Question: After completing these three rounds ask "what are you feeling, thinking or noticing now about the issue just addressed?"

This new thought or feeling replaces the previous statement. Repeat the three hand shifts with 3 quiet breaths on each hand movement, using the new feeling or thought such as:

> "I am okay even though... *(I dislike what I am doing and that position would have been a perfect change for me.")*

Keep following the new thoughts repeating the technique until the original upset defuses. Your statement will change to a neutral or positive thought or feeling. Finish the technique by repeating this positive thought or feeling in the same 3 Times 3 format.

> "I am okay even though... *(I did not get that position as it does require mandatory overtime which is difficult with my young family.)*

As stated, this "3 Times 3" technique is also a good remedy to quell anger burning in your body or to quell your reaction to the issue that made you angry. Using the same method, you would keep asking yourself –

> **What am I thinking, feeling or noticing about my anger at that person or situation?**

After several rounds, your statement will be neutral or positive. Go ahead, try it and be pleasantly surprised at how simply you can calm yourself and your issue. This technique probably uses the powerful but soothing electricity coming from your heart and the many bioelectrical meridians that flow through your hands.

> ### Review and Emotion Worksheet
>
> 1)   Do you remember how to form a Reminder Phrase (RP)?
>
> It is the (emotion about the issue).
>
> Say your issue out loud and then pick up the emotion about the issue.

2)   What is the SUDS rating?

Subjective Unit of Distress Scale is your opinion of how upset you are.

3)   Why   is   the   SUDS   rating   be   important?
_____.

EFT is so quick and easy, people actually forget how upset they were. It's helpful to review the rating and remember the SUDS was initially higher.

4)   Do you remember where the 11 acupoints are located?

You will after a few more practice sessions and there are pictures and graphs to remind you in this chapter.

5)   Try to quiet a nagging issue using Technique 30, the 3 Times 3 method. Remember after every three rounds, ask yourself what am I thinking, feeling or noticing now about this upsetting issue?

Repeat 3 Times 3 until a neutral or positive emerge.

Emotion Worksheet:

1) Chief Complaint –what is bugging you?

How much does it bug you 0 to 10? SUDS =_____

2) Aspect –What about this chief complaint is the worst?

Or What am I willing to work on first?

3) Reminder phrase   (emotions about this aspect))

What emotion do I feel about this aspect?

4) EFT - Add the reminder phrase to the following table for 3 rounds or more until it just does not bother you much anymore.

Touch or tap these acupoints while saying the Reminder Phrase (the emotion about issue)

Emotion Worksheet Optional Set Up: I am okay even though ....reminder phrase (RP)

RP = (*Emotion* about the *issue*)

Karate chop	(_____about_____)
Top of head	(_____about_____)
Inner Eyebrow	(_____about_____)
Outer Eye	(_____about_____)
Under the eye	(_____about_____)
Under the nose	(_____about_____)
Under the lip	(_____about_____)
Collarbone	(_____about_____)
Under the arm	(_____about_____)
Gamut Point	(_____about_____)
Heart hold	(_____about_____)

Figure 3.6. Emotion Worksheet

What is my SUDS level of intensity now? Should I do more rounds of this? Should I consider another aspect from Step 2?

5) **S**pontaneous insight. Since my upset has changed, what do I want to do about this issue in a productive manner?

Good job! You now have a great tool in EFT and Tapping for when stress irritations, annoyance, problems, pain and more gets the better of you.

In Chapter 4, I will answer typical questions about EFT that I have received from clients and trainees. They may be the same ones you have as well. Chapter 4 will fine tune this skill. Then, for the adventurous, Chapter 5 will take you into the "deep cleaning" of your old issues.

CHAPTER 4:

REFINING EFT (aka Tapping)

"Creativity is intelligence having fun."

- Albert Einstein

Refining Your EFT Experience:
STRESS RELIEF, aka EFT and Tapping

You learned how to do bare bones EFT, Tapping and meridian therapy in the last chapter. Here we will refine the concepts. Hopefully, any questions you have will be answered here and the next few chapters.

So here the scoop about how this works.

When we experience an upsetting event in our lives, negative feelings occur and attach themselves to the memories. Even negative body sensations which is talked about extensively in Chapter 6. Each time we remember the incident we re-experience the unpleasant emotions. Perhaps you witnessed a terrible car accident. Every time you think back on it you'll also re-experience the horrible feelings associated with having seen people injured or killed. You may even vividly recall the sounds of crumbling metal or need to cover your eyes with your hands to "block out" the images. Our brain contains old emotional issues and events. It is as if a pattern was installed at the event.

These negative experiences in our lives create the stress we live with. Maybe it's over an upset at work, a failed relationship, or the apprehension about an adolescent child with substance abuse problems. Stress is uncomfortable, debilitating, bad for our health, and simply makes life that much harder. Stress clutters our minds and stresses every system of our body, leaving us feeling uneasy.

Sometimes, stress will continue to reverberate within us even after a considerable amount of time has passed. It's as if we don't know how to turn off this lingering stress.

One event can remind of another. Negative feelings can be triggered in similar circumstances, even when the connection is vague. You may sob at the funeral of a colleague's father - a man you never met because you remember the funeral of your family member. You may become upset by a song, because it reminds you of a failed relationship. You may get uncomfortable in an art museum, because a picture reminds you of your deceased, beloved grandmother. Perhaps your tears at the movie had deeper causes than the main character's dog. Sometimes you are aware of the triggers involved, and sometimes you aren't.

EFT directs you to think about those negative stressful thoughts while you are stimulating the acupoints. This creates a profound relaxation instead of the usual upset connected to the issue. EFT defuses, releases, and desensitizes the charge of the issue, the corresponding emotions, and the connected physiological discomfort. EFT returns control to you of your body and emotions. 3 Times 3 (Technique 30) does this too.

EFT and all meridian therapies also treat physiological hyperarousal and affect dysregulation. Physiological hyperarousal is when you feel like you stuck your finger in an electrical circuit, when you're panicky, and when you are freaking out. It is when you are too restless to sit, your heart and mind are racing, you feel tremulous throughout your body, and/ or your stomach is doing somersaults. It can be felt as a tightness or tension in your body. A panic attack is an example of this.

Affect dysregulation is when you feel unable to control your emotions. You may be labile, flipping quickly between the extremes of emotions. You may fluctuate from tearful to angry, to giddy, to remorseful. You may feel stuck in a negative emotion and be unable to find peace. It is the opposite of peaceful. Continue applying the EFT acupoints even if you cry as that crying will stop soon.

The next several chapters are designed to teach you how to break the stubborn connection between an event, troublesome feelings, and any lingering stress, so they no longer interfere with your daily living nor influence your life choices. Once understood, this is usually only a 5 minute release.

I'll discuss ways to delve deeper into belief patterns that may be limiting your true potential. True de-cluttering of your life!

The Leap into a Gentler Treatment

The meridian techniques, including EFT, are fun, funny, unique, and cutting edge. While cutting edge in the USA, they are centuries old in China and Asia. They are quite accepted in England.

In China, we would visit with one acupuncturist who would work with and re-balance our body as a whole, recognizing all our body systems are interconnected. The Eastern focus is on the mind-body connection. It is as if there is a blockage in our human electrical system that interferes with optimal functioning. But for us in the West, this is an unusual thought, a paradigm switch from what we have been raised to believe is right. (However in the West, we also recognize electrical charges in the heart by performing EKG's, in the brain by testing with EEG's and even the horrible EMG to test nerve functioning.)

The essence of Complementary and Integrative Medicine is the combination of Eastern and Western practices. The idea is not that one is better than the other, but that when used together they have the strongest and longest lasting results. Humans are complex creatures, and sometimes different approaches are needed to solve a single problem. Thus, the material in Chapter 2 - typical Western psychological tools - combined with EFT surpasses each other alone.

Acupoints, Acupressure and Acupuncture

Meridians circulate throughout your body and are often named after the major organ that sustains the meridian. Meridian techniques, used in this psychotherapy and in EFT, are associated with three body areas: the face, upper torso, and hands. These directly correlate to acupuncture meridian points, discussed in the last chapter. You can recall where those acupoints are by the "Body Locations of Acupoints Diagram" in Chapter 3 (Figure 3.2), the Emotion Worksheet (Figure 3.4) and photos of these acupoints in Figure 3.3 of Chapter 3.

In my experience, I've found that including the gamut point on the hand (see Figure 3.3, picture10) is a powerful tool, although some EFT professionals have eliminated this point. I include it because the gamut point is the estimated acupoint for physical and emotional pain (depression). Many of my clients have both. It is also known as the triple warmer or thyroid meridian. The triple warmer interfaces with those systems that regulate the thyroid.

> **Interesting Aside:** Thyroid functioning is tested in psychiatric hospitals, because thyroid disease can mimic severe depression.
>
> It makes sense that physical and emotional pain are wired together. Hurting physically (being punched) or emotionally (yelled at) elicits the same response—crying. Further, many depression medicines are also used for physical pain management. While the specific wiring may not yet be understood, this is certainly evidence of a connection between physical and emotional pain and the gamut point addressed both.

Technique 31: Tap, Touch, or Camouflaged Application of the Acupoints

The minute I say *acupressure,* the entire world hears me say *acupuncture.* Don't worry; needles are not involved in any way with this. Using your own two fingers to gently touch or tap on acupoints works because they use the same meridian as acupuncture. Stimulation of the acupoints is the basis for EFT and many other meridian-based therapies.

Almost everyone in the field is stimulating the acupoints with about 7 light to medium taps on each point. Tapping is a common name for this. This works fine but can look a little strange. Think about it. You're nervously sitting on the subway, tapping various spots on your face and hands and mumbling all the while. Guaranteed you'll have vacant seats next to you!

There is another way that looks more normal and is therefore more comfortable for many people. A light touch on the acupoints is inconspicuous, gentle, and portable, as opposed to tapping which is very attention grabbing. Either of these methods works well to activate the acupoints. For the last twelve years I've applied a gentle touch rather than tapping. This is every bit as effective. Gentle touch is my adaptation of John Diepold, Ph.D.'s "Touch and Breathe" approach. (http://theamt. com/touch_and_breathe.htm)

This light touch on the acupoints can be applied inconspicuously anywhere, anytime. I call it "Camouflaged EFT." Pictures of body language in Chapter 7 will give you ideas of how to camouflage your touch. Reposition your touch slowly so movement is not discernible; calming yourself anywhere, anytime. For example, camouflage EFT if you are called to your supervisor's office. Tapping in his waiting room on these acupoints would raise even further concerns about your employment stability!

The challenge is to go slowly, because it is easy to pick up speed. If I am going too fast to the next acupoint, I add a count of five to seven to slow down. Some acupuncturists leave the needles in for a full twenty minutes. Thus, slow it down. You want your body to register and disseminate the flowing benefits of the touch for ultimate soothing results.

Going through one round of each of the 11 acupoints from the Emotions Worksheet in Figure 3.4 takes about thirty seconds. Repetitions of 3, 6, or 9 rounds—all under 5 minutes—are still quite rapid solutions for desensitizing most upsets.

Why repeat the touching or tapping so many times? Like many things, the more the better. One bite of dinner, one jumping jack, or one quick peek at the television needs repetition to obtain the benefit. A long hug feels better than a quick pat. Activation of the acupoints with their soothing benefit is enhanced with repeated application.

Other than its effects in early childhood, little is written about the benefit of touch in mainstream journals. Ever have a massage and feel relaxed beyond description? Ever have a caring person hug you when you were upset? Ever notice a screaming baby calm immediately when lifted to their parent's bosom? Notice the profound calming effect these have on the raw nerve ends. Perhaps this effective self-touch falls into this same category.

Tip to Demonstrate EFT to Another

Sit at a comfortable therapeutic distance, perhaps four to six feet apart. I demonstrate on myself—touching my acupoints while repeating the reminder phrase. I instruct the client to copy me and play "Simon Says," and I get to be Simon, because I know the acupoints. Both as a teaching tool and to maintain appropriate boundaries, this increases the chance others will apply these techniques independently whenever needed. It also simultaneously desensitizes me, thus avoiding my own professional burn-out and compassion fatigue. I always do a demonstration first, often on a chore they dislike. I want the person to be comfortable with the method BEFORE going into their real issues.

Technique 32: Wording - the Art of Capturing the Reminder Phrase (RP)

At this point, I've discussed the main principles of EFT, and the fact that light touch works well as a way to stimulate acupoints while remaining inconspicuous. The next step is to attach specific wording to each issue, which enables us to focus on exactly what we want to desensitize. Wording is key and capturing the words to develop the Reminder Phrase (RP) is an art.

For example, let's say you feel stressed over your mother-in-law's controlling ways. You begin using EFT by thinking of your anger at your mother-in-law, but your mind quickly jumps to what you're going to make for dinner. You're going to desensitize any stress related to cooking dinner, not your mother-in-law if you don't stay focused.

The *RP* is what will keep your mind and therefore the benefits of EFT on target. While activating your acupoints with a light touch, you will state the RP to desensitize the upset and calm down your angst about that particular issue.

The *emotion* about *the issue* is described by the reminder phrase. The key is the more specific you are, the better the results. I will give you many examples of what to say. You can create the formula! It does not have to be perfect. Here are the questions to ask.

 and Ask

- **What exactly about this issue is bothering me?** Go deep. Be as honest as you can. It may be the largest part of the problem or surprise you by being something so small and petty. If it bothers you, it matters. Asking yourself, even out loud, what bothers you the most about an issue can guide you to capture the reminder phrase.

- **What emotions do I feel?** What part of this makes your blood boil? Again, go deep. Is it hurt, embarrassment or fear? Anger? Humiliation? Grief? Write down all of them. Nobody will see this but you. If you're working with someone else, choose a trustworthy person so you can be completely honest.

Don't worry if you don't get it exactly right the first time. You can do the EFT circuits as many times as you like. Try to be as specific as possible stating the *emotion about the issue*. The more finely you can attune the reminder phrase to what you're feeling, the more directly you will clear the stress. By ridding yourself of the stress you'll gain a clearer mind.

Further Ideas on Finding the Reminder Phrase

If you're having trouble coming up with your reminder phrases, this section is for you. If not, then skip to the next section on The Subjective Unit of Distress rating scale. You do not need to create a reminder phrase

91

if you are experiencing the upset right now, in this moment, as the upset is overriding all else. Just go with your upsetting feeling.

Otherwise, EFT wants you to be as specific as possible, in order to experience the emotional issue you wish to desensitize. The reminder phrase creates focus. Otherwise, you would desensitize yourself to whatever random thought you were experiencing. The reminder phrase is one of the major differences between this technique and its sister, acupuncture. In acupuncture, no specific thought is used.

If you are unable to experience an emotion or physical discomfort, the issue is probably already desensitized and really does not bother you much.

The only exception is when events are so severe, as in Post-Traumatic Stress Disorder that our emotions and sensations become blunted, protectively keeping the lid on the issue. In this case you should work with a professional therapist to help you resolve the associated stress.

So you have lived to the grand old age of 15, 20, 50, or 65? You have emotional clutter. No age is too young; no age is too old. My sweet 6-month old great nephew just went through corrective surgery. He now has emotional clutter. When he is older, he may struggle to visit a hospital. He may have to desensitize. Here's a reminder phrase he may need to use in the future: *Scared about imagining how I felt about my surgery.*

Below are some examples that are taken from typical life situations. The Reminder Phrase is italicized. Use the Worksheet at the end of Chapter 3 (Figure 3.6) to desensitize if any anything similar applies to you. The reminder phrase is an *emotion* felt about *the issue.*

A kid in class called you "stupid."

How did that make you feel? *Tormented (emotion)*

What made you feel tormented? *Being called stupid (issue)*

The RP is – *Tormented about being called stupid.*

Your parents had an awful argument with swearing and loud hurling insults.

What bothered me? (Issue): *the fight my parents had.*

How did it make me feel? (Emotion): *Scared.*

The RP is – *scared about the fight my parents had.*

Here are more examples.

To find the issue ask: *what bothered me?*

To find the emotion ask: *how did it make me feel?*

You forgot an assignment at home.

The RP is - *worried about being in trouble at school.*

The restaurant is serving very slowly.

The RP is – *greatly annoyed about waiting.*

You stub your toe.

The RP is - *ouch, achy about my toe is killing me.*

During your commute, you get stuck in traffic.

The RP is - *nervous about being late for work.*

You are told to work late.

The RP is – *upset about not wanting to work late.*

Figure 4.1. Creating Reminder Phrases

Technique 33: Systematic Desensitization- A Hierarchy of Reminder Phrases

Another way to think about digging deeper with EFT is to borrow from Cognitive-Behavioral Therapy (CBT), which I discussed earlier in Technique 25, page 25. In CBT you create a hierarchy of progressively more difficult situations. The higher up on the hierarchy, the greater the intensity of the event. Each level is progressively more difficult. This is also called Exposure Therapy. Just use EFT to desensitize the progressively more difficult steps.

For instance, let's say you're too anxious to fly. Do these in your imagination.

Begin by imaging driving to the airport. Next imagine going inside a terminal and using EFT until calm. You may next imagine heading toward a gate using EFT. Progress to getting on an airplane, take off and more - all while applying EFT. If you have a severe case, you can actually do these actions as a dry run while using EFT to calm your jitters.

EFT is one way to desensitize the hierarchies. The hierarchy list becomes the *reminder phrases*.

Example:

Nervous about *driving to the airport.*

Feeling dread about *entering the terminal*

Racing heart about *seeing the gate.*

Or if your issue is fear of seeing a dentist, the hierarchy may begin with imagining walking into his office calming yourself with EFT. Next, actually make an appointment and use EFT to calm yourself. Then imagine sitting in the dental chair applying EFT until calm. Imagine these steps while calming yourself.

The point is as follows: you can work through your stressful issue by using EFT in small steps, rather than going after it all in one big chunk.

Unlike many positive therapies that tell you to change your negative thoughts to positive ones, EFT says bring up the negative feelings and thoughts. "Bring them on!" Bring them on so they can be released permanently. You don't have to control negative thoughts, because they are gone!

When you actually think about and re-experience the emotions surrounding the issue that's upsetting you, you will be able to desensitize them. This is not cruel, since you are thinking about the upset for a mere 5 seconds! Five seconds is all that is needed to bring the upset into view! Because many people try to cope by putting the upsetting thought out of mind, EFT can appear to be paradoxical. This is because you do ask the person to think of the worst. But EFT then takes the emotional power out of the upset!

Next, let's look at a severe case of mental illness and how EFT is applied and beneficial.

CASE Chronic Mentally ill Clients Benefit from Using EFT – Example 4.1

For the past three years a client with bipolar disorder incorporated EFT to reduce stress. These are the only three years of his adult life that he was not hospitalized at least once a year. He uses EFT whenever he feels overwhelmed by life events, thus avoiding extreme stress, rocketing emotions, and subsequent hospitalizations.

Below are some of the situations where he used EFT:

> I am ok even though *I am upset my father took my money.*
>
> I am ok even though *I am angry the pharmacy did not have my medication on file.*
>
> I am ok even though *I am worried my landlord is selling this house.*

His case is truly an example of complementary medicine. EFT was used to calm stress, talk therapy was used to emphasize realistic decision making and self-care, and traditional psychotropic medication was employed to stabilize his moods. All three therapies were necessary, in order to help desensitize upsets and maintain this severely ill person's stability!

Below is an Emotion Worksheet example of an EFT round with which this same client treated himself. Light touch was applied sequentially to each of the 11 acupoints, while he repeated the *Reminder Phrase*. As instructed, he did these three or more times for each stress reducing session, until he became calm.

Emotion Worksheet	
Touch Acupoints and Say the *Reminder Phrase*	
	(*the emotion about the issue*)
Karate chop	*upset about my father taking my money*
Top of head	*upset about my father taking my money*
Inner Eyebrow	*upset about my father taking my money*
Outer Eye	*upset about my father taking my money*
Under the eye	*upset about my father taking my money*
Under the nose	*upset about my father taking my money*
Under the lip	*upset about my father taking my money*
Collarbone	*upset about my father taking my money*
Under the arm	*upset about my father taking my money*
Gamut Point	*upset about my father taking my money*
Heart hold	*upset about my father taking my money*

Figure 4.2. Example of Acupoints Coupled with the Reminder Phrase.

His spontaneous insight: "I am okay. I cannot let my father's behavior put me over the edge. I have a friend and can borrow some money until my check comes."

Next let's elaborate on a rating system and its other uses.

Technique 34: The SUDS (Subjective Units of Distress Scale)

As mentioned in chapter 3, the SUDS is a common tool used by the medical and psychotherapy world that measures either emotional upsets or physical pain. The SUDS (Subjective Unit of Distress Scale) is based on your personal evaluation of the effect a certain issue is having on you. This rating originated in cognitive-behavioral therapy and is also used by the medical profession to obtain your impression of your current physical pain level. For our purposes, it is used to as a gauge to assess the level of change of your emotional upset. Thus, there is an initial rating and then subsequent ratings after completing each 3 rounds of EFT.

The SUDS intensity fluctuates from 0 to 10, with 0 meaning no upset exists and you are completely calm, neutral or happy. At the other end of the range, 10 means the worst possible upset and you are on the verge (or past the verge) of hysteria.

Here are some simple examples to give you the idea. Assign numbers to the following phrases based on the above scale. This is basic but will get the point across. What is your SUDS numeral reaction to the following descriptions?

- Your best friend is at work today. _____

- Your best friend left for work late again. _____

- Your best friend had a fist fight with a co-worker. _____

Obviously, the SUDS level increased as you went down the list. Furthermore, in life what upsets one person may not upset another. The event may be the same, but the emotional reaction can be quite different.

Examples:

The Red Sox lost to the Yankees.
The disappointment for me was a 1, my husband was a 6, and my son was a 9.

Our overgrown grass was not cut today as promised.
My anger scale was a 6, my husband was a 9, and my daughter was a 0.

How do you measure your SUDS level? One way is through body sensations. Heart rate, stomach, nervous tremors, body tension, eye pupil dilation, shaking foot or hand, and every body language movements are clues. Another way to determine your SUDS is being aware of difficult emotions that are out of normal control. We might cry, feel angry, sad, worried, etc.

Rate your emotional upset now on any issue. Also, rate the intensity of your physical discomfort on the issue.

and Ask Yourself:

Choose an issue that's currently causing you stress, and ask yourself the following questions:

- How upsetting is this issue for me right NOW on a scale from 0 to 10, where 10 is the worst possible?

Or...

- How intensely do I feel this issue right NOW on a scale from 0 to 10, where 10 is the worst possible?

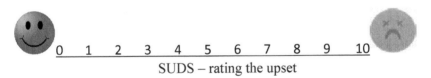

SUDS – rating the upset

Figure 4.3. Subjective Unit of Distress Scale (SUDS) Graph

SUDS Notation

Below is a notation formula for recording SUDS levels as they drop. This is an easy way to note your progress. The benefits of EFT occur so fast that you can forget how badly you felt. The SUDS notation is a good reminder.

SUDS: 8 →4→ 0 or you can skip the interim rating and just record SUDS 8→ 0.

Thus, I may write in my record:

> "Desensitized John from his upset over his argument with his employer SUDS 8→ 0. He now plans to schedule a meeting for the two of them to have a discussion about this so this does not reoccur every time there is mandatory overtime."

> You might write, "Desensitized myself SUDS 8→0 on my argument with my boss and will meet with him to discuss better ways to handle mandatory overtime."

Tip - Another use for SUDS in your life

Using a SUDS level in navigating relationships can also be useful as a shared communication tool.

"I'm an 8 on this topic, give me an hour to calm down so I can think and act rationally." Or

"You're yelling like a 7, let's take a break and discuss this later after we both calm down."

This is a great improvement over intimidating our family members with our body by groaning, rolling our eyes, shouting, or sarcastic rebuffing. It reduces uncomfortable and disrespectful drama!

It can also be used to let others know your pain or fatigue level. Used on a recent trip, it was easier for others to understand that I was a "6" after climbing to that hilly monastery and needed to sit a bit.

When our most stressful issues happened they were all a SUDS of 9 or 10. Time, venting, and problem solving lessen the intensity of the issue. The meridian therapies including EFT or 3 Times 3 will quell whatever is left-over from the event by focusing on how you feel <u>NOW</u>

REVIEW True or false?

1) T or F   The SUDS (Subjective Unit of Distress Scale) is an intensity meter used by psychotherapists, pain managers and even in your family to let them know just how unhappy, hurt or stressed you are.

2) T or F   The activation of the acupoints can be done by tapping, rubbing or touch. The touch can even be concealed and inconspicuously camouflaged.

3) T or F   The trick of obtaining major benefit from the repetitive touching of the acupoints is in formulating a Reminder Phrase to focus on desensitizing a specific upset.

4) T or F   Persistence and repetition of EFT rounds are important.

Chapter 5 will show you some ways to become unstuck when addressing more serious issues.

(By the way, all the answers in the review box are true.)

CHAPTER 5:

CLEARING OLD STUFF

Until we are all free, we are none of us free."

- Emma Lazarus

Old emotional clutter maintains your painful past as well as the childish, tactless, reactive and counterproductive behavior in your current life! In other words, past hurts may contribute to ineffective drama in the present. Ridding oneself of emotional clutter creates potential to flourish. You grow up emotionally and act maturely.

Technique 35: Going Deeper – Clearing Emotional Clutter with EFT

In the previous two chapters, you learned the ins and outs of using EFT to help you get rid of stressful issues in your life. So, you may ask, why go deeper? And certainly, why devote an entire chapter to the subject?

The reasons are twofold. First, old, deep-seated issues that have been left untreated can be triggered by everyday events in the present. Some of these issues you may have become so used to that you don't even realize they're bogging you down. We learned lessons from these difficult events, some beneficial, some not. Some of the lessons may even be unnecessary and outdated–such as never cross the street without an adult. Thus, we may unconsciously apply these outdated lessons where they are no longer needed. Other issues are just plain stubborn and extra effort is needed to get rid of their negative effects.

Second, if you don't treat new upsets as they come up, over time they become triggers too. Reducing stress and its aftermath in your life is not a one-time occurrence. Because of the world we live in, stress is a constant, and we need to be continuously vigilant about getting rid of the damage it leaves behind.

These lingering effects of stressful events in our lives are what I call *emotional clutter*. I'll provide you with an easy, five-step process for ridding yourself of emotional clutter, as we go deeper into your old issues.

First, I want to cover some background about emotional clutter, so you understand exactly what's happening to you that you may not be aware of.

Emotional Clutter Explanation

Emotional clutter is what's left over after we've taken an emotional punch. Picture a prize fighter in the ring. Notice how his head slams back with each punch taken. Emotional punches happen to us all day long in varying degrees - as if our heads are getting hit with disappointments.

These punches can leave us feeling irritable, nervous, and out of control, if we don't effectively calm ourselves. For example, you could be stuck on a roadway, where the traffic has slowed to a stall and is making you late for a meeting. In the future, you don't even remember why you avoid this convenient road. This small experience leaves a mark on you: emotional clutter -that detracts from the mighty mind's effectiveness.

Maybe a co-worker snaps at you and you feel off for the rest of the day. Or your paycheck doesn't clear in time and you're late with your bills. All of these experiences leave marks on us.

Many of these punches occur when we're children and don't know how to deal with negative remarks and rejection. Perhaps your mother was hard on you when you made a mistake. Now you cringe at the thought of messing up, and are indecisive and timid.

Perhaps you were told you were ugly during an argument with an angry child, and you've been overly conscious of your appearance ever since. You forgot that the angry child wanted to hurt you at that moment, and you have incorporated that criticism into your self-perception.

Maybe you were in a car accident and are reticent to drive certain places. These experiences leave a memory trail.

These are all punches, affronts to our bodies, minds and emotions, and can leave us feeling overwhelmed. Many times the effects are completely unconscious, but they exist nonetheless. Our physiology is activated and we feel stressed. Too many emotional punches leave you worn, dismayed, and beaten down. Untreated, they sap your motivation, resolve, and energy. These fuel present problems, making them bigger!

Extreme forms of emotional clutter can even lead to all the psychiatric diagnoses, including: depression, anxiety, panic attack, phobias, obsessive-compulsive traits, acute stress disorder, and post-traumatic stress disorder. Emotional punches and the emotional clutter they leave short-circuit our effectiveness in our jobs and family lives. They hold us back from personal fulfillment. They can even cause us to look physically run down.

But it doesn't have to be this way. EFT and all the Meridian Therapies can help clear the clutter so we can function at higher and more productive levels. Emotional clutter happens at all phases of life, and by going deeper with EFT we can reduce its effects.

Triggers

Have you ever noticed how you overreact to something that you realize in hindsight wasn't that big a deal? This happens when we are stressed in our current life, and something triggers our old emotional clutter. This clutter raises its ugly head and awakens the pain of an old injury, which causes us to overreact to the new situation. Our response is out of proportion, because it has been affected by old emotional clutter.

Now let's go deeper into emotional clutter. Below are 3 examples of difficult events, also called defining moments, and continue to trigger ongoing emotional stress. These defining moments were dangerous and the struggle with them (emotional clutter) continues even if their danger no longer applies.

> I am jumpy near that park. What happened there? A bully chased me in the park.

> I hate going by that hospital. Why? My friend died there.

> I am reminded of my overly-stern mother whenever someone speaks condescendingly to me.

A trigger can even be vaguely related. When our old emotional clutter is triggered, our brains short-circuit, reducing our ability for rational thought, sometimes drastically. We begin to function from our reactive limbic system. Four "f's" dominate—"fight, flight, freeze, and foggy brain"— not the most mature executive thinking system! We struggle to subdue this intensity, because we want our reasoning brains back. EFT will bring it back. Remember that triggers are frequently unconscious and elusive.

In short, old emotional clutter can be triggered by a recent event. We overreact and are left wondering what the heck just happened? How was I so out of control over such a small incident? Why did I overreact and yell at my co-workers over a simple joke? The answer is Emotional Clutter, left over unneeded emotional stuff!

Discussed next is another type of emotional clutter; a limiting belief.

Limiting Beliefs

A particularly insidious form of emotional clutter appears in the form of limiting beliefs. Limiting beliefs grow from an event (or a series of events), where we generalize a negative event into a larger belief system about ourselves. One or two unfortunate events happen, called defining moments, and we forever see ourselves in this negative view. For example, we believe we're not smart enough and not worthy enough; we're certainly not ever going to amount to anything - all traceable to failing a math test in school. Limiting beliefs are so powerful they are also termed core beliefs or core values.

Limiting beliefs create distorted responses worthy of de-cluttering. In order to weed them out, you need to search your past for awful events that you broadened into, a generalized, and possibly not useful, conclusion about yourself and your life. Most of these come from childhood, but not all of them. Many come from a negative event that left a mark, especially the "first or worst" problems, like the break-up of your first love or the first time you lost a job. But they can arise from any time things went poorly.

Below, I have examples of common limiting beliefs which grew from *specific defining moments.* We all have them, and they don't mean anything is wrong or unfixable with us. These beliefs grow out of reactions to the emotional clutter we've accumulated throughout our lives. We have formed erroneous beliefs, because we generalized a defining moment and gave it greater meaning.

We want to desensitize the defining moment using EFT to collapse the limiting belief.

Once we identify a limiting belief, we want to identify the defining moment.

Ask yourself:

When was the first or worse time I felt like this?

Limiting Belief:	I am not smart enough and shy away from my potential.
Defining Moment:	Did not get accepted to my first choice college.
Limiting Belief:	I may be too cautious and afraid that people are troublesome.
Defining Moment:	I was punished for a crime my sibling committed.
Limiting Belief:	I am squeamish about my sexuality.
Defining Moment:	I was told about graphic sex by a young neighbor.

☹	
Limiting Belief:	I am not a good cook.
Defining Moment:	I was told by my older brother that he needed a hack saw to cut my very first attempted cake I baked.

Figure 5.1. Examples of Limiting Beliefs and Defining Moments

So now that we've looked at the causes and effects of emotional clutter, let's look at how we can easily use EFT to clear it. Below are five steps to use, along with an example to help illuminate the process.

Five Steps to Going Deeper Using EFT

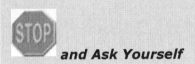 *and Ask Yourself*

Step 1) Limiting Belief.

The first step is to find a limiting belief and rate its SUDS.

- What negative belief do I have about myself that hinders my personal growth?

_____

_____

Hint:I believe I will never_____
What I dislike about myself is_____
I am too _____

- SUDS – On a scale from 0 to 10, where 10 is the worst, how strongly do I hold this belief? SUDS = ?   (Example. I distrust all people. SUDS = 8)

(Ex. I think people are out to get me and cannot be trusted.)

Step 2) Defining Moment.

Locate the event or events that led to this limiting belief. Use the questions below to help you drill down.

Usually there is one significant defining moment. Occasionally, the belief may have settled in your head through repeated exposure to a negative outside influence. Once you have identified the event, rate it using the SUDS level of intensity. Here are some good questions to help you find the event that led to your limiting belief.

- What happened in my past that made me feel like (limiting belief)?

- What in my life reminds me of (limiting belief)?

- What is the first or worst event that made me feel like (limiting belief)?

- What experience did I have to lead me to believe this way?

- What is the earliest I can remember feeling this way and what happened?

_____

_____

_____

(Example: My brother did not admit he did it so we were both grounded all day. SUDS=9)

Rank this belief using the SUDS rating. How upset am I about this (defining moment) as I remember it now, on a scale from 0 to 10, where 10 is the worst? SUDS = _____

Frequently, these questions will lead you to remember a defining moment—an old event that changed the way you view life. What we learned from these moments is often outdated by adult standards. For instance, adults can leave unhealthy situations where a child may not have a choice. By desensitizing these old issues, you de-clutter and you clear the way to live freely.

Step 3) Reminder Phrase.

Next, create the *Reminder Phrase* (chapters 3 and 4) It is the *emotion* about *the issue*, i.e. the *upset* about *that event.*

(Example. *furious I got punished for something my brother did.* SUDS = 9)

Step 4) Desensitize.

Complete three EFT acupoint rounds (see Chapter 3 if you need to remember where the acupoints are located), lightly touching of each of the 11 acupoints while repeating your *Reminder Phrase.*

Persistence When you have finished the three rounds of EFT, check back to see what level the SUDS rating is when you think of your limiting belief. If it has not lowered to a 2 or below, go back and look for more defining moments or negative events related to the limiting belief and cycle through these steps again.

(Ex. *"furious I got punished for something my brother did"* is repeated while touching the acupoints until you no longer are upset about this. It is in the past, desensitized, and is a SUDS of 2 or below.)

Step 5) Spontaneous Insight.

Once the upset is desensitized, the brain works differently and freely, i.e., you have renewed emotional freedom. Your brain sees old constraining issues in a new light, and spontaneous insights occur.

Example. My thoughts now are that this all happened a long time ago. As an adult, no one will punish me again.

My brother was just trying to get out of trouble. I now forgive him and the situation, and it is time I move from this issue. My family was good but not perfect. And I no longer think people are out to get me.

A client's spontaneous insight will often be, "This feels silly now." Actually those are liberating words that allow the individual to go forward. This insight is not really silly at all!

Therapists often create these spontaneous insights for clients – called reframes - but they are even more powerful coming from you.

Let's go back to our first examples. We will watch the progression from a limiting belief, identification of the defining moment, and the generation of the Reminder Phrase that is used for as many rounds of EFT acupoints as you need. When the event and emotions are desensitized, presto! Up comes a spontaneous, liberating insight opposite to the limiting belief. And there it is: emotional freedom!

Below are examples of the typical sequence of how a limiting belief is desensitized. They can help you apply the sequence to your own issues. Remember to rate the SUDS level of the reminder phrase and treat it with as many rounds of the EFT acupoints as you need. Each round is 30 seconds, so 3 rounds are very quick and adding another 3 rounds, if needed, is only another minute and half.

Limiting Belief:	I am not smart enough and shy away from my potential.
Defining Moment:	Did not get accepted to my first choice college.
Reminder Phrase:	*upset about getting rejected*
Desensitize:	Using 3 or more rounds of the 11 acupoints until calm (SUDS 0-2)

111

Spontaneous Insight: I did okay and am happy teaching. Maybe I will chair a committee.

Limiting Belief: I may be too cautious and afraid that people will get me into trouble.

Defining Moment: I was punished for a crime my sibling committed.

Reminder Phrase: *furious about punished for my sister's crime.*

Desensitize: Using 3 or more rounds of the 11 acupoints until calm (SUDS 0-2)

Spontaneous Insight: People may criticize me, but it will not be physical or dangerous. I can use EFT for any comments that I take to heart.

Limiting Belief: I am squeamish about my sexuality.

Defining Moment: I was told about sex by an uptight parent (or too graphic neighbor).

Reminder Phrase: *freaked out about sex.*

Desensitize: Using 3 or more rounds of the 11 acupoints until calm (SUDS 0-2)

Spontaneous Insight: Many people are excited about sex. I will go slowly, with a loving partner, and explore my sexuality.

Limiting Belief: I shy away from cooking

Reminder Phrase: *hurt* about *my brother mocked my cooking*

Defining Moment:	I was told by my older brother that he needed a hack saw to cut my very first attempt to bake a cake
Reminder Phrase:	*hurt about my brother mocked my cooking*
Desensitize:	Using 3 or more rounds of the 11 acupoints until calm (SUDS 0-2)
Spontaneous Insight:	This was only sibling rivalry and mocking as a child. As an adult, I will take a fun cooking or baking class.

Now try to fill in your issue

Limiting Belief:

Defining Moment:

Reminder Phrase (RF):

Desensitize with EFT and the RF:

Spontaneous Insight:

Figure 5.2. From Limiting Beliefs to Spontaneous Insight

It is a basic human need to be able to handle stress, endure what has happened and bounce back into life. This is resiliency, important in everyone's life.

| CASE | **Self-Sabotage - Example 5.1** |

A bright business woman shies away from all promotions. She tells herself she likes to be behind the scenes, but it is actually a limiting belief in how she views her abilities.

Step 1) Limiting Belief

This person thinks she is not smart and shies away from promotions. This is *her* limiting belief and because of it she had many opportunities over the years she has not pursued.

Her SUDS rating of this belief is 10!

Step 2) Defining Moment

She did not get into her first choice of four-year college after high school. This was a long time ago for this thirty-five year old, talented employee. Yet she still shies away from promotions.

Step 3)   Reminder Phrase

She created a Reminder Phrase from the ***emotion*** about ***the issue,*** based on the emotion her limiting belief caused.

> *upset* about *getting rejected from my first choice four-year college after high school.*

Step 4) Desensitize

She completed three rounds of EFT acupoints while stating the Reminder Phrase. She took another SUDS rating and found her intensity was still a high 8. However, it had dropped the predicted 2 to 4 SUDS points, so she knew it was working.

She continued with several more rounds of EFT until her SUDS rating lowered to 1.

Remember, even if you have a very similar issue, your defining moment is likely to be different from the example.

Emotion Worksheet

Touch and	say the emotion	and the issue
Karate chop	*Upset* about *being rejected from my first choice college*	
Top of head	*Upset* about *being rejected from my first choice college*	
Inner Eyebrow	*Upset* about *being rejected from my first choice college*	
Outer eye	*Upset* about *being rejected from my first choice college*	
Under the eye	*Upset* about *being rejected from my first choice college*	
Under the nose	*Upset* about *being rejected from my first choice college*	
Under the lip	*Upset* about *being rejected from my first choice college*	
Collarbone	*Upset* about *being rejected from my first choice college*	
Under the arm	*Upset* about *being rejected from my first choice college*	
Gamut Point	*Upset* about *being rejected from my first choice college*	
Heart hold	*Upset* about *being rejected from my first choice college*	

Figure 5.3. EFT Emotion Worksheet Example

Step 5) Spontaneous Insight

Once desensitized, she had a typical "aha" moment—a cognitive shift.

She said, "That event changed my life, but in retrospect it was probably lucky. My alternative plan has been fulfilling, because I went to a community college, saved a bunch of money, and finished my bachelor's degree in teaching later. I could have been drowning in debt if I went straight to a four-year college as an engineering major. Furthermore, I am a very capable teacher. I can easily mentor, and supervise others, and consider chairing a committee in my department."

Thus, limiting beliefs occur because we overgeneralize significant defining moments and they create negative belief systems. Once these moments are desensitized, we are free to think creatively without the emotional clutter from our past. True emotional freedom for and by our mighty mind!

Here is another common situation.

| CASE | **Upsetting Colleague - Example 5.2**

Let's say you had a flare-up at work with a colleague. Consciously, you recognized the other person's bad qualities and responded to them. But step back for a second and ask yourself what old button this person might have pushed. What similar situation does this remind you of, and how much of your reaction was from connection to a negative past event?

Begin by establishing the normal EFT Reminder Phrase in italics below, (*the emotion* about *the issue*). Your co-worker just does not listen and instead does what she wants. This infuriates you and makes you feel powerless to intervene in an effective manner.

> *upset that I feel powerless around Mary and can't get a word in edgewise.*

Now, dig deeper by going back in time:

When have you felt this [powerlessness] before?

And before that?

You want to get back to as early a time as possible. Try to find the first or the worst time you felt this. Often the first or worst time an event happens will muck up your system and get stuck.

- Was your relative, teacher, parent, clergy, or coach overbearing like that?

- Does that memory cause you to feel the same powerless feeling that your colleague does?

- What if your mother was a whirlwind, always on the move and rarely letting you finish what you wanted to say? Here are some possible reminder phrases:

    feel apathetic about *my mother who never listened;*

    upset about *how futile it was to get my mother's respect;*

    feel invisible about *others ignoring my feeling*

You begin to realization that you gave up trying to tell her things, since it was futile. She never listened, so why bother?

Below are more examples of possible events and their corresponding *Reminder Phrase*:

    furious about *my mother ignored my protests that I did not want to sing in front of my cousins.*

    angry about *my mother didn't believe me that my teacher rejected my 6th grade science project and she had to call the teacher herself.*

Desensitizing these old defining moments frees you to address the current issue with the emotional intensity relevant to the present situation. This is because the raging fires from the childhood experiences are extinguished lessening emotional clutter. (More difficulties that occur at work are discussed in Chapter 12.)

Next, here is another example about a car accident. Whether serious or just a fender-bender, car accidents scare us and create clutter in our emotional system.

| CASE | **Car Accidents- Example 5.3**

Many upsets originate in childhood. Maybe you have a memory that summersaults in your belly from when a classmate was killed driving home from the prom. At the time, you were stunned this could happen and your mind and body recorded that outrage and it is activated in similar circumstances. Now, even though it's years later, this emotional clutter comes to life as your teenager is learning to drive. This is the negative power of emotional clutter.

> (*feel sick* and *stomach somersaulting* about *my classmate getting killed*).

Perhaps you felt as if you were punched emotionally when you skidded on black ice. Stunned that you did not die as your car veered recklessly toward a tree, you are now unable to drive in the winter.

Or maybe you were in an accident and are too frightened now to drive to work. This clutters up normal functioning. A possible Reminder Phrase is:

> (*terrified* about *thinking I was going to die.*)

As with so many stress-related experiences, EFT can work wonders on emotional clutter. Using the above example of a car accident, here are some sample reminder phrases you might use to begin desensitizing yourself. Pick one or create one that encapsulates your issue:

---

feel sick about remembering my classmate died driving home from the prom

still upset about my car accident

always freaked out about that intersection

worried about any car that is behind us

> *scared about being a passenger in my friend's car*
>
> *afraid to be near big trucks*

So if you have worries about driving, plug those worries into the emotions worksheet at the end of Chapter 3. More is written about auto accidents in Chapter 9. Desensitize your emotional clutter from past auto accidents and build renewed trust in your driving ability.

Get out the EFT shovel and dig yourself out of your emotional turmoil! Emotional clutter makes you overreact to small stuff. Displaced anger or exaggerated responses also arise from emotional clutter. They are risky if they flow into relationships, school, or the workplace. If you freak out, how effective are you? Try to find the *first* or *worst* time you got angry over a similar event to desensitize with EFT.

Another type of issue arises from health concerns and experiences. We all have worries about our health. Sometimes these are connected to medical events. Some people experience "white coat syndrome", where their blood pressure rises during a medical office visit because of anxiety. Dig deep to see if you can find an event or a fear attached. Here is an example from someone who grew up with a chronic medical condition.

CASE | Old Medical Memories- Example 5.4

A woman spoke of lack of confidence and fearfulness in most situations. This woman had lots of medical challenges as a child.

When we searched her memory, there was little upset about all the surgeries and treatment she had. Thus, she discounted that her medical troubles were a contributor. However, we kept searching.

She remembered her family used to tell her that her medical issues were "too much bother." (She needed specially prepared food and had frequent hospitalizations.)

We began with the set-up phrase, "I am okay even though *my mother told me I was too much bother.*"

From this, we developed the shortened Reminder Phrase:

"upset my mother considered me too much bother."

Other additional specific aspects that emerged included:

upset I was too sick to go on that spring vacation

angry she held it against me that I was hospitalized

hurt that she was angry about my relapse

She coupled these Reminder Phrases with persistent EFT acupoint sessions until the emotionally charged punch was gone. Her goal was to feel confident and capable. This negative limiting belief that she was "too much bother" and therefore "undeserving in life" interfered often with her self-perception and self-esteem. She held back in life, yet she desired to go forward. After clearing these defining moments, she felt calm and strong. (There are more stories about medical worries discussed in Chapter 9.)

Many limiting beliefs come from well-meaning family members expressing a frustration unaware of the longstanding impact on you. I am sure some hurtful words are stuck in your head from your childhood. Once you locate them, desensitize them with EFT. They are from another time, and other circumstance, probably said in a fleeting moment of anger and not meant later, and they have no right to follow you into your present life!

Read the next example about being uncomfortable sexually. We all know that sexual abuse is outrageous, but smaller events and hurtful words leave an impact too. EFT can downgrade the lingering effect on you.

| CASE | **Sexual Advances- Example 5.5**

An event that happened to me in my early twenties left me with a huge dose of emotional clutter. This is a common event in many young women's lives. My mother had choreographed a weekend ski trip with college students, who attended the college where she worked. But the married owner of the chalet pursued me relentlessly, and he was my mother's friend! This does not qualify as major trauma. However, it is a small "t" trauma-like experience, which left a distrust of men and fearfulness about being an attractive (and naïve) young female.

overwhelmed about my mother's married friend "hitting" on me.

upset about him trying to kiss me when his wife went upstairs

freaked out about him insisting we go out to get food for the group.

Cleaning away this clutter allows one to interact more freely with the opposite gender. Plug your sexual misadventures into the Emotion Worksheet at the end of Chapter 3.

Issue Sleuth

In many cases, the core of the problem may be unconscious or coming from a different angle than you thought. You may need to dig beneath your current words to understand where this issue began. We talked about "limiting beliefs". What we are talking about now are any old issues, any early emotional punch that leaves emotional clutter. These may or may not develop related limiting beliefs. Emotional clutter bogs you down, interfering with your actions, behavior, attitudes and decisions. Let's be sleuths to find it and then desensitize it.

 and Ask Yourself the following questions.

Good Questions to Find the Issues

Let's try to work this for you. These questions are "fishing" for issues and emotions. When you find the question that gets a serious answer, stop and work on it. In other words, if you bring up a whopping whale, stop and work on that. But if it is just a tiny minnow, keep fishing for the big one.

- What about my job, family, living situation, friends, relationships, politics, is bothering me today?

_____

_____

- What happened to me as a child that was upsetting and remind me of how I feel about an issue now?

_____

_____

- What still stings when I think of my relationships with my brother, neighbor, cousin, aunt, mother, father, grandparents, etc.?

_____

_____

- When did I feel like this before? What happened before that reminds me of this feeling?

_____

_____

- What happened to me at age one, age two, age three, etc.?

_____

_____

- What did I see on television or the movies, hear people talk about or read, that upset me on a personal level?

- What am I afraid about trying to do this?

- What is in the way of my success in this?

Fine Tuning

Answering the questions above and writing down your answers can be therapeutic, just as venting on paper can be. However, treating them with EFT is the dimension that will desensitize their current impact. Pick one from your list, and ask the following questions, in order to dissect it for treatment aspects.

What part of this issue do I want to work on first?

What part of this issue bothers me the most? Or, if the issue is huge, what part do I feel comfortable working on first?

Now that you have a list, choose just one to work on at a time. You can choose to work on the worst part of the problem first or the easiest part.

The CARES recipe. Here is a reminder for how to proceed.

    Figuring out each step.

C 1)	**C**hief complaint (issue) and SUDS level of upset thinking about it for 5 seconds. SUDS intensity=____.
A 2)	**A**spects: what parts of this bothers me? Select one aspect you want to desensitize.
R 3)	**R**eminder Phrase (RP): is drawn from the emotion about the issue

E 4)   **E**FT: - eleven acupoints are touched or tapped while repeating the RP until the initial SUDS decrease to 0-2. (EFT will desensitize any other aspect identified in step 2 by repeating the steps on each for each aspect.)

S 5)   **S**pontaneous Insight: liberating, and intelligent insights emerge!

The Voice of Reason dominates!

Technique 36: Positive Affirmations - A Nice Finishing Touch

Here is one to add quality finishing to our work.

Affirmations and Self-Talk – To Like Yourself

Self-talk is not mumbling and bemoaning your down-trodden self. It is motivational, positive talk you repeat to yourself. Here are some examples, but there are thousands of them. You can find more with an Internet search using "affirmations."

"I can do it. I am fabulous and deserving of this. I can handle this. They are lucky to learn from me. I am an exciting person. I am honest and hard worker. I eat healthy food. I study and comprehend quickly. I am capable of making more money. "

TIP: Say an affirmation as a positive statement, because the brain does not get the word "not".

Thus, if I say "do not think what day today is", you think: it is Sunday. Do not think about the color of the clothes you have on. You immediately note the color. The brain does not get the word "not." Therefore, self-talk and affirmations need to be said in positive language only. Rather than stating "do not worry", say- "I am calm, cool and collected!"

And if you are trying to alter a behavior such as excessive alcohol or food consumption, say what you intend to do, rather than what you intend not to do. Examples:

> I am going to eat lots of vegetable today.
>
> I am going to drink club soda and lime at that party.

"I am well, I can cope, I am special, I am worthy, I am safe, I am happy, and I am capable" can all be added to the last few rounds of EFT, but only after you have collapsed the upset with EFT. Come up with your own ideas of what you want and add them in too. They are the opposite of what you started with. Instead of *I am stupid*, they transform *to I am smart, clever, and talented.*

Super Technique 37: **Forgiveness -- the Ultimate Antidote to Anger**

"Resentment is like drinking poison and then hoping it will kill your enemies." - Nelson Mandela

This sentence is going to surprise you and you may need to read it twice. Forgive people for *your* sake as when you forgive them, you feel better and let go of resentment and anger, and feel better. So do it for you!

When you resent someone, they don't suffer, you do. This works without actually saying it to the person.

Forgive people for not being the way that you want them to be. Forgiveness is a powerful antidote to anger. Through forgiveness, you let things rest and stop obsessing and being agitated. It does not even have to be sincere. When I forgive someone for being an idiot and cutting me off in traffic, I really do feel better and have no need for road rage.
I forgive them for *my* sake, not theirs, so that I can settle and find peace. When I hold onto the hot coal of anger, I get burned!

If forgiveness feels stuck because the affront was too big, try forgiving 5%. It seems to generate some peace and in time, you may be able to forgive even more.

And now a word about important forgiveness with couples and EFT.

Men are from Mars, Women are from Venus – With Some Forgiveness Thrown In

People are Different *and* Equal

My mantra is: <u>We are all different *and* equal.</u>

I am convinced the world would be a better place if everyone adopted this phrase as their own mantra for living. Difference excites us, difference annoy us. If everything and everyone was vanilla, it would be a boring world. Patience, tolerance and curiosity are virtues when it comes to valuing differences. Sometimes EFT is also needed.

Marriage is one example of this. We tend to marry or stay in committed relationship with people whose characteristics are the opposite of our own, the complement of us. One example is a highly anxious and conscientious person often marries someone very laid back. In the beginning that opposite quality is adored as it is our missing characteristic. We feel this other has "completed us and made us whole".

A year later, we will argue about that very same quality that attracted us. For instance, the highly conscientious person will want their laid back partner to take things more seriously. The laid back person will want the other to just chill out a bit! A good relationship has both people move toward the middle of the road of these opposing characteristics.

Married couples do influence each other's thinking. When you cannot agree, three possible solutions to this common problem are as follows: "agree to disagree;" learn to laugh at the differences; and use EFT to calm down the frustrations of this predictable dilemma.

Battles over our differences are predictable. *Men are From Mars and Women are from Venus* many truths and a book by John Gray (1992) also point out differences between men and women's thinking and behavior.

An upset wife released her anger about her husband's differences using EFT. Some of her aspects and Reminder Phrases were as follows:

> *angry about him forgetting to come home early to set up for the party*
>
> *furious about him talking down to me when his father is around*
>
> *upset about him yelling at our son for spilling milk*
>
> *scared about him getting so upset when the dog misbehaves*

An Optional Positive Last Round

As mentioned, some EFT practitioners add an optional round of EFT using positive words. Here are examples related to forgiveness, given the predictable opposites couples bring to the relationship. Apply these after calming down the upsets. After a wife calmed down on each aspect of this issue using EFT, the following words were added on the last round (or last few rounds) of EFT.

> "I forgive him for not being what I want him to be. He tries, but he does not always get me. As a male, he takes too much offense to my rambling, because he wants to fix it. He cares about me. We are different but equal. I can forgive him for having a male mind that sees things differently. I forgive him for prioritizing his job and yet appreciate that he is a good provider. I forgive him that his father unnerves him and he overreacts. I forgive him for being tired and without patience around our son and dog. He is my complement, my opposite in characteristics, and we balance each other's attributes. Now that I am calmer, I can wait for a good opportunity to discuss these issues with him, so we can learn how to handle them better in the future. He is a good man, a good father, a good provider and I love him."

Before using EFT, this woman refuted anything positive about her husband. Once calmed by this technique, she absorbed their intellectual differences and laughingly understood the reality and benefit of their differences. As mentioned, one slogan should be universally accepted, and that is: All people are different and equal. Viva la difference!

After calming down upsets the husband may have, his positive statement might be this:

> "I forgive her for not being what I want her to be. She tries, but she does not always get me. I wish she would be concise and just get to the point, so I could fix her problem. We are different, but equal. I forgive her for having a female mind and seeing the world differently. I forgive her for being tired and impatient with me. I forgive her that her mother unnerves her and she overreacts after talking with her. I forgive her for prioritizing relationships, and yet I appreciate how amazingly she takes care of all of us. She is my complement, my opposite in characteristics, and thus we balance each other's attributes. Now that I am calmer, I can wait for a good opportunity to discuss these issues with her, so we can learn how to handle them better in the future. She is still the pretty girl I married, I love her, she cares for me and the kids and works hard. I love her. "

- Write out a similar positive and forgiving statement for your spouse/partner. Read it as you touch the acupoints.

- You may want to reach more serenity by writing out a positive, forgiving statement about yourself, your parents, friends, co-workers and others in your life. Calm down your upset first with EFT and then read this statement as you continue to lightly touch or tap the acupoints.

Technique 38: **Scripts and Choices Wording**

Some people embellish the Set-up Statement and the Reminder Phrases more than I usually do. Dr. Pat Carrington created "Choices" wording. You can read about Dr. Carrington and get a free download on this method at www.masteringEFT.com. Her wording may look like this.

> "Even though I had an impoverished childhood with lots of trauma, I choose to be happy and find a good place for myself in my world."

Others in the EFT field use scripts. A script starts the EFT round with a compassionate Set-Up Statement. Then at each of the following acupoints, a different concern is stated, and the statements often become more positive toward the end of the round. CJ Puotinen is a master of this, and I recommend her brilliant workshops which can be found at www.taptheworldeft.com.

Here is an example of a script. You can work with this script, devise your own, or do a computer search on the phrase "Scripts EFT" to find one that you like.

Karate Chop (KC) - Even though I am an unhappy person... I deeply and completely accept myself or

KC - Even though I focus on what is wrong ... I've decided to forgive myself

---

EFT Sequence of Activating Acupoints and Saying:

Top of Head - I am never content

Eye Brow –   I always think something will go wrong

Outer Eye -   I even worry about worrying too much

Under Eye -   I only see dark clouds

Under Nose - Why can't I just live in the present?

Under Lip -   Being this way is who I am used to being

Collar Bone - What if I thrive on doubt?

Under Arm –   What if I had to learn to be a calmer person, how could I adjust to that?

Gamut Point -Just maybe I could change, but maybe not. That is a tall order

Heart Hold – Maybe I could just postpone my worry to another time and day

I still prefer to specifically focus on one issue and one emotion, in order to effectively clean out that issue. I just want to inform you of tapping with scripts and they do have a value. I recommend you collapse your issue first and then add scripts.

Many in the field are branching out to include deeply profound and loving words. A book with many scripts was number 5 on the New York Times Best Seller List and number 1 on Amazon in 2013, is *The Tapping Solution: A Revolutionary System for Stress-Free Living* by Nick Ortner.

Technique 39: **Metaphors and the Movie Technique**

Metaphors and the movie technique are other ways to title your reminder phrase and summarize your issue. Sometimes a summary of the event can be turned into a metaphor or a movie title that captures the essence of the issue nicely. It becomes the Reminder Phrase.

Here are some wonderful metaphors or movie titles used to progress an issue rapidly.

- My mother had it wrong!

- This was a nightmare!

- Living Hell!

- Ain't right what happened!

- Cheated!

- Lost!

- Tormented!

- Unforgiveable!

- My dad was a bully!

- Stop staring!

If one of these fit your situation, use it as the Reminder Phrase in your EFT reminder phrase. You can also create your own movie title. Be sure to see if there are more specific issues remaining to be desensitized once these are defused.

REVIEW

Lots to review as this was a busy chapter

1) Do you have emotional clutter that gets triggered by current interactions?

2) Triggers- what or who does this remind me of?

3) Do you limit yourself because you believe a view of yourself that may be outdated?

4) What do I believe I am not capable of doing? I will never....

5 Steps to debunking Limiting Beliefs. - Now try to fill in your issue

Step 1) Limiting belief:

Tip: What do I believe I cannot do?

Step 2) Defining Moment:

Tip: What is the earliest example of this? Rate a SUDS level =____.

Step 3) Reminder Phrase (RP):

Tip: *The emotion about the issue*

Step 4) Desensitize with the 11 EFT acupoints while saying the RP:

Tip: Repeat until calm, SUDS intensity = 0 - 2.

Steps 5) Spontaneous Insight:

Tip: What do you think or feel now and does that feel freeing?

We have looked at serious issues and ways to find them. In the next Chapter, we will look at an alternative focus to calm the situation, the "Mind-Body Sweep". Read on for more fascinating 5-minute stress management!

CHAPTER 6:

MIND-BODY SWEEP – THE TOUGH STUFF

"Life's sharpest rapture is surcease of pain."

- Emma Lazarus

Is there a softer way to tip toe into serious stress? This next gentle technique goes to the issue through targeting body discomfort.

Super Technique 40: **The Mind-Body Sweep**

In the previous chapters I've covered how to deal with various levels of stress using Emotional Freedom Techniques (EFT), coupled with innovations from many others in the field. You've learned how to reduce both recent and deeply rooted stress. You've also learned how stress triggers operate as a warning device, letting you know you have an emotional issue that needs to be dealt with.

EFT often focuses directly on the emotional aspect itself. EFT can also focus on a physical issue, if that is the complaint. There is another even gentler way to proceed, when an issue is still activated and awful. You can *intentionally* shift the focus onto the body's physical reaction to that stressful thought, in order to lessen the intensity quickly. This is the physicality of stress. (Chronic pain may be different as explained in Chapter 15.)

I call it the *Mind-Body Sweep*, or to just the *"Sweep."* Imagine a feather duster or a whiskbroom sweeping down the body from head to toe, cleaning out the physical discomfort manifested when thinking about the problem. This is the essence of the Sweep.

The key to the Sweep is that it concentrates on the physical manifestation of the stressful event. Have you ever noticed when you have a tough day at work and you end up with a stiff neck? Maybe the kids misbehaved, the dog got sick, and the plumber didn't show up. At the end of the day you have a headache, when normally you never get them. If you have a stressful interview or speech to make, does your stomach tighten up? You might even get heart palpitations.

The difference with the Sweep is the actual issue is temporarily pushed off to the side, in order to focus *just* on the physical symptoms. This gentler approach can facilitate work on some pretty rough issues.

Thoughts Create Responses

To obtain an understanding of how the Sweep is beneficial, give the following exercise a try. We often create physical discomfort by thinking of upsetting thoughts.

Imagine this:

> Imagine opening a broken refrigerator to find rotten food left in there for several weeks. Picture the blue– green mold covering the cheddar cheese, and imagine that ooze from the black hamburger meat is dripping down the shelves. Everywhere you look, food is crusted to the walls. The pungent smell overwhelms you. You dare not even go close to the milk container, because you just know chunks

of curdled spoiled milk live within. Imagine it is your job to clean this smelly mess.

What do you notice about yourself? For me, my nose crinkles up, I shudder and my stomach churns. When I think of that hamburger ooze, I get nauseous. Also, the idea of the milk container makes me want to physically take a step backwards.

BUT, there is no broken refrigerator in front of us, it is only a thought. The point is that when you have a thought, your body often reacts, consciously or unconsciously.

What's happening is that you are experiencing the physicality of stress. It happens all the time. You argue with a family member, and your shoulders tighten up. Maybe you even develop a headache, a stiff neck or tightness in your gut. Your thoughts are unhappy and you're at a SUDS of 10, because your body hurts.

You can certainly treat your emotional upset with standard EFT, but I've found that with more sensitive emotional wounds, it's even gentler to approach it from the physical side first. After you've calmed your bodily discomfort, the emotional SUDS intensity is usually half of what it was when you first thought about it. You will then be better able to tolerate directly addressing the emotional upset. The Sweep produces a generalized relaxed state.

In traditional psychotherapy, the issue would be discussed for much of a 50 minute session. The person may or may not leave calmly. In the Sweep, the focus is on the upsetting issue is for only 5 seconds, and then locate where this is felt in the body. Then the body discomfort is calmed.

Let's look at how problems grow and are manifested in your body.

How Events Gain Emotional Momentum

Consider this event. You look outside and notice the tree limbs in your back yard are swaying. Mesmerized, you enjoy their leafy dance. Suddenly another thought intrudes, "We're about to get a storm." This thought progresses to an awareness that your children are at a friend's yard playing outside. Your emotional safety alarm goes off with fear, "I better go get them." Then your physiological alarm goes off. You may notice tension throughout your shoulders or chest, have trouble swallowing, or develop a hand tremor.

You make a phone call and learn they're playing in a protected basement. Your shoulders, chest, and tremor relax as the fear dissolves. Sometimes these physical discomforts do not relax. You can't settle down. You either go get your children anyway, overeat, take a drink, clean an already clean house, or employ other coping mechanisms, some beneficial, some not. You still feel anxious, tense, and stressed; you have a racing heart, a tight neck, and are edgy. These physical discomforts may linger for quite a while, even days or longer, sometimes developing into more physical problems. Your protective alarm went off, but it is just not willing to resume to its normal quiet!

What happens if no one answers the telephone where your children are playing? You may even be triggered by remembering a dangerous storm from earlier times. You kick up another notch in your alarm system, grab a coat, and run to that neighbor. Nothing else is in your mind. You are now hypervigilant, scanning for the sound of children as you get closer, and every other noise is blocked out. Your adrenaline is bubbling, moving you toward high alert. Even after discovering the children are safe; your body may forget to shut down all this stress. You want to calm down, but just don't know how. You may vent to another person and find some minor relief, but your body is still activated, achy, and off kilter.

You are not alone in this struggle to quiet your body. Many people are trying to recover from years of abuse or accumulated stress. Some have chronic stress on their jobs, such as many first responders like police, firefighters, emergency medical technicians and medical staff. And of course, the military.

Imagine the level of stress and the internal physical agitation of children living in violent neighborhoods. While the teacher is trying to teach multiplication, the child is distracted and his body is trembling as he worries why his teen-age brother did not come home last night. Bullying also takes its toll on a child's concentration ability.

During a psychological assessment, a person is always asked about his physical symptoms. But the focus of counseling then moves to a discussion of the issues and the ensuing emotions. However, what if after a calamity, the focus stayed on desensitizing the physical body's memory—the uncomfortable physiological sensations that occurred with the event? This is the principle behind the Sweep.

Here I will give you a feel for the process so you will clearly see what the Sweep is all about.

Below are three Reminder Phrases. The first two are based on the standard EFT formula. Phrase A identifies the issue, and Phrase B describes the emotion associated with it. The third phrase, C, is the physical expression of the stress caused by A and B. Phrase C is the one to use in the Sweep. Find where in your body you feel the most discomfort.

   A) Thought or issue Reminder Phrase is: *"don't know where my kids are in this incoming storm."*

   B) Emotional Reminder Phrase is: *"worry about my kids."*

   C) Physical Discomfort Reminder Phrase is: *"pressure in my chest."*

All of these phrases will work. However, with serious upsets, intervening first on the physical discomfort has the benefit of releasing the pressure rapidly.

Here is an example.

| CASE | **First Responder Horror: A Preview of the Mind-Body Sweep, Example 6.1** |

Here is a scenario. At the scene of a car accident, a fireman recalled being haunted by the horror of seeing a terribly injured dog. A former Marine, he is a stern, no-nonsense type guy, but he has a tender spot for animals.

He explained that he was "gearing down" after the car victims were air lifted to the hospital. He was startled by nearly stepping on this tormented dog, which had obviously been thrown from the car. As he talked, his physical agitation was immediately visible: tears on his cheek; restlessness in his chair; and the clenched eyebrows of despair. He was stressed, and distressed, by what he experienced when he saw the injured dog, and he was uncomfortable being in psychotherapy.

I asked him to think about the injured dog for only 5 seconds and then to stop. I then asked him where he felt the memory in his own body. He determined he felt a *"weight on his chest."* I knew from his demeanor that his SUDS intensity was high and when asked, he indicated it was a 10.

To avoid thinking about the intense upset of the actual incident, we placed the accident images of the injured dog on an imaginary shelf off to the side and out of mind. Sometimes, I even request that they throw the issue out of the room we are in, (such as into the waiting room) so the focus is only on the physical discomfort.

The focus became to think *ONLY* of the *weight on the chest*, while lightly touching the 11 acupoints used throughout this book (see Chapter 3 for chart and photo reminder of where these acupoints are located).

The weight on his chest diminished dramatically (SUDS 10→5) after 3 rounds of slow, light touch on the acupoints. Less than 5 minutes later, after 9 rounds of the acupoint sequence, he discovered the weight on his chest was gone. We stopped every 3 rounds, to re-assess where his weight on his chest. His recovery looked like this: SUDS 10->8->4->0.

After these nine rounds of the Sweep, he re-focused on the image of the dog in the accident and found himself far more composed. He said his upset was around a SUDS rating of 3. He actually said, "I'm ok, it's what I do for a living". This was his "spontaneous insight". As often happens, relieved, he laughed about the unusual therapy technique.

Because of his extreme physical discomfort and yet reluctance (or inability) to get closer emotionally to the experience, the Sweep became the ideal tool to help him regain his balance. If I had dealt directly with his emotional issue using traditional psychotherapy, it most probably would have increased his stress to highly uncomfortable levels. (And he may have dropped out of psychotherapy.)

How's that for powerful?

At the next session, we checked our work to see if this event still haunted him. Sometimes issue come back up but the SUDS or the power of the issue is less than half it was from earlier session. We re-treated any of it that re-occurs.

Once that issue was gone, he brought up another memory he had, from age 7. While walking to school, he remembers a dog that was hit by a car. That dog howled in agony, and it deeply agitates him to think of it even now, 30 years later. He felt it as an *electrified chest;* the Sweep calmed that physical discomfort too (SUDS 9→4→2→1). (The SUDS numbers here note each 3 rounds of the acupoints, and the necessary persistence to keep taking the upset lower.) It is common that past memories are stirred by current events. So keep checking for more associated memories!

The Mind-Body SWEEP – 5 Steps to Quieting the Body's Storm

Performing the Mind-Body Sweep on yourself or someone else is easy and fast. The key is, as always, to be gentle in its application, because you're dealing with memories of serious stressful events.

I will list five steps to perform the Sweep for easy reference. Then I will go into each step in deeper detail, to help you understand the best ways to use this fabulous stress-relieving technique. Later in the chapter, you will find a chart for using the Sweep, a suggestion about wording the *Physical Reminder Phrase* and some suggestions of questions to ask yourself.

The first example was traumatic. You will see how lesser issues may have a physical hold on us. These physical memories often reappear in similar circumstances. The goal is to be rid of the lingering physical discomfort associated with issues, which also prevent it from reoccurring and adding to physical distress should those issues come up in the future.

Now for the **Five Steps to The Sweep,** using an example of being yelled at by your supervisor. This technique starts the same way as any EFT example, but notice the deliberate shift to the physical sensation of discomfort. Temporarily put the issue on the shelf or tossed in another room for later treatment, and go in through the body. It is interesting that the issue and its physical manifestation usually quiet down together, even though there is no intentional focus on the issue in this technique.

CASE | Yelled At by a Supervisor. - Example 6.2

STEP 1) Chief Complaint -Identify Issue and Rate

Tune into the stressful situation for only 5 seconds. Then rate the intensity on the SUDS system, where 10 is the worst possible upset. Write this down.

Example: *Yelled at by my supervisor*, SUDS = 8

STEP 2) Aspect of the Physical Discomfort and Rate

Locate where in your body you feel physical stress while thinking about the upsetting event. Rate this physical discomfort using the SUDS rating. Most people point to the pressure on their body. Figure 6.2 on page 150 helps finds the words to describe these physical discomforts.

Example: *Tight throat*, SUDS = 5

Pressure in my chest, SUDS = 8

STEP 3) Reminder Phrase of the Physical Discomfort & Combined with the Acupoints

Chose the worst-rated physical discomfort first, since the lesser one may also resolve once the more intense one has calmed. Use the physical discomfort description as your *Physical Reminder Phrase*, and do 3 rounds of the 11 acupoints reviewed in Figures 6.1 and 6.4 at the end of this chapter. Be sure to focus ONLY on the *physical discomfort* as the Reminder Phrase. Be persistent and do as many rounds as needed to bring the SUDS rating as low as possible.

Example: *Pressure in my chest* (the worst physical symptom). SUDS=8

This is typical about the way SUDS rating often drops, corresponding to each 3 rounds of the 11 acupoints. The lower   SUDS   number   representing   increased desensitization is the payoff for persistence!

SUDS 8→5→3→1.

Repeat steps 2 and 3 to see if there any other physical symptoms until all physical discomfort associated with the stressful event is significantly lower.

Repetition and Persistence

This means think about the awful issue for 5 seconds and then note where you feel it in your body. Repeat this step using the EFT acupoints while thinking about the new physical discomfort. Continue doing this until there is no physical discomfort when thinking about the awful issue.

Repeat the EFT process on all physical symptoms until they are gone. Sometimes the physical discomfort moves to a different location in your body. Gary Craig labeled a similar phenomenon where pain discomfort moves as "chasing the pain." It moves! Be sure to address this new physical discomfort the same way you did the others. You may need to start the whole process again, if new physical aspects emerge.

Example: *Pressure in my chest*, SUDS 8->4->1

Tight throat, SUDS = 5->3->1

STEP 4) Review the Original Upset

Now that the physical discomfort is gone or very insignificant, think back to the original upset you chose in Step 1. What is the SUDS rating now when you think about it for 5 seconds?
____

Example: Yelled at by my supervisor. Current new SUDS = 3.

Usually the upset has lost at least half of its initial SUDS rating, because you treated the physical discomfort associated with the upset. It is a gentle way to delve into serious issues.

Then continue to STEP 5, to use EFT with a switch to the emotional issue to complete the desensitization of this upset.

STEP 5) EFT for the Remaining Upset

When all the physical discomfort is gone but there is still some upset remaining on the original issue, return to the Emotion Worksheet at the end of Chapter 3 to desensitize it with the standard EFT. In our example, the remaining upsetting *Reminder Phrase* is:

Upset my supervisor yelled at me, SUDS=3

Notice the SUDS of the upset dropped 8→3 using the Sweep on the body discomfort *of tight throat* and *pressure in my chest*. This upset diminished without ever directly addressing the issue but by only focusing on the body discomfort.

In this example, when the issue is desensitized, the spontaneous insight might be:

"I was arguing about the project's deadline and my boss is under stress from his manager to get this done. Let me arrange a time to have a review of what happened and how we do it better in the future."

The five steps are pretty straight forward, aren't they?

Here is a worksheet on the Sweep and then there are a couple of charts to help you establish the Physical Reminder Phrase and to see how the Sweep looks.

Mind-Body Sweep Sample Worksheet

Example of Coupling the Acupoints and Reminder Phrase

Light touch on	
ACUPOINT say	**REMINDER PHRASE**
Karate chop	*pressure in my chest*
Top of head	*pressure in my chest*
Inner eyebrow	*pressure in my chest*
Outer eye	*pressure in my chest*
Under the eye	*pressure in my chest*
Under the nose	*pressure in my chest*
Under the lip	*pressure in my chest*
Collar bone	*pressure in my chest*
Under the arm	*pressure in my chest*
Gamut Point	*pressure in my chest*
Heart hold	*pressure in my chest*

Figure 6.1. Example of Mind-Body Acupoints and Wording

You have a choice. You can continue to calm the pressure in your chest (SUDS now a 4) or go to the most serious physical discomfort now which now is the *tight throat* (SUDS is a 5). Continue applying the 11 acupoints while stating the physical reminder phrase until the SUDS rating will not go any lower.

Then switch back to earlier chapters of EFT and desensitize your remaining emotional upset to being yelled at by your supervisor.

Describing the Physical Discomfort

Some people have questions about exactly how to go about forming the *Physical Reminder Phrase.* First, you must find the physical sensation, the body's discomfort. Ask yourself to experience your emotional upset issue for ONLY 5 seconds, and note where you feel any discomfort in your body.

Most people feel it immediately, and they easily point to the spot. They grip their throat, shoulder, neck, stomach, back, chest, head, legs, etc., and show where they feel tension.

Most people find it hard to capture the expressive word to describe their discomfort. Physical descriptive words listed below in Figure 6.2 are an aid to find the often elusive description of your physical sensation. Attach these descriptions to the part of the body that is experiencing physical discomfort, e.g., *stabbing* temples, *aching* shoulders, or *butterflies* in my stomach. In other words, notice what part of your body is involved and add the right descriptive words from this list that suits you.

churning	burning	stabbing	aching
tight	clenched	prickly	pricking
tension	tingling	nauseous	weak
choking	lump	knot	jarring
cramping	shooting	splitting	butterflies
squeezed	pressure	sour	gassy
too excited	thrilled	exuberant	dizzy
pounding	throbbing	pulsating	radiating

Figure 6.2. Possible Descriptions of Physical Discomfort to be Attached to the Body Ache

Note how descriptive words from Figure 6.2 above emphasize the physical discomfort. When I think of the distressing image, my body reacts in the following ways:

Distress	Physical Reminder Phrase for treatment	
Bloody car accident	makes	*my throat tighten*
Dead animal	makes	*my skin crawl*
Dead six foot snake	makes	*pressure on my chest*
Gruesome TV rape	makes	*tingling in my arms*

Attacked outside office	makes	*my heart pounding*
Road rage	makes	*my teeth clench*
Rudely insulted	makes	*my fist tense up*

Figure 6.3. Incidents and Possible Resulting Physical Discomfort

The Physical Reminder Phrase is repeated at every acupoint to keep you focused while defusing a specific physical sensation.

It is important to know how to formulate a *Physical Reminder Phrase* as well as an *Emotional Reminder Phrase,* because not all issues elicit a physical sensation. Therefore, the emotional wording from the previous chapters is useful for finishing an intervention, once the Sweep has lessened the intensity.

When you are stressed, your system is out of balance. The bigger the upset, the less you will be able to use your intellect, reasoning, problem solving skills, and personality to cope with the situation at hand. Every SUDS point that you can lower your upset will increase your ability to use your intellect, with composure, and diplomacy, to deal with problem situations and difficult people. In other words, when your issue is a SUDS intensity of 9 or 10, your thinking ability, reasoning ability, and personality is inversely related, reduced to a meager 1 or 2.

Back Into Relief through the Body - Summary

Most people enter traditional psychotherapy because they have been unable to rebalance their lives on their own. People come into therapy because they feel badly. These individuals are physically and emotionally uncomfortable, and they suffer from a myriad of issues and complaints. Despite having tried everything, they could not cure themselves. The symptoms still persist. This isn't anyone's fault. Their reactions often are a normal reaction to a horrible event.

Traditional psychotherapy addresses the issues and emotions in one's life, but often neglects the physical symptoms. (The symptoms might be headaches, insomnia, pain, body tension, appetite changes, exaggerated startled response, etc.) Actually, clients are accused of "somaticizing" their issues; this means that they are converting their stress into physical symptoms. The Sweep suggests they coexist.

Psychotherapy favors clients obtaining insight, such as understanding that an upset stomach means they are nervous. The Mind-Body Sweep targets relief of the upset stomach - with or without insight. The Sweep creates a generalized calm, even when thinking about the mishap.

The Sweep works with any stress, but it is particularly beneficial with serious stress. Serious stress may be a trauma, critical incident, or any ordeal. The common denominator is that the mere thought of the issue is distressing beyond the realm of words. Rather, there is agony, expressed with tears, rage, silence or screams. Physical activation is often noticeable such as rocking, grimacing, pacing, tapping or jigging movements of hands and feet. Focusing on the body's discomfort first, relief happens in a gentler, less invasive way. With the Sweep these psychosomatic symptoms are the points for treatment.

Thus, the Sweep is one more important intervention in this growing field of Energy Psychology and Meridian treatments. It quickly restores your emotional balance and personal composure, and creates a generalized calm. It takes less detective work than standard EFT. Using the Mind-Body Sweep to calm down the body and then EFT to calm down the left over thought and emotion create the most effective interventions!

 REVIEW

We have learned 3 ways to address our stressors:

the emotion

the thought of the event

the body sensation of discomfort

When experiencing upsetting issues and emotions, ask

where do I feel this in my body?

Label the physical discomfort with the adjective from Figure 6.2 above and plug in into the chart below.

The Mind-Body Sweep Worksheet

Light touch on	
ACUPOINT while saying the PHYSICAL REMINDER PHRASE	
Hold for one breath or to a count of 7	
Karate chop	*Your body sensation.*
Top of head	*Your body sensation.*
Inner eyebrow	*Your body sensation.*
Outer eye	*Your body sensation.*
Under the eye	*Your body sensation.*
Under the nose	*Your body sensation.*
Under the lip	*Your body sensation.*
Collar bone	*Your body sensation.*
Under the arm	*Your body sensation.*
Gamut Point	*Your body sensation.*
Heart hold	*Your body sensation.*

Figure 6.4. Mind-Body Sweep Worksheet

Perhaps you are thinking these techniques are odd or too weird, even though they are considered mainstay in Asia. But do we use them here? We now venture to the next chapter where the question is, "Do these acupoints show up in everyday body language we all use?" You may be surprised in the next chapter. The answer is, "Yes."

CHAPTER 7:

IS EFT BODY LANGUAGE?

"And now, presenting right in front of your own eyes..."

ACUPOINTS AND THEIR RELATION TO BODY LANGUAGE

Technique 41. **Are the Acupoints Actually Body Language Points We Use All the Time?**

Are the acupoints discussed throughout this book actually body language? How mighty and amazing is this mind of ours if that is true?

Could we possibly be using these acupoints—meridian theory acupuncture points—unconsciously and all day long to soothe ourselves, maintain balance, and re-establish equilibrium? Let's explore this as well as the *estimates* of what emotions are attached to these acupoints.

Observe people's body mannerisms. We know that touch soothes us. We instinctively hug a sad family member. Perhaps not coincidentally, several significant meridian points run down the front of our torso. You can even slowly glide down the front of your own body with your hands, (hand over hand) neck to belly, for comfort. Many of my widowed or divorced clients like this slow chest glide, possibly because they are missing their partner's touch. (See Massage, Technique 59, on page 292.)

We even hug in happiness when exuberant. Is it random touch or are we unconsciously activating meridian acupoints? Are we taking the charge out of intense emotions and creating calm?

Hugs and Touch: Soothing Jittered Nerves

We hold crying babies close to our bodies. Any parent knows that transitions - moving from one activity to another - are stressful for children. Children tend to resist transitions. The child does not want to come into the office and does not want to leave later. A parent (and dog owner too), will ease those transitions with touch - a hug, hand holding or a gentle guiding hand on the back or shoulder. Healthy touch is important, but not written about as much as it deserves. We adults use touch too by greeting people with a hand shake, a hug, a pat on the shoulder.

We need affection daily. Think about those who do not get much touch, such as older children. Do they get physically aggressive or wrestle to be touched? Does that touch become a reward, making them seek out more physical aggression? Of course, a possible solution is respectful touch (on the shoulder or the forearm) or shaking their hands to hit that Karate chop point (pictured below figure 7.1 and 7.2) to rebalance them.

The science of understanding the brain is developing rapidly. We know that a hug, which probably hits most of the meridians in the front of the body, releases oxytocin, the bonding hormone. We know that light touch releases serotonin. Prozac, and her sister SSRI (Selective Serotonin Reuptake Inhibitors) medications including Zoloft and Lexapro are other ways to increase serotonin too.

We know that EFT reduces cortisol, the stress hormone. (Dr. Dawson Church. Journal of Nervous and Mental Disease. 200(10), 891-896. doi: 10.1097/NMD.0b013e31826b9fc1). Elevated cortisol levels are connected with rapid aging, several diseases, and psychological diagnoses including depression and anxiety.

Using a toy Energy Ball, (www.safari.com) a ping pong ball that includes a battery with two medal nodes attached, demonstrates the body electric.

When two people touch one node each and hold hands, the ball lights up – demonstrating humans conduct electricity. While this may feel farfetched, just remember that EEGs and EKGs are also specific measure of the body electric.

My suggestion is that touch, even self-touch is soothing. Watch sports fan when their team is losing. They are holding their faces or torsos, probably activating soothing acupoints. I believe we touch intuitively, because we have experienced the reward of comfort from this. Thus, we learn and remember this physical calmness and do it unconsciously when we need it. Are we actually activating the soothing meridians that soar throughout our body?

As you've seen, acupoints soothe our discomfort. When we're overly emotional and reactive, we feel off balance, uncomfortable, or embarrassed.

In the words of one of my clients, acupoints might be our "re-set buttons." For example, I often sit in staff meetings with a finger resting under my eye, believed to be the point for anxiety. It quells my tight stomach when we discuss problems.

My brilliant colleague agrees with my observation. "Human beings naturally touch certain parts of the body that bring them comfort, and those parts of body normally have acupuncture points that corresponding to certain meridians that serve certain mental and physical functions," according to Dr. Jingduan Yang, M.D. Director, Acupuncture & Oriental Medicine Program, Jefferson (Hospital) Mryna Brind Center of Integrative Medicine in Philadelphia.

Let's look at which emotions may be associated with each acupoint. Ask yourself if they feel accurate. Good questions to check out your observations are mentioned later in this chapter, after the photos.

If we use acupoints intentionally, one's often associated with body mannerisms; they can help calm our reactions to a tense situation. Experiment with the acupoints and see if you find a few that you use automatically. Consider intentionally using those acupoints when you are upset and see what happens.

The acupoint meridians run thorough the body similar to the nervous system. They are invisible to the eye. But so is your wireless internet connection, even the very oxygen you breathe are invisible, yet we know they exist.

Using the adaptation of light touch EFT, you can easily see the relationship of acupoints and body language. The photos in this chapter illustrate this relationship of acupoints and body language. This means you can apply these calming techniques publicly. I call this *Camouflaged EFT*. Position your hand and hold for several normal breaths when using Camouflaged EFT in public, in order to avoid notice of movement. Some acupuncturists leave the needles in twenty minutes; slow down and hold a point for as long as you like.

The nomenclature of where these acupoints are located is how they are portrayed in Chinese medicine. Thus GV-20, top of the head, stands for Governing Vessel, point 20. I explain first how they are used in meridian type therapies including EFT, and subsequently how they appear in body language.

Here is the body language associated with each acupoints used in EFT acupoint with some explanations. We start with the side of hand, Karate Chop.

KARATE CHOP OR SIDE OF HAND

Location: The Karate Chop acupoint is the one you've been using to start rounds of EFT throughout this book and used when you state the set-up statement. It is the first acupoint activated. It's easy to find. While making a fist, it is the thickest crease on the outer side of the hand and is next to the baby finger. You can use either hand.

In Chinese medicine, the body is viewed as lined throughout with bioelectric energy channel, called meridians. These are like the electrical wires in your home, where a switch on the wall activates a circuit, which then turns on a distant overhead light. By activating a meridian at any point (flipping the switch) the entire meridian circuit is activated, generating a soothing effect throughout your body.

The Chinese name these meridians from body organs they flow through. For example, the Karate Chop point is also known as the small intestine meridian (SI-3).

THE ACUPOINT: Karate Chop

Figure 7.1. Karate Chop Acupoint – next to little finger, cover the fat crease you found when making a fist

Body language Interestingly, and right in line with my hypothesis that we use acupoints unconsciously all the time, the Karate Chop point is activated whenever we shake hands with someone. The acupoint is known to calm excessive emotions, to facilitate re-balancing the emotional system (called psychological reversal), and to simply take the edge off tense emotional situations. And we've been doing this all along without realizing it.

A military client pointed out the Karate Chop acupoint is held in both the "at ease" military position (one hand on top and wrapped around the second hand resting on the front of the midsection) and in the "parade at ease" military position (hands positioned behind the back covering this acupoint).

Handshakes, which automatically touch this acupoint, have profound, sometimes world changing significance in international diplomacy. Even the reluctance to shake hands may be an unwillingness to concede, an act of resistant.

Perhaps we should we start a meeting or corral a rambunctious classroom with this karate acupoint to take the edge off. Families may want to interrupt a parent-teenager conflict with this acupoint via a gentle handshake. This handshake, touching the side of hand acupoint, may re-balance an oppositional child or just lower the emotional thermostat of the individual, family or classroom. It helped raising my children in difficult times!

The handshake of peace is included in several religious ceremonies. I recently found it quite soothing at the end of an emotional funeral.

There is no way to know how effective and far reaching this acupoint may be. However, with no harm to anyone; it is worth a try to slip a handshake into your family interactions, particularly at edgy moments.

BODY LANGUAGE Possible Meanings:

"Ok, we can make-up."

"You may have a point."

"Maybe I am being too stubborn about that."

"I'm satisfied. We have an agreement."

"Well maybe this will work out eventually"

Are we rebalancing ourselves? Are we lowering resistance? Or calming each other? Even shaking the hand of the overjoyed winning contestant helps her think straight, bringing her back to reality. Shaking hands with a losing opponent creates a more balanced and appealing humility-beneficial to both winner and loser! Families and teachers might consider a handshake intervention when a child is gearing-up! Add it to a game of "Simon Says" and take the edge off the classroom.

Figure 7.2. The Handshake naturally activates the side of hand acupoint

Example in Real Life

Two boys are intensely fighting on the playground. The principal pulls them apart and gives them two choices: detention or shake hands. Their SUDS emotional level clearly is at a 10! For no other reason other than not wanting to be in detention, and with great reluctance, they shake hands. They now appear more resigned, perhaps their SUDS is 6, and they are able to be on the same playground without an imminent re-attack.

TOP OF HEAD

Location: Simply place your hand on the top of your head and you've found it.

In ancient Hinduism this point is also known as the crown chakra, and represents spirituality and intuition. It's interesting how ancient healing techniques from around the world have many things in common. Both men and women of many faiths cover this part of their head when engaged in their spiritual practice. Is this humility? Does covering this area protect and/or activate spirituality? Interestingly, several other acupuncture meridians pass through this point, forming an electrical intersection of sorts. Chakras and meridian represent areas of the body where life energy can be found.

In Chinese medicine the Top of Head acupoint is called the Governing Vessel (GV-20). It is one of the main meridians.

THE ACUPOINT: Top of Head

Figure 7.3.

155

Body language How many times have you scratched or held the top of your head when puzzled or unsure? Does it calm you? Does it help you think? Does it give you pause to consider? Revitalized I scratch the top of my head when I am confused, pondering or looking for some information stored in my head somewhere! Putting your hands on your head may even mean you are amazed. Or have you ever seen someone who is devastated or enraged with both hands on their head? This intersection of meridians is a powerful acupoint. Consider activating it when you want to open your mind to counter a sense of feeling baffled.

BODY LANGUAGE Possible Meanings:

"Hmmm, I don't know, let me think." (see figure 7.4 below)

"I wonder."

"I'll never fathom all the wonders of the world."

"Boy oh boy, go figure, I never expected that."

"Oh no!"

Figure 7.4. Wonderment

INNER EYEBROW

Location: The Inner Eyebrow acupoint is located, on the inner side of your eyebrow, close to the nose. Some people use the point on the side of the nose, just below the eyebrow.

In Chinese terminology it's known as the Bladder Meridian (BL-1), because the energy channel or "wire" runs through the bladder.

THE ACUPOINT: Inner Eyebrow

Figure 7.5.

Body Language

This acupoint is thought to be the acupoint for trauma or serious upset.
If we get dreadful news or are intensely worried, we often hold or rub our eyebrows and press this acupoint specifically. Donna Eden, international lecturer and author of <u>Energy Medicine,</u> calls this the "Oh my God" point. I agree with her!

If you are upset or feel the need to immediately calm yourself and get back on track, try holding this spot. You may be pleasantly surprised at the results.

BODY LANGUAGE Possible Meanings:

"Oh no, that is bad news and tremendously upsetting." (see Figure 7.6 below)

"I cannot deal with all that."

"I'm really worried"

"Oh my g-d"

Figure 7.6. Upset

OUTER EYE

Location: This acupoint is located just on the side of the eye. It is very close to the eye. It lies right on the edge of the eye socket bone.

In Chinese terminology it's known as the Gall Bladder (GB-1), because the energy channel or "wire" runs through the gall bladder.

THE ACUPOINT: Outer Eye

Figure 7.7. Side of the Eye

Body Language

The Outer Eye is the estimated point for anger, rage, irritation, and serious thought. In expressing anger we may even say, "That person had a lot of **gall** to do that." Thus, gall is even connected in our language with anger.

158

BODY LANGUAGE Possible Meanings:

"Pretty angry" (see figure 7.8 below)

"Concerned"

"Annoyed, frustrated"

"Pensive"

"Serious thought"

Figure 7.8. Irritated and Annoyed

Example:

Years ago a colleague was angry about being in court and wasn't sure she could contain her fury while listening to "lies." She used this acupoint to get through the trial. Using this acupoint did not make her happy. However, she was able to sit through the court sessions without shouting at the witnesses and being able to camouflage her disdain. She improvised by rubbing both sides when she was really furious and it contained her.

Give it a try!

UNDER THE EYE

Location! This acupoint is located just below the eye on the edge of the eye socket bone. Use slight pressure to locate the eye socket the first time. Afterwards, only use extremely light touch.

In Chinese medicine this acupoint is referred to as the Stomach meridian (ST-1).

THE ACUPOINT: Under the Eye

Figure 7.9.

Body Language

This acupoint is a huge one for me. I had been overly anxious my entire life, until I learned about these meridian acupoints used in EFT. This one is the acupoint for anxiety and the stomach. My stomach has always been the gauge for my feelings. It tightens and churns, has butterflies, twists, drops, and sinks when I worry. I either want to eat too much or eat too little. I may even experience nausea.

BODY LANGUAGE Possible Meanings:

"Pretty scared and stressed?" (see figure 7.10 below)

"Anxious, worried, and nervous"

Anticipating the worst; doomsday and catastrophic thinking, called "what if thinking". What if bad things happen?

Figure 7.10. Anxiety and Worry

Example: Asked about fears, many people will grip their stomach. If I think I am running late, my stomach has heaviness, a drop, and even a squeeze. My stomach is a barometer of my comfort level; it is not always a welcome barometer.

UNDER THE NOSE.

Location: This point is located under the nose in the slight indent.

In Chinese medicine it's called the Governing Vessel (GV-27). This major meridian begins under the nose, goes up through the head, and down the back to the tailbone. It's a significant one.

THE ACUPOINT: Under the Nose

Figure 7.11.

Body Language

Often these acupoints effect physical functioning. I have asked over 400 people to breathe normally and rate their breathing. I have subsequently asked them to touch all the acupoints. The average gain is a 20% deeper breath. I believe this acupoint is one of the more significant in this experience and can be used independently to increase breathing.

Activating this meridian appears to bring up *diaphragmatic breathing*, a common anxiety-relieving technique. Diaphragmatic breathing was explained to me in a 1987 Harvard-Mass General Hospital workshop. The diaphragm is the large muscle that separates the chest and the abdomen. Its function is to expand the chest and creates the pressure changes that pull air into our lungs. Movement of the diaphragm is assisted by the abdominal muscles. Expanding and contracting the abdominal muscles help the diaphragm fully expand the chest and this allows oxygen to be pulled all the way down deep into the lungs. Diaphragmatic breathing is also called "belly breathing", because the abdominal muscles play such an important role.

Diaphragmatic breathing is taught to anxiety clients, in order to interrupt shallow breathing and give them stress relief. It is also taught to singers, cheerleaders, news reporters, and preachers to open up their lungs and give them more volume. You automatically "belly breathe" laying on your stomach – it may slow you down and help get to sleep or rest. I believe this deep breathing is what cigarette smokers are seeking - to calm them.

This is estimated to be the acupoint for calming feelings about: not having control of a situation; or being embarrassed.

BODY LANGUAGE Possible Meanings:

"I don't know that answer, let me think." (See figure 7.12 below)

"I don't have control of this."

"I want to understand what is needed."

"I'm embarrassed."

Figure 7.12. Seeking Control of the Situation or Embarrassment

Example:

The finger across the top lip or under the nose is commonly seen in everyday life. I watched a televised college basketball coach hold this point, when his team lost their focus. When it got really bad, he switched to the point under the lip possibly indicting not feeling good enough, feeling unsure, or not knowing. I have no idea what this coach was actually thinking, but this is what his body language showed when his team was faltering.

(In person, I would have checked in and asked if he was worried about his team at that moment, and not assumed it.)

UNDER THE LIP

__Locations:__ This acupoint is located under the lip midway to the chin.

Chinese medicine refers to this point as the Conception Vessel (CV-24), one of the main meridians for the smooth flow of the all-important, life carrying Chi. It runs from its origin under the chin down the front of the body. Interestingly, a hug probably activates a soothing response from this meridian that goes down the front of your body.

THE ACUPOINT: Under the Lip

Figure 7.13.

Body Language People may unconsciously activate this point when they have feelings of uncertainty, not feeling being good enough, of not knowing something, of feeling shame, unworthy or when they're experiencing self-doubt.

BODY LANGUAGE Possible Meanings:

"I am not sure. Let me think." (see figure 7.14 below)

"Hmmm. "I don't know."

"I am not good enough."

"I am not worthy."

Figure 7.14. Unknowing, not sure

Example:

Aguste Rodin famous statue, "The Thinker," is holding this point. According to the Wikipedia, it "depicts a man in a sober meditation battling a powerful internal struggle."

Or is this calming him with this acupoint position as he contemplated his situation? The Thinker (or Le Pensuer) is located outside the Rodin Museum in Philadelphia.

COLLAR BONE

Location: This point is just under the collar bone a few inches from the sternum, and it is below the shoulders. Technically, it's in the indent below the collarbone, not on the bone. The point seems to be effective in the general vicinity, even if it's not pressed exactly right on the spot.

In Chinese medicine, this is known as the Kidney Meridian (K-27).

THE ACUPOINT: Collarbone

Figure 7.15. Index finger activating the Collar Bone acupoint, just under the collarbone

Body Language Common body language for this point may mean you're being too hard on yourself, that you're extra punitive, or that you have fears. I will joke with perfectionists and tell them to keep their fingers on their collarbone until the next session. Are perfectionists hard on themselves, or have they internalized their fear of criticism from others? This acupoint alone or if activated on both sides is quite comforting!

BODY LANGUAGE Possible Meanings:

"I am sorry that I ruined your day." (see Figure 7.16 below)

"Too hard on myself"

"This is scary"

"I'm overly responsible for everything and full of guilt."

Example:

I often see older depressed ladies holding this point if they have made the smallest transgression, such as being a few minutes late for an hour appointment. They clearly are too hard on themselves. They say, "I'm sorry for ruining your day - by being a few minutes late."

Figure 7.16. Too Hard on Oneself

UNDER THE ARM

___Location:___ For women, it occurs where the bra strap is located under the armpit. For men, it exists four inches below the armpit and parallel to the nipple.

This is the Spleen Meridian (SP-21).

THE ACUPOINT: Under the Arm

Figure 7.17. 4" Under the Arm pit where the thumb is placed in this photo.

Figure 7.18. Worried about the Future

Body Language This acupoint is associated with worry about the future. It is activated when we fold our arms. We might be unconsciously calming worries about the future. Some people consider this a "closed off" position, which makes sense if you are worried or fearful.

BODY LANGUAGE Possible Meanings:

"Worried about the future"

Closed off to be self-protective

Example:

After the horrible Columbine School shooting, a second school shooting occurred in Georgia. The newspaper had a large photo of three terrorized girls. The first one had her head down and her hands on her inner eyebrow—estimated as representing *traumatized*. The second girl also had her head down with her hands covering her mouth and above the lip area—estimated as representing *not having control of the situation*. The third girl was looking up, but she had both hands under her arms (as above); this is estimated as depicting *future worry*. All these emotional estimates made sense to me.

THE GAMUT POINT

Location: This point is located in the gully (or indention) between the little finger bone that extends into the back of the hand and between the ring finger bone that extends into the back of the hand.

In Chinese medicine this is the Thyroid meridian (Th-3). It is an important acupoint. Dr. Roger Callahan, founder Thought Field Therapy, named it the gamut point.

Body Language

The Gamut Point is the estimated acupoint for emotional and physical pain. This makes sense. If you hurt me emotionally I will cry. If you hurt me physically, I will cry. Thus somehow physical and emotional pain is wired together noted by the same response, to cry. Interestingly, antidepressants are often used for pain management.

As I mentioned in a previous chapter, when a depressed client is admitted for an inpatient hospitalization, the thyroid is tested because thyroid disease can mimic depression. The Gamut Point is on the thyroid meridian.

This acupoint can be activated to relieve physical and/or emotional pain. I complete all dental work holding this acupoint; I do not use any other anesthesia or pain management. My dentist is more nervous than I am. He always leaves shaking his head, incredulously telling me I am the best patient.

To use for pain management, hold this acupoint for 15 to 20 breaths to see if your SUDS pain level drops. If it does, then stay here until the pain is gone or the benefit stops. I also recommend that you rest your hands on your lap in a comfortable manner. If the pain does not drop, do some re-balancing using the pretzel or the brief energy correction, explained in the next chapter. Then activate this acupoint again. If this pain short-cut does not work, try applying the whole recipe of 11 acupoints. I needed the whole recipe when my mouth throbbed after a tooth was pulled.

THE ACUPOINT: Gamut Point

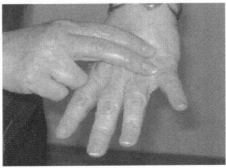

Figure 7.19.

HEART HOLD

This point is not part of the original EFT protocol, but is my addition and can be used alone or in combination with EFT.

Location: Place both hands across your heart area. This is also used in several cultures as part of a respectful bow.

According to reflexology and hand massage charts, the hands house most of the meridians and flow through the hands. Furthermore, it is the heart chakra position, symbolic of compassion, tenderness, unconditional love, and feeling grounded and a sense well-being. In Yoga, a heart chakra meditation releases sadness and fear, and it brings in compassion and love.

I sometimes call this "A tranquilizer in your hands," because it is so calming.

Body Language The bowing position with hand across your heart implies respect and greeting. It's also noted in everyday life to express sincerity, genuineness, seriousness, and honesty. It is often described as a gesture "to follow one's heart". People often use only one hand to cover the heart area. My clients tell me this position feels "very peaceful."

THE POSITION: Heart Hold

Figure 7.20.

TYPICAL BODY LANGUAGE

The following photos mimic many upsetting moods that people exhibit and acupoints they are activating via this body language. Perhaps you will see how the 11 acupoints used in EFT are a part of everyday body language.

The pictures that follow hit many of the above mentioned acupoints. My hypothesis is that people use these acupoints unconsciously, because our bodies remember that they calm. An important recommendation of this book is to use theses acupoint *intentionally* in the EFT sequence, in order to calm, self-soothe, reboot, re-balance, recharge, desensitize, self-regulate, and get on with your life.

Body language (accidentally or not) hits many acupoints. Look at the photos of the body language and the EFT acupoints. Consider the connections. Do some situations seem more closed tied to one gesture than another? Interpreting which gesture connects with which emotion will vary from person to person.

Here are some situations to consider and may be represented in the photos below as you watch. Make a guess which of these emotional situations are reflected in the face photos below.

A person whose favorite sports team is losing;

A person who is in a scary movie;

A person whose family was called with the worst possible news;

A person who has witnessed a fatal car accident; or

A person who is remembering a traumatic event in their life.

The commonality is the recognition that each photo shows a reaction to distress. And there is no exact answer to what event brought up which picture, because people experience situations differently.

Acupressure Face Lift – an Unexpected Gift of these Acupoints

Jingduan Yang, MD, Director of Acupuncture and Oriental Medicine at Jefferson Hospital in Philadelphia, told me that the acupoints employed here in EFT are the equivalent to his treatment as an "acupressure face lift." So maybe you will even look younger, using the acupoints mentioned in this book! That alone could be a motivator to use these daily. Interesting, the same method takes down stress and enhances your beauty. I see a correlation, do you?

Emotion Estimates and an Educated Guess

> "I've learned that people will forget what you said, people will forget what you did, but people will never forget how you made them feel." -- Maya Angelou

These normal body positions probably represent emotional statements. When you observe them, you can ask empathetic questions to determine their actual meaning. Even if your guess is incorrect, the person will probably perceive your concern and tell you what the meaning to them is. Either way, you are offering a considerate and compassionate discussion.

I was always amazed as a young therapist at how specific people use their own idiosyncratic language. I could say,

> "Gee, that must make you angry".

They corrected me saying:

> "No, not angry, just mad!"

I did not see the difference between angry and mad, but they did and that is what mattered. I learned to worry less about the actual verbalization and interpretation of the body language and to appreciate the concern expressed and that language use varies person-to-person.

If I see a client holding an acupoint spot while telling me a story, I note it. I subsequently *check out* what they're actually feeling in their own words. I never assume I am correct until we discuss it. Below, imagine a person is holding or scratching the acupoints in the second column. Here are some examples of my questions:

Possible Checking-Out Questions	Body Part held by the Person
Are you confused by this?	(*top of head*)
Was this terribly upsetting for you?	(*inner eyebrow*)
Were you angry/concerned this happened?	(*outer eye*)

Are you worried about something?	(*under the eye*)
Did you feel as if you did not have control or were you embarrassed?	(*under the nose*)
Did you feel like you did not deserve to have that or did you not know anything about it?	(*under the lip*)
Were you too hard on yourself or too anxious about it?	(*collar bone*)
Were you trying to bring up your energy and concentration?	(*collar bone*)
Are you worried about this happening in the future?	(*under the arm*)
Did this make you sad/depressed or cause physical pain for you?	(*gamut point*)
Did you feel it deeply or does it sincerely affect you?	(*heart hold*)

Most times, clients agree with the above questions and perceive them as empathetic inquiry. In exploring peoples' well-being, these are also wonderful observations and questions to portray your interest. These questions are less open ended than that typical question, "How did that make you feel?" They imply a deeper level of understanding and may evoke more meaningful exploration.

Summary

I submit my hypothesis that the acupoints used in theses similar meridian treatments - Emotional Freedom Techniques, Thought Field Therapy, Tapping, Meridian Therapies and Energy Psychology - are common human mannerisms. They are brought into play by the body language we commonly use to calm and self-soothe. These acupoints are right before our eyes, and we can engage them when our awareness is attuned.

Furthermore, my guess is that since meridians run throughout the entire body, people holding other areas may be activating soothing meridians too.

Use these acupoints intentionally when you need to desensitize upsetting events. It is thought that your body chemistry changes, lessening stress hormones. You heal. We discussed Dr. Dawson Church's empirical study earlier that cortisol, the stress hormone, decreases when applying these acupoints. (Stressproject.org). The burden of carrying the residual damage from life's worst events can be mitigated via the change that occurs with these techniques.

The emotions associated with the acupoints above involve common observations. They are viewed over and over in peoples' mannerisms. Research is validated by the following question: "Is this finding easily reproducible?" The answer with self-soothing and acupoints is an emphatic, "Yes". Do your own research. Watch people today at work, in the park, or on television. Observe particularly the losing fans in any sports stadium. You will see these acupoints instinctively accessed all day long. Interestingly even actors utilize these acupoints in their portrayal of emotions.

Various *estimates* of the emotions are expressed by touching these acupoints. Many people agree that certain acupoints express an emotion but there is no need to have absolutely conformity. When I am treating myself with EFT, I use all the acupoints. However, I know that without even being aware of it (because I catch myself), I instinctively activate acupoints in my daily life. Perhaps use of specific acupoints is part of our outward expression of inner emotional life.

Some think humans are capable of healing themselves, of regenerating good physical and emotional health. In this healing puzzle, acupoints are one possibility.

Donna Eden (Energy Medicine, www.innersource.net) said when she has created something she finds it later in literature or in different cultures. I am not alone in noting that these acupoints are connected to emotions.

Even an internet search on "acupuncture and emotions" highlights the Chinese traditional medicine view that body organs and emotions are inseparable entities. Chinese traditional medicine sees the mind-body as one, not separate. We can observe Chinese medicine acupoints possibly in their simplest form: *body language*.

The next chapter will add more finishing touches and additional tools, in case EFT gets stuck and needs some more refinements.

CHAPTER 8:

IF EFT GETS STUCK

We ask ourselves, who am I to be brilliant, gorgeous, handsome, talented and fabulous? Actually, who are you not to be?"

— Nelson Mandela

Persistence and Repetition

The meridian-based stress relief techniques you've learned in the preceding chapters are faster and more thorough than anything I've ever seen. One round, when done slowly, takes 30 seconds of time. The normal expectation for speed of recovery from the upset is that the issue/emotion/body sensation will drop 2 to 4 SUDS intensity points with every three rounds–or 1 ½ minutes of application. This 2 to 4 point SUDS drops continues with every three rounds of the application of the light touch or tapping on the meridian acupoints. So even if you have a huge upset and apply the rounds 20 times, this amounts to only 10 minutes time to attain calmness, balance, and to feel recharged.

Persistence is important! You need to repeat the rounds until your issue is as calm as possible. Hopefully you have a spontaneous insight too. Like exercise or medication, you get the benefit only if you use the techniques. Be sure to use them as you become aware of new aspects of processed issues as well. Jack Canfield, author and editor of the <u>Chicken Soup</u> book series and professional business and life coach, (www.jackcanfield.com) recommends to his coaching clients that they use EFT 15 minutes a day to curtail whatever is currently in your way! Remember too that you can apply it in any circumstances as Camouflaged EFT, as discussed in the last chapters, so that only you know you are stressed.

Among EFT practitioners, there is a conservative estimate that these meridian-based stress relief techniques are about 85% effective. Some insist they are 100% effective, if applied well. Occasionally, there can be some stuck parts that do not resolve even with repeated application of these techniques. This chapter covers what to consider for that resistant 15%. Most people using EFT never need any of the following methods. However, these refinements are included in case you get stuck. You will know you are stuck if you go through several rounds of EFT and your SUDS rating scale does not drop or only drops 1 point.

Beginning with the basics, let's look at what can get tangled. This chapter describes four simple roadblocks that may interfere with effective EFT techniques. These include:

1) *massive psychological reversal*;

2) *topic too global*;

3) *switching aspects*; and

4) *early aspects or old clutter driving the upset.*

Corrections for each of these issues are also provided below. An easy-to-use worksheet, which summarizes these *four issues* and their *corrections*, is included at the end of this chapter.

Roadblock 1
Massive Psychological Reversal

In Chinese medicine, Chi is defined as life energy and circulates in our bodies much like in-home electric circuitry. Turning on a light switch on the wall activates the wiring to turn on the distant overhead light. Similarly, touching an acupoint on a meridian activates the entire meridian that flows throughout your body, which is soothing and energizing. Sometimes at home, the circuit breaker trips and needs to be rebooted. Similarly, sometimes the body's energy flow gets reversed, mixed up or clogged and needs to be rebooted and re-balanced. In this technique it is called a *massive psychological reversal*. It is easy to correct and not dangerous, so don't let the terminology scare you!

There are two easy ways to re-balance Chi--our life energy: the "pretzel" and the "brief energy correction". Use either the "pretzel" or the "brief energy correction" techniques, described below in the next two sections, when the SUDS level refuses to drop.

Technique 42: The Pretzel – a Rebalance

An easy–to-remember way to Correct Massive Psychological Reversal

The pretzel can be used as a correction for massive psychological reversal caused by over-energy. In other words, when you're hyped up due to either positive or negative emotions (i.e. energy), the pretzel works well to rebalance your energy into a more natural, calmer state. I believe it also corrects negative energy, which is energy that persistently holds you out of balance. Even though you usually feel nothing, sit in the position for *one minute* or more to rebalance your energy.

Three points of light touch are involved in the pretzel. The fingers are interlaced and held comfortably across your abdomen with your forearms resting as much as comfortably as possible on your torso. Now cross your ankles. Hold this position for one minute. Figure 8-1 on the next page, provides two optional stances illustrating the "pretzel".

My anxious clients often note subtle relief, perhaps a few points drop in their SUDS rating. People who are anxious are typically overcharged and overly sensitive; and they have too much nervous energy.

A few clients with Post-Traumatic Stress Disorder (PTSD) have reported to me that the pretzel position reintegrates them when they are beginning to dissociate. A Vietnam veteran client told me that this position gave him relief when he begins to dissociate; he could actually feel himself refocus in his body. It substantially removed the haze and the growing distance he felt from whatever situation had arisen. Another veteran reported a similar response; as has another - a childhood abuse survivor.

Interestingly, the "pretzel" can often be seen in normal body language similar to the body language discussed in Chapter 7. This "pretzel" position was taught to me as a young girl on how to sit when wearing a skirt! I see men in this position with their legs sprawled out. As with so many other aspects of body language, perhaps the pretzel is intuitively invoked when needed.

You can talk, watch television, or do any sedate activity - while holding this position for one minute or more. A few of my clients report they do this at night and it helps settle them for sleep. This familiar body position appears natural and is not awkward.

Figure 8-1. The Pretzel. Interlace your fingers and rest your hands on your abdomen or chest with your inner arms comfortably resting on your torso. Cross your ankles. Hold for

one minute or more. Most people rebalance nicely in this position. Either of these pictured positions work just fine, use the one you prefer.

Again, this is simply a re-balance of your energy system.

For those with experience in Energy Psychology, the pretzel is my adaptation of Wayne Cook's Hook-up. In Cook's Hook-up, the hands are more twisted with pressure on the wrists. My adaptation came into being because a colleague misunderstood my description of Cook's Hook-up and actually ended up with this more user-friendly version.

Technique 43: **Brief Energy Correction**

A quicker way to correct Massive Psychological Reversal

The "brief energy correction" technique is quicker than the pretzel, but it is a tad harder to remember. The pretzel works nicely for many people. However, those who don't receive any benefits from the pretzel should give this brief energy correction a try. It's another posture that can help realign unbalanced Chi, life energy. So if the SUDS level still does not budge when you are applying EFT, you can try using this quick brief energy correction.

The brief energy correction technique is initiated by placing one hand over your belly button. This hand stays stationary. You move the other hand to four positions holding for one full breath at each position. If you prefer, you can hold each for a count of 5. Place the second hand so the fingers stretch across both sides of the collar bone and hold for one full breath. Then place two fingers under your nose and hold it for another full breath. Then do the same with two fingers beneath your lips. Finally, cover your tailbone with your hand and hold it for a full breath or 5 seconds.

A review of the brief energy correction to a count of five below:

1) place one hand on belly button over clothes and do not move it,

2) place other hand across the collarbone-hold for one breath.

3)   move two fingers to under the nose –hold for one breath,

4)   move two fingers to under the lip -hold for one breath and

5)   reach to the tailbone with your hand - hold for one breath.

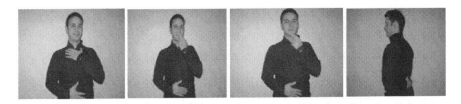

Figure 8.2. Brief Energy Correction – hold one breath at every point

After using either of these two corrections (i.e., the pretzel or the brief energy correction), go back to EFT from Chapter 3 and try again.)

Technique 44: **Cross Crawl – For Brain Rebalance**

Here is another technique, which is somewhat related to the two massive psychological reversal techniques described previously (i.e., the pretzel and the brief energy correction.) This technique is the "cross crawl", which is useful for "brain rebalancing". You have your tires rebalanced; don't you wish you could have your brain rebalanced? Here is one way to do that. It can also rekindle your mental energy when you are tired. It simply involves crossing the vertical mid line of your body by swinging your right hand to your left knee, releasing it and then swinging your left hand to your right knee. Avoid crossing your own hands while doing this by keeping your hands about 8 to 12 inches apart. You are alternating swinging one hand at a time to your opposite knee and vice versa. Repeat 5 or more times. The recommendation is that you do this standing, thus you raising your knees as in marching positions. You can do this sitting, if you prefer.

This method is common in many techniques, including Donna Eden's Energy Medicine, (www.innersource.net). This activity may be helpful all by itself with Attention Deficit Disorder (ADD), oppositional situations, or some neurological deficits.

Roadblock 2
Topic Too Global

Another reason EFT might get stuck or not be fully effective is taking on too large of an issue at once. The goal is to break down the upsetting issue into smaller, specific parts or aspects. Energy Psychology, including Emotional Freedom Technique (Craig), Thought Field Therapy (Callahan), Evolving Thought Field Therapy (Diepold et al.), and other derivatives of the meridian therapies, are effective methods. But it is essential to recognize these techniques clear one small part or *aspect* at a time. They usually do not multi-task! It may take work on several aspects to clear your upsetting issue.

To combat this weakness (in the words of Ann Adams, LCSW),

"To be terrific, be specific."

This means that after you have selected an issue to work on, keep asking yourself:

What in particular about this issue bothers me?

Also, remember that what's most important is your *impression*. If you are working on yourself, it is your impression of the emotions involved that are the most important. If you're working on a friend or client, it's *his* take on the emotions, not yours. A useful guideline when helping another is to use her/his words and impression, not your own.

For example, I received a call from a colleague wanting to use EFT on her child for an immediate school upset. She asked me for the wording for the reminder phrase. I had to explain to her that it was her daughter's words that were important; not my words or even hers.

When helping someone by using EFT, we are the guide and the sleuth to uncover the specifics about the issue that bothers the other person.

Questions to dig deeper and find the specific emotional aspects could look like the following:

- What in particular, is bothering you about the problem?

- What aspect of that bothers you?

- What part of that bothers you?

- And what aspect of that is the problem?

CASE **School Upset Example 8.1 from the school upset just mentioned:**

>   Q. What is bothering you about school?
>   A. Science

>   Q. What is it about science that bothers you?
>   A. The teacher is mean.

>   Q. What is it about the mean teacher that affects you?
>   A. I'm afraid to ask a question when I don't understand.

>   (This is a clear aspect to work on: an *emotion* about an *issue* and a *reminder phrase* has even been created as well.)

Adding in the Set-up statement: Optional. The setup statement is

>   "I'm ok even though... I am *afraid about asking a question in science class.*"

The Set-up statement focuses you on the problem. You can repeat this entire statement, while you are holding the karate spot on the side of hand. The set-up statement is often useful to focus the person on the problem when the person is not actually in the problem that minute.

Next the reminder phrase which is a shortened version of the above.

Reminder phrase is *"afraid about asking a question in science class."*

>   Repeat this phrase on each acupoint, as you go through the EFT sequence for 3 rounds or more until the upset and the SUDS level are very low.

Often when the SUDS level is 3 or below, a revelation, an "aha moment," a spontaneous, liberating insight will commonly occur. This is because all of a sudden, the emotional piece is no longer clouding the view.

In this example the student's spontaneous insight was stated:

"It is my teacher's job to answer questions, so I plan to ask when I don't understand." This is both true and an expression of liberation from an inhibition.

| CASE | **Typical Mother-Daughter Conflict-Example 8.2** |

Here is one more example of drilling down to find the core issue and the reminder phrase.

> Q. What is it that bothers me when I visit my mother's house?
> A. She always asks me personal questions.

> Q. What is it about my mother asking me personal questions that bothers me?
> A. I am so sensitive to her slight disapproval.

> Q. What is it about her disapproval that bothers me?
> A. I get flustered and doubt my decisions.

So here we have the reminder phrase, *flustered about my mother's disapproval.*

> **Reminder phrase** is *"flustered with my mother's disapproval"*
> Repeat this phrase on each acupoint from the worksheet at the end of Chapter 3, repeating the sequence for 3 rounds or more. Take a new SUDS rating after every 3 rounds with the goal of lowering your intensity to the point you are no longer bothered.

> **Spontaneous Insight** Once the SUDS level is 3 or below, a new spontaneous insight can emerge. Here the person said "She is just worried about me because she loves me." This different perspective made it bearable and liberated her in the relationship. She even repeated this insight to her mother, and they laughed and hugged. What a lovely scenario compared to gruff rebukes!

As an aside, no relationship is more intense than the mother/daughter relationship. Women tend to focus on details which can result in nit-picking. This is followed closely by the father/son relationship. In fact, family relationships, while loving, are also loaded with expectations and disappointments. It is so important to recognize that all people are "**different and equal**." If we could be wholly at peace with that, so many frustrations would fade away: in families, at school, at work, in places of worship, even between nations. Differences make people interesting!

Roadblock 3
Switching Aspects Too Quickly

Let's say you are working on an issue by yourself (or helping someone else), and you're progressing and getting good results. Every 3 rounds of acupoints the SUDS rating is dropping. However, at some point this progressive reduction of upsets and corresponding SUDS ratings begins to climb higher. Out of the blue the SUDS might have gone up from a 3 to 6!

Initially this is baffling. You have probably switched to a new aspect. As you calmed down the original aspect of the issue, you may begin thinking of a new aspect that has not been addressed. You may not even realize that it's happening. For example, if you are working on sadness over losing a pet, you might switch to thinking how annoyed you were at veterinarian. Annoyance at the vet is a new issue. The solution is to go back to the sadness over the pet and stay with it until calm evidenced by a low SUDs. Then start anew: create a reminder phrase on the annoyance at the vet and desensitize that.

Put that new aspect on hold until you complete the first aspect. I often ask clients to put the new aspect "on the shelf", up high and off to the side of their peripheral focus, a technique from gestalt therapy. I promise them we will get to it next and, indeed, it is the next aspect of the problem that we address.

This phenomenon is often present in clients with Attention Deficit Disorder and also in people who are accustomed to multi-tasking. Be aware of the necessity of staying with one aspect of the problem. Emphasize different words or use more dramatic tone of voice stating the reminder phrase to help you stay focused. Sometimes I say "ONLY thinking about sadness of losing your cat," the emotion about the issue.

A good metaphor for this is vacuuming a large room. If you slide the vacuum for one sweep in each corner of the room, the room remains dirty. It is better to vacuum each quarter of the room thoroughly before moving on to the others. We must "vacuum" each aspect thoroughly before we move to the next aspect.

If you are working alone and you realize you notice this shifting aspect, write the reminder phrase on a piece of paper. Make yourself read the paper as you stimulate each acupoint.

| CASE | **Frustration About Work Changes – Example 8.3**

A news reporter is frustrated with the weekly changing of her day off. The reminder phrase we are using is:

"frustrated with my days off changing every week."

She is calming down, with each round diminishing her upset until the last round. Her SUDS scores taken after every three rounds were 7-> 4-> 2 -> 6. We stop here to look at what she is thinking about. She reports that her husband acts annoyed when her work schedule changes, even though she made it clear that would happen when she went back to work. She had shifted to a new aspect of the situation.

Let's ask her to put the second aspect on the shelf for now, and to only think about her own annoyance with the weekly schedule change. That SUDS is a 2. Continue with the acupoints and take it as low as it will go. I often say to a client when we are at SUDS of 2, "I am being greedy, let's just see if we can get it even lower."

After completing the desensitization on the first aspect, we move to the second issue where the reminder phrase will be:

"frustrated about my husband acting annoyed by my schedule change."

Her final spontaneous insight was: it goes with the territory of being a news reporter and that her husband wants her to bring income home too.

She understood about the scheduling when she took this job. In other words, she cleared the negative emotional charge on this issue and calmly explains, "This is how it is and I love the work!"

Roadblock 4
Early Aspect Cluttering the Way: Go for the Gold!

Clearing specific aspects of the problem you're working on with EFT is a strong technique. However, it can be more powerful when you find the *first* or **worst** time a deep-rooted similar experience affected you. Furthermore, it has been observed that when we are triggered to old events, our emotional response is consistent with the developmental age we were when they happened. If you get teased at work, for example, you surely don't want to act like your inner 3-year old child crying and trying to slap your tormentor. By using EFT to clear clutter, you have a better chance of responding with maturity and maybe, a witty remark!

CASE   Co-Workers Frustration Cluttered by the Past –
Example 8.4

A client reported being frustrated with co-workers in her office, because they would use her computer and pens without asking her, and sometimes they absentmindedly kept the pens. She was unwilling to confront them, because she was afraid she would scream and rant endlessly about feeling disrespected, which she knew was an exaggeration. So we began to pull apart the various aspects.

Here are her results:

> *Upset about her using my computer* SUDS = 9

> *Upset using my pens* SUDS = 3

> *Upset she does not return my pens* SUDS = 7

Begin treating the worst - the highest SUDS rated - because the lesser upsets often defuse during the treatment of the most severe issue. Here we will use "upset using my computer." SUDS =9.

Once these three aspects were defused, we needed to see if there was any stubborn clutter left from the past. I asked her if anything else about her co-workers using her stuff or anything from her childhood felt similar.

She told me, "Yes, it reminds me of when my little brother would tear up my bedroom and my parents would only yell at me for getting upset as he was just 'a baby'. I couldn't yell at him, because he was seven years younger. So it was futile."

There now appeared two more connected aspects from her past. The reminder phrases desensitized are given below. The decreasing SUDS levels are noted for each 3 rounds of EFT acupoints.

"upset about remembering my brother tearing up my room."
SUDS 8→4→ 1

"feeling helpless (futile) about getting my parents to help me make him stop." SUDS 6→3→0

Our goal is not to numb people out, or to stop caring about real life. The intent is to clear outdated emotional clutter so that we can address the current problem with tact, compassion, and intelligence.

The final step in the example above was her enlightened spontaneous insight.

"These items actually belong to the company so she has a right to use them too. I will schedule a private time to meet with her about returning what she uses and putting them back where I can find them." This person can now use her mature thought processes that were clouded by her emotional upset.

To reiterate, it is more thorough to get to the emotional clutter from the *first or worst* time you experienced a similar negative emotion. When you clean something, you must start with the deep dirt. Then you can dust and polish. We are doing the same with EFT. Our *first or worst* events lay the ground work for our future reactions to similar events.

Review and Worksheet-- Cheat Sheet for When EFT Needs More Focus.

1) **MASSIVE PSYCHOLOGICAL REVERSAL** - Use when you are working on an issue without benefit, such as the SUDS level dropping only one point or less. Try either of these:

Pretzel – Fingers interlaced resting relaxed on the abdomen, inner arms resting comfortably on the torso, ankles crossed. Hold *one* minute or more.

Brief Energy Correction – One hand holding and covering the belly button. Other hand moves sequentially to the collar bone, under the lip, under the nose, and tailbone. Hold each approximately one breath.

2) **TOPIC TOO GLOBAL** -- "To be terrific, be SPECIFIC" –Ann Adam, LCSW. Find several aspects for each problem and ONLY work on ONE at a time. (What is it about this issue that is bothering you now?)

3) **SWITCHING ASPECTS** – A good clue this has happened is if the SUDS rating goes up rather than down. 99% of the time when I see this with clients, we discover they have switched their thoughts to a different aspect. They get some relief and are ready for another part of the upset. I often have them "put that next part on the shelf" temporarily and promise we will get back to it. We then focus on the original issue and finish it first.

4) **EARLY ASPECTS OR OLD CLUTTER DRIVING THE UPSET**

Ask: what might be lying deeper beneath this problem.

Ask: What early experience does this remind me of?

Ask: When was the *first or worst* time this happened?

Be careful when you are working with other people, because you often don't know where they are going. If it gets too intense, stop using the upsetting words and just calm them with acupoints and grounding them by describing the current time and place to them.

Timing is important. Do not ask about an issue unless you have the time to work on it.

The following chapters discuss situations where stress thrives and how to remedy them, including learning more communication techniques. I bet you can identify with a few of them! There are lots of everyday examples of which you might relate.

CHAPTER 9:

GRIEF & LOSS

"Do not judge me by my successes, judge me by how many
times I fell down and got back up again."

— Nelson Mandela

Introduction

The following chapters focus on stressful issues that commonly creep into
our lives. Perhaps you are dealing with one of these issues. This chapter
deals with the most common and difficult issues; grief or loss that
destabilizes us. The common stages of grief are reviewed because it can be
helpful to have some expectation of what grief may look like.

Other everyday concerns addressed in Chapter 10 are anger and conflict.
Chapter 11 addresses common bandits that steal our zest for life including
automobile accidents, medical worries and then, sleep problems and
couples conflicts. All of these issues create stress and are a part of living
but can be overwhelming.

Cases are offered to lead by example with the hope that you can change the details and find relief for your personal situations. Cases are composite cases with identifying data changed.

We will approach these situations with many effective techniques to help you cope, as well as EFT. With EFT, as usual we begin by identifying the issues and clearing the associated emotional turmoil. We can then go deeper to identify the defining moment from the past that made the triggering event so powerful in the present.

Reminder Phrases are listed in *italics*. Feel free to create individually personalized reminder phrases and follow along. If you want to, you can add the clause "I am okay even though" or "I deeply and completely love and accept myself even though..."to the reminder phrase to create the set-up statement. Stated first, the set-up statement is optional (but perhaps useful) in focusing on the issue, and adding a component of self-acceptance.

You may need to refer to the Emotional and Mind-Body Sweep Worksheets located at the end of Chapters 3 and 6. Once the issue is desensitized, a liberating, spontaneous insight emerges.

You'll see that the lists of aspects here are abundant. This will enable us to cover the issue comprehensively. Don't worry that you need to eliminate all of them. Usually, the removal of 1 to 5 of the aspects collapses the entire issue. A few stubborn issues can require the treatment of additional aspects. This was true for many of my anxiety issues.

A way to remember the 5 steps is that the steps spell the word CARES. Indeed, the goal is that EFT *cares* for you and your issues, so they become desensitized and you are whole again

Also included are steps and stages of processing different issue so you can also, head back to Technique 3 on page 20 and utilize the 5 steps of verbally processing your upsets.

GRIEF

"Give sorrow words; the grief that does not speak knits up the o-er wrought heart and bids it break." — William Shakespeare, Macbeth

A hugely upsetting event in all our lives is the death of a loved one. I see people who would never enter therapy otherwise. Divorce also involves grief, except there are some additional issues of rejection, a failure, and a struggle for closure. Death, divorce and other losses (job, relocation, a pet, or even a friend moving away) follow some predictable stages of grief outlined next.

Grief from the Death of a Loved One

The stages of grief listed below represent my adaptation from expert Elizabeth Kubler-Ross. These stages can be experienced in any order, and these stages can be re-visited in a random way. Knowing these stages will help you understand a number of different intense emotions are normal. Also, people grieve in different ways, so try not to judge others even if you are grieving the same person.

Technique 45: **The Stages of Grief**

STAGES - These stages identify strong yet common emotional reactions to loss and offer empathy and reassurance that they are normal. You can use EFT to lessen their intensity. The bereaved think they are losing their mind. Normalizing this process can help the bereaved know these are expected reactions to grief. As mentioned, these stages also apply if the loss is not a person, but is a job, an opportunity, a home, etc. Here are the stages of grief.

Shock/denial

When notified of the loss of a loved one, a common response is "You're kidding", even though no one jokes about this. It is just unbelievable! There is a struggle to grasp the ramifications. Shock/denial can last a few days, weeks or months. It can even return months and years later. Sometimes, I think denial may be a way to help the person to be able to do what they have to do, i.e., drive to the hospital, arrange a funeral, or cancel work. It is probably compassionate psychological anesthesia, allowing the reality of the loss to seep in slowly.

Crying, sadness

Everyone understands sadness in grief. Normalize it, offer tissues and provide empathy. Actually encourage it through empathetic listening. There are some chemicals released with tears that make one feel better. People acknowledge they feel better after a "good cry." It is necessary grief work.

Anger

This stage needs explanation because it can be unexpected or upsetting. Anger surfaces that the person died, that they died in the way they died, or that the person left them. It can be free floating anger too, anger at God or a person involved like a doctor. Sometimes, if this stage is not understood, people feel guilty about feeling angry at the poor person who died. Anger is normal and to be expected. Anger has little cousins that may appear too like edginess, irritability, impatience, snappishness and annoyance. It is better for anger to be expressed outwardly at the situation, than inwardly at something you think you should have done.   Anger turned inward can fuel depression.

Guilt

We all think we could have done more. Guilt is the flip side of responsibility. Only responsible people feel guilt. Sometimes - similar to trauma- the moment, day or week before the death is intensely frozen in memory. We have more ammunition with which to beat ourselves. When an event as serious as this happens, it is normal for us to think "if we had only done more". We remember everything we did not do! Rather, we need to remember everything we did do!

Bargaining

The goal of bargaining is "I cannot change what happened, but in their memory, I can make the world a better place." We feel better by DOING something in their honor and memory.

Society also benefits from this stage. Examples include memorial parks, planting trees, donations to a favorite charity, and even political action to solve problems. Examples of benefits to society from grief include: Megan's Law, adding street lights to dangerous intersections, and the movement for new gun laws spurred by the awful Sandy Hook School tragedy. Making the world a better place is a wonderful way to memorialize loved ones!

Acceptance

"No one gets out of life alive."

This stage occurs when grieving people find the ability to move on and to reconnect with life. They begin to establish a "new normal" life. They also are free enough of sadness to enjoy memories of the deceased person. They can tell you stories of that person without feeling tormented. You can ask about their beliefs in the afterlife. I often wonder if my parents are dancing and playing cards up there.

People move unpredictably between these stages, such as going from acceptance back to denial to rethinking bargaining. This is very normal.

Goals of Grieving

By working through grief, it is possible to enjoy the lifetime memories of the deceased. This is because you are not stuck in the pain of her/his death. You can share pleasant and funny memories.

As stated earlier, people need to grieve so that they can move on, reconnect with others, and establish a new way of life without the person. People need to create a "new normal," meaning a new way of interacting again in the world. I have been told that if people who lost a limb do not grieve, they rarely will use the prosthesis.

Also, you may already have experienced that one death reminds you of another. So while the funeral may be for a friend's parent, a person you barely knew, it may actually remind you of a significant death in your own life. This is normal, since new grief may activate an old loss. This is true for trauma too. An example of this was during the crisis of 9/11; those people with previous trauma struggled even more than the general population.

I believe that people want to be remembered for how they lived, not the way they died. It is suggested we offer sympathy first and later begin to reminisce about the deceased person's earlier life. This will begin a pattern of sharing those life-enhancing memories. Initially, the grieving person may be tearful, but it gets easier and sets a trend to think of the deceased person as he/she lived. I know of a grief group, where they actually bring in the deceased person's favorite food to share. Of course, the fun memories flow from this activity.

If the deceased is older, I suggest to the person grieving that the deceased got the "whole package or most of the package." The bad news is that they died at 71; the good news is that they did not die at 61, or 41, or 21, or 11. They got childhood, early adulthood, mid-life, senior years, retirement, family, children, and grandchildren. They got the whole package, even though we wanted them here longer. It follows then that grief of a younger person is more difficult.

If the deceased is a child, any accidental death or sudden unexpected death (including suicide or homicides) it is considered traumatic grief and is more difficult to endure.

Length of Grief

The first three months of grief involve constant upsets. Also, the first year is the toughest. This is because every new event without that person can trigger a new cycle of grief and loss. These new events can include holidays, birthdays, planting the garden, shoveling snow, not being at a school play, or other shared events.

Typically, it helps comfort the bereaved if you send cards, attend the wake or funeral, and donate to memorial funds. Check if these are culturally sensitive, i.e., you do not want to send a Christian Mass card to a Jewish person.

Here is a case of traumatic grief, after a fatal car accident.

| CASE | Death of a Young Husband -- Example 9.1

The Mind-body sweep on grief was used (from Chapter 6), because the intensity and pain was high!

Georgia is one year out from the death of her husband, who died unexpectedly in a car accident. She wants to be whole again and just cannot get there. She started by discussing missing him intensely at night. When asked where she felt this physically, she described it as a "heavy heart." But as this is a common metaphor we changed the words to be descriptive of a physical sensation to: *heaviness or pressure in her chest*

She agreed this was how she experienced it. I only wanted her focused on her physical symptom.

> **C 1)** **C**hief complaint: Missing John intensely at night
>
> **A 2)** **A**spect: Physical discomfort, heaviness on my chest
> SUDS rating = 10
>
> **R 3)** **R**eminder phrase: *heaviness on my chest*
>
> **E 4)** **E**FT: Do 3 or more EFT rounds of the 11 acupoints
>
> (using the Mind-Body Sweep Worksheet at the end of Chapter 6) while repeating the Reminder Phrase until calm.
>
> -- Cycle from steps 2 through 4, finding and desensitizing new aspects and defining moments.
>
> **S 5)** **S**pontaneous insight: "I still miss him at night, but think I can distract myself by reading, watching television, and playing with the dog."

Next we discussed that she felt as if half of her was missing because they had a very close relationship. After thinking about it for 5 seconds and having tears well up, she described the physical sensation as a tightness in her throat. So we used that as the RP.

Tightness in my throat

Thus we repeated the same steps but plugging *in tightness in my throat.* Here is her Step 5 Spontaneous Insight once we completed this.

> **S 5)** **S**pontaneous Insight: "I wish it were different, but I know I can and will find new things to fill the hole I feel."

Again, saying what you are missing out loud helps to find the new aspect and reminder phrase. Yes, talking to yourself here is acceptable.

It is good to know that if you are with other people, EFT can also be done silently; you think the reminder phrase silently in your head while using the camouflaged application of EFT described in Chapter 4.

Here are some possibilities for reminder phrases that may spark your creative thoughts. J is substituted for John. If any of them resonate with you, stop and work on one. If you get overwhelmed reading this list, identify where the pain is in your body and desensitize that physical discomfort (Mind-Body Sweep from Chapter 6.)

Here are some possible reminder phrases for EFT, the Emotion Worksheet from Chapter 3. Just pick one or create your own RP of your upset.

> *Sad J is unable to be at my graduation*
>
> *Sad J cannot hold me anymore*
>
> *Sad that J is unable to help me carry in groceries*
>
> *Angry that J had to leave me at this point*
>
> *Angry that J was too young to die*
>
> *Angry that J's doctors did not figure out his illness earlier*
>
> *Angry that J blew off going to the doctor for so long*
>
> *Miss that J does not help me with errands*
>
> *Miss that J is not home when I get there*
>
> *Miss J's smile when I have had a bad day.*
>
> *Miss J balancing our checkbook*
>
> *Miss sexual intimacy*

What aspect from the list above or other specifics of him/her are you missing?

What did he/she do for you that you miss?

What about him/her do you miss?

_____

_____

After writing your upsets down, try the CARES steps of EFT to desensitize the pain of grief that you are experiencing. Pick one at a time to work on.

Be gentle on yourself if working alone, and go into these areas gradually. You are in no hurry to process each aspect.

If you have too much time alone or are lonely, see if you have www. meetup.com in your area. It is not a dating site, but an activity site where you can forge new connections through participating in common interests. You might find a board game group, a hiking group, wine tasting, and even some EFT groups! Like all websites, caution is urged in sharing personal addresses and any private or financial information. However, I hear stories of renewal of interests from folks who have successfully connected with a "meetup group". One young mother found a play group in her new community and told me that meetup.com gave her the needed courage to relocate with her upwardly mobile husband. A widow found a movie group. I found a writer's group and a board game group.

REVIEW - Grief

Grief can take anyone out of their normal functioning. Review the stages of grief. While there are similarities in how people deal with grief, it is different for everyone. The goals of grief are to let go of the hurt so pleasant memories are available, and to get back into the life you have. The deceased would want you to live again and not be in pain. Use EFT to calm what is bothering you.

Some people are perplexed that in grief they are angry too. It is one of the stages. Thus let's look next at anger and ways to curtail its excessive fury.

CHAPTER 10:

ANGER AND CONFLICT

> "I'm so angry I could explode, I wanted to slug him. I'm so
> pissed I could punch a wall."

Ever felt this way?

Your internal temperature is rising, you feel the slow burn in your body mounting to the surface, and you are seemingly helpless to quell it. You have been here before, and you know that the release is not pretty. You will shout, scream, and intimidate those closest to you, and you'll end your tirade with deep remorse.

But it will be too late. Those around you feel verbally abused and traumatized by your furious release. Their SUDS will be a 10 when they recall your outburst. They do not understand how helpless you feel. They do not comprehend that the level of expressed rage caught even you by surprise. You wish you could intervene, but you don't know where the anger dwells when unexpressed. You sense it's just below the surface. You actively work to hold it down.

Simple issues become exaggerated. Afterwards you're demoralized that you couldn't contain yourself. You liken yourself to an emotional time bomb. Others tell you that you are verbally abusive which you deny vehemently, but inside you know it is true. You are unsure how it got to this level.

Does any of this sound familiar? About you or someone you know? This type of barely suppressed or uncontrolled anger is the result of layers of emotional triggers accumulating throughout a person's life. You can use EFT to calm anger quickly as it arises. Another solution is to go deep with questions and try to locate those defining moments that first created the feeling of powerlessness and rage.

Ever experience anger's little cousins of irritability, annoyance, sarcasm, quick to attack, constant slow burn and frustration? Do any of these situations apply to you?

Did one of your parents scream and punish a lot?

Were you in the military or the police and see or do horrific things no one should witness?

Do you feel others got more than you did?

Were you the underdog of an aggressive sibling?

Did you somehow learn early in life that powerful rage intimidates others and gives you influence?

Is what worked earlier in life not working now?

Have you lost a job or spent more time with superiors or Employee Assistance Counselors because you just can't contain your rage?

Does your family hide or threaten to leave?

Does your family cringe when you come home?

Do you feel the slow burn without being able to change it?

Were you called "stupid" or humiliated by a family member?

If you answered yes to any of these questions, write down the issue. Then you can break it down and list specific aspects to desensitize using EFT or 3 Times 3. This will eliminate your underlying volcano! It is a bit of work, but what worth having is not a bit of work? A garden, a room painted, exercise, shopping and clearing old issues are worth a bit of work!

CASE | Angry Guy –Example 10.1

Andrew had a chip on his shoulder. He was a volcano, ready to erupt at any time. He was frequently rude, sarcastic, and edgy. Finally, both his employer and his wife had enough and told him to get counseling or else! He knew he was verbally abusive at times, even though he denied it to his family.

This is what we uncovered working with Andrew using the CARES format.

C 1) **C**hief Complaint: "I will never control this anger"

A 2) **A**spect/Defining Moment: Angry that while his parents were at work, his older brothers ganged up on him.

SUDS = 9

Mind-body Sweep - Where did he feel this in his body?

R 3) **R**eminder Phrase: *Tight fists* SUDS 9-> 0 using the Mind-Body Sweep Worksheet

E 4) **E**FT: Apply light touch on the 11 acupoints

(using the Mind-Body Sweep Worksheet at the end of Chapter 6) while repeating the Reminder Phrase for 3 or more rounds, until calm, and the SUDS on this aspect is as low as possible.

--Cycle back through steps 2 through 4, finding and desensitizing new aspects and defining moments.

S 5) **S**pontaneous Insight: "We were all kids and kids often fight. I can and will get over this. I can always excuse myself and calm down alone in the bathroom."

Once the physical upset was quieted, he finished the issue with the standard EFT using the Emotion Worksheet at the end of Chapter 3, as you will see next.

Is there more? Going deeper by repeating steps 2-5

C 1) **C**hief Complaint: "I will never control this anger" (Same as above, just a new aspect)

A 2) **A**spect: Upset my parents worked so much and my brothers got away with this. SUDS = 5

R 3) **R**eminder phrase: *Upset about my brothers getting away with this because my parents worked so much.* SUDS = 5

E 4) **E**FT: Apply light pressure on the 11 acupoints (using the Emotion Worksheet at the end of Chapter 3) while repeating the Reminder Phrase for 3 or more rounds, until calm, and the SUDS on this aspect is as low as possible. Suds = 5-> 0 using the Emotion Worksheet

--Cycle back through steps 2 through 4, finding and desensitizing new aspects and defining moments

S 5) **S**pontaneous insight: "I really don't want to hurt others. I can use EFT to calm myself. Or I can excuse myself until I am in better control."

You can also plug in the simple 3 Times 3, Technique 30 from Chapter 3, page 80, and use the very same reminder phrases to defuse anger. Remember to place your hands over the heart, repeating the phrase and taking 3 breaths, then switching your hands and repeating the process for a total of 3 times. After calming the first thought, ask "what else is bothering me about this?" Then repeat 3 Times 3 on that too. Repeat until calm and feeling neutral or optimistic about the issue.

There were several more aspects, some current and some from the past, which he listed and worked on daily for half an hour for several months. He regained his composure, kept his job and wife, and became more diplomatic. So there is a bit of work needed, but much less than the consequences of losing a job or wife!

Anger is an emotion that is played out in the mind and the body. The mind interprets something as aggravating, and the body tenses and begins the burn toward eruption. Anger has value as a defensive posture if threatened, but good judgment often disappears once in the middle of anger. Anger activates the reptilian part of our brain that does not do higher functioning thinking!

In summary, remember that EFT has a cumulative effect. The more you use it, the quieter the storm underneath. Once you have quieted your body via the Mind-Body Sweep of Chapter 6, then calm down the issues.

Here are some examples of reminder phrases to plug into the Emotion Worksheet. The emotion might be angry, ballistic, furious, or pissed off. Pick out those that apply to you or create your own so you can desensitize them. Work on one at a time. These upsetting issues and the resulting reminder phrase are the *emotion* about *the issue*. You may note that as you calm several, others quiet too even without direct treatment - as evidenced by a low SUDS score when thought about.

> *Irritated about slow drivers*
>
> *Hateful about that car that cut me off*
>
> *Angry about dumb things people do*
>
> *Pissed about losing my temper again*
>
> *Irked about my boss lecturing the group*
>
> *Annoyed about my wife not appreciating me*
>
> *Frustrated about my kid's homework not being done*
>
> *Furious about my employer piling too much on me*
>
> *Ballistic about the house being a mess when I get home*
>
> *Furious about my mother telling me something I already know*
>
> *Pissed off about another rainy day when I planned a cook-out*

What makes you angry now? Or what memory from your past still ignites your anger?

All of these angry issues and emotions should be plugged into the Emotions Worksheet. You can also choose to use the Mind-Body Sweep Worksheet, if thinking about the anger for 5 seconds brings up physical discomfort in your body.

Afterwards you may have an "aha moment," a spontaneous insightful experience, where something positive shines through because the negative is not clouding the issue. It may even be empathy for the person you're mad at, other insights or a more highly evolved level of maturity. Here are some spontaneous and liberating insights possible once EFT has defused your anger. What is different is that the spontaneous insights emerge from you and you actually believe them rather than trying to convince yourself to think this way.

Examples of liberating Spontaneous Insights

"Poor thing, it must be awful to be so slow."

"It isn't so bad; there are many more serious issues."

"Not sure why this made me so crazed."

"I can handle it and may even learn some patience."

"I can live with this."

"I will be a better parent than my father."

"It was a long time ago and it's time to let it go."

To be comprehensive, here are other anger management tools that many people find useful. Several have been mentioned before; only new ones rate a new Technique number.

MORE ANGER and CONFLICT MANAGEMENT TOOLS

Anger is an emotion that often needs a physical discharge. The Mind-Body Sweep can be effective in these situations to quell the physical manifestation of anger.

Anger can be held, even for hours. It should be expressed appropriately so as not to come out as displaced anger (i.e. kick the dog or overreact to small things). Verbal venting also helps, which you can review on page 20. There are more communication tips later in Techniques 50-53 to help you learn better ways to handle conflict.

Learn to recognize your body "temperature" to know when anger is growing. Sense the tension in your stomach, arms, fists, shoulders, neck, etc., and then use one of the next techniques.

Intensity

Use the SUDS intensity rating to assess your anger on a scale of 0 to 10. When your anger is high, your brain's reasoning and judgment are probably poor. As your anger goes down, your reasoning, judgment, and diplomacy get better. Begin to do a self-assessment so you recognize when your SUDS level is climbing, and use one of the coping tools below or EFT.

Technique 46: Leave the situation to Get Composed

Get some distance between you and the problem _before_ you do something stupid, criminal, abusive, or dangerous. Go for a walk, go to a different room in the house, or pull off to the side of the road. A socially appropriate way to get out of a stressful situation is to excuse you to go to the bathroom.

Exercise to Burn it Off (at the gym, in the community or at home)

Walk, vacuum, polish furniture, jump rope, run stairs, swing a bat/ tennis racket (safely), jog, shoot basketball, ride your bike, tighten and loosen fists repeatedly... move!

Write it Out to Let it Go- a reminder of Technique 2, p20

Write letters about your upsetting thoughts. **NEVER** mail them, NEVER mail them and NEVER mail them. Do not write them on the computer as they can be retrieved. Destroy the paper letters of your angry thoughts right after writing and thinking about them. These angry thoughts are how you felt in a moment of time and should not be discovered by anyone. The goal is to reduce your intensity, so that you will not create a problem down the road.

Technique 47: Empty Chair Technique

Vent all You Want and Tell Him Off

This comes from Gestalt therapy, which is very interactive. Imagine someone sitting in a chair. When alone, yell, scream and tell that someone off. Muttering under one's breath helps if done when you are alone. People tell me they do this all the time when alone in their cars. Some people even scream in their cars. I also recommend you use rolled newspaper and hit the chair. The slapping of a newspaper is loud and makes you think you are really exerting force. Do not do this if you might scare your pets and only do this alone.

Acupressure point

The estimated acupressure point for anger is close to the outer edge of your eye(s). It will help calm you. Use any and all of the Emotional Freedom Techniques acupoints to lessen your intensity.

Humor

I believe anything you are able to laugh at does not hold power over you. Comic relief is real! You have to laugh at human errors so you don't take yourself or life too seriously. Are you still single and Charles Manson is not anymore! You laugh, it is crazy this 80-year old cult murderer is about to have a 26-year old bride! Comic relief - just laugh about it. Watch the monologues on late night television to experience comic relief about the world today. Find the comedy in your mistakes.

Furthermore, I believe the best interventions among family members have a bit of humor in them. If you are furious because your partner does not take the garbage out despite multiple discussions, change where you keep the garbage for a day. Move it to the living room so it sticks out like a huge ostrich. Draw a funny card and post it on his side of the bathroom. "The garbage loves to go out with you." My favorite is pointing out how lonely the dishes in the sink are, because they are not in the dishwasher with all their friends! Humor takes it to a different part of the brain; and is creative and healthy for both of you.

Forgiveness

The antidote to anger is forgiveness, as mentioned in Technique 37, page 125.

Example: If I apologize because I lightly hit your grocery cart in a food market, you will forgive me and not think about it. If I do not apologize, you might be angry about it all day. You did not get a chance to *forgive* the incident and release your anger. So forgive that person without the apology, for your sake.

Forgive people for being human, for being in a rush, for being male/ female/youthful, for not being thoughtful, for not being what you want them to be, etc. *You* feel better when you forgive, because *you* give up the anger. Thus, do it for *you!*

Technique 48: Be Grateful

Make a daily list of 3-5 things you are grateful for. There are always people better off than you, but there are also many people worse off than you. Switch your equation to focus on the positive things in your life and to be grateful for what you have. These positive things include health, shelter, food, a pleasant day, a friend, a family, a television show you enjoy, or anything you appreciate. Value today. This technique also stops you from fretting about the past or worrying about the future. It also makes you focus on the present and be positive – a double win on the road to happiness and contentment.

Technique 49: 80/20 Rule –Focus on the Positive

Consider an 80/20 rule. It means that in life if 70-80 percent of what occurs is good and only 20-30 percent is pretty darn annoying or awful, and then you are one of the lucky ones. Life has ups and downs and the sooner you accept this, the better your view of life becomes. By the way, this equation may fluctuate with many things going wrong balanced later by many things going right. Briefly vent about your frustrations, but then focus on the 70-80% of what is good. Positive thought calms you. (However in that 20%, there may be some "deal breakers" such as: child abuse, addiction, criminal activity, violence, etc. that override staying in that situation.)

Deep Breaths

Take several slow, deep breaths, holding each for a count of 5. Release each breath slowly and longer than your inhale. It actually is what cigarette smokers do in order to create their relaxation. Mentally only allow yourself to focus on the breathing. Think: I am breathing in... and breathing out.

Music

Most any type of music can help soothe and distract you. Choose music that has always perked you up, calmed you or your family down or made you happy in the past. This can provide some immediate relief. Many televisions even have music videos located at their on-demand section. Enjoy!

Reading, playing on the computer, and television

These can also be distracting. It is a safe place to get lost in another story and take a break from your woes.

Counseling or Psychotherapy

Psychotherapy addresses underlying and often forgotten causes of current anger. Clear it out. It is the only place in the world where the focus is on just you for 50 minutes. It is a gift to you!

Imagery

Imagine yourself in a fabulous place, such as a beachfront, a mountain, a luxurious garden, or a theme park for kids. In other words, change your thoughts quickly to something relaxing and wonderful to lessen your preoccupation with your upset. You can even pick one spot and go there mentally for 15 seconds. For me, it is Newport, RI and Cape May, NJ. Where is that place for you?

Technique 50: **Surrender Position to Not Argue**

The "Surrender position" is shrugged shoulders, hands turned outward in that *I don't know* position. The body position says *–I do not agree with you and I am not going to argue with you.* It is a way to avoid engagement in futile conflicts or when someone is being demanding of you. I first read about this to avoid arguing with drug abusing, angry teens. (These teens try to pick fights so they can storm out of the house and use drugs.) It's also is useful if bullied, even by an older, insistent superior. (You do not want the bully to know they have upset you). It is the body saying "whatever, I do not agree with you and am not going to argue".

Sometimes you need to stand up for what you believe and deal with conflict. Here are 3 appropriate ways to be heard without violating the rights of others. Try to get a partner to practice a few times.

Conflict Management Techniques

Technique 51: I-Statement

Own and address your 50% of the problem.-

Conversation goes around and around. He said, she said, he said, on and on. Here is a formula to own your 50% of the responsibility. This avoids shaming or blaming. I-Statements have 4 parts:

(1) I

(2) feel (how) ex. upset, confused, etc.

(3) about what and

(4) either the effect it has on you or your preference for a better way.

Here is an example where the young adult did not want to bother to put on safety equipment when his mother needed his help cutting down a tree. She avoided an argument using I-Statements.

(1) I

(2) get nervous

(3) when you cut trees without any safety equipment

(4) so please put on boots and safety glasses for me.

This was effective because the young man did put on safety equipment; even if the only reason was to appease her.

Here is another way to address conflict directly and diplomatically.

Technique 52: **Facts, Impressions and Talk - Stay FIT**

F is for facts and only facts.

I is for your impression of the facts and

T is for talk it out, by asking a tentatively phrased question to invite them to respond.

Here is an example.

F – You have been late all week

I - I don't think you prioritize this job

T – I wonder how you see it?

Of course, watch your tone of voice so there is no irritability or sarcasm.

Another communication tip: pay attention to timing and to potential safety issues if someone is very angry. Not everyone can spontaneously discuss difficult topics. You may want to take a time-out to give them a chance to collect them. Respect includes allowing them time to compose themselves. You may remind them that you both want the best for your organization, family or even friendship. A common mission binds people for the greater good!

Now, for a way to get specific with others about what we need or want from them.

Techniques 53: **The Business Letter Communication Style**

Sometimes we are baffled by how others misperceive what we want or need from them. This technique quickly advises them of what we are looking for. It is not a guarantee, but the chances of feeling more satisfied are significantly improved. In a business letter, the first sentence tells what we want and then we give the details. (I want a refund, because here is what happened with this product.) Do the same thing - say what you want BEFORE giving the details.

It looks like this: Something happened today, I want to tell you but what I need from you is:

a hug and say "poor baby"

make suggestions on how I can handle this

just listen and nod so I can talk it out

handle it for me

I need help with...

Then, give the details about what happened.

Veterans and First Responders and Counseling Worries

I mention veterans and first responders in this section, because so many struggle to manage their emotions and angry outbursts. If you are veteran, contact the Veterans Administration. You will find colleagues there who have walked your walk and understand what you're going through. If they can ask for help, so can you. Bring this book with you to share EFT treatment possibilities there too.

Another option is to look for an organization called Give an Hour, www. giveanhour.org. Therapists around the country have agreed to treat a veteran free for one year. They may even treat disaster workers. It's a way that therapists use their expertise to give back to the country.

Look at Dr. Dawson Church's web site, www.Stressproject.com where you can find help beyond the V.A. Consider watching the movie on working with veterans. I must warn you that this serious movie can be intense and might trigger you; but at least it will give you hope that there are available approaches to curb your misery. This movie is not staged and really does happen using the Emotional Freedom Techniques and Energy Psychology. Dr. Church's research is also published in The *Journal of Nervous and Mental Disease, 201, 153-160* and entitled "Psychological Trauma Symptom Improvement in Veterans Using EFT: A Randomized Controlled Trial".

Look at www.energypsych.org, www.emofree.com or www.eftuniverse. com for therapists who use the methods described in this book.

Remember, it's never weakness to acknowledge problems. It's strong and intelligent to recognize something needs to be fixed. If your car was sputtering, you would address that. Don't let yourself "sputter" and hurt those around you. Ask for help for yourself. Do it for others who you might pick on, if you cannot do it for yourself.

Don't worry about your reputation. This country values overcoming adversity and redemption stories. Ted Kennedy, Rodney King, and Reality Show edgy characters are examples of being revered by overcoming their dirty laundry.

When I worked with high ranking Navy officers in Newport, Rhode Island, occasionally Military Police would arrive at my office. They brought a client-signed release for confidential information. They asked only if my (military) client could be blackmailed. They wanted no details; they were just making sure that the military member was" taking care of their personal and family issues." It was surprising how little information they really requested.

Therapy is not a punishment. It is a gift where someone focuses their interest on you for fifty minutes. See if you can find that in any other relationship. Even with a good friend it will be a give and take of five minutes each. Get past the first two therapy sessions and you might decide your pre-conceived prejudices were ill-conceived. Why two sessions? Any reputable therapist will use the first session or two to conduct an assessment to determine what you need. Assessment is not therapy. Usually in session 2 is when you begin to pull apart an issue.

Help Is Available

If your anger is out of control, find an Energy Psychology Therapist, Tapping or EFT therapist NOW. You must get treatment. If this type of therapist is unavailable in your area, find any available therapist. Every community has a mental health center to work with indigent or uninsured clients. Do an internet search using your county name and then attach "mental health center." Or call the local hospital to speak to the social work department, the emergency room, or the closest mental health team to inquire where to get mental health services. You may even like it once the initial wariness resolves.

In the next chapter look at other events that may alter your life including a motor vehicle accident, medical worries, sleep problems and couple conflict.

CHAPTER 11

COMMON STRESSORS

Automobile Accidents

Medical Worries

Sleep

Couples Conflict

Auto Accidents and Nervous Driving

A motor vehicle accident can alter your life. Driving comes with inherent dangers, and being in an accident or near miss can leave marks on your confidence in driving.

First a perspective: Driving a car is a privilege. It is the only common, day-to-day activity that requires participants to carry insurance. Why? Because risks are involved and history dictates you may experience an accident or two in your lifetime. The most likely outcome is that your car will take the impact and you will walk away only shaken up a bit.

Furthermore, near misses happen every week. Accept that driving is not a perfect science and that it is a privilege, not a right.

An earlier example, (Example 5.3, Chapter 5) discussed how early driving disasters continue to clutter up your current driving. You may want to review that example, if you have driving worries. Use the additional examples presented below as a format for you to plug in your specific driving issue.

People get emotionally triggered by driving in situations similar to their accident. This could be driving near the location, in similar weather, or in similar congested traffic. For example, I get nervous rounding the bend where I spun out in the rain. Making a turn in the rain now makes me a tad nervous, too.

Victims of car accidents often visibly shake when in a car; they can be horribly frightened and become annoying passengers. They often over react to any minor situation. These car accident victims might even scream, or demand the driver brake thirty feet before any normal person would. They are hyper alert, hypercritical and paralyzed by fear.

Once the trigger (original) accident is desensitized, these stressed out survivors and their family members are so grateful they often exuberantly hug me. They appreciate the profound release of these emotional and physical expressions of terror. Family members are glad to have a more serene passenger, as they too "caught" the anxiety of their frantic backseat drivers

Treatment can use the Emotion Worksheet located at the end of Chapter 3, page 84, or focus on the body sensation using the Mind-Body Sweep Worksheet, page 147, at the end of Chapter 6. If you are the guide or therapist, proceed by the most benign way possible. If you or the person you are working with had a serious body injury, you can desensitize through the Emotion Worksheet. Do not get confused and use the Mind-Body Sweep on an actual injury. Use it only when the sensation is a manifestation of the emotions. It is too intense to focus on an actual physical injury obtained in the accident as the reminder phrase.

| CASE | Car Accident –Hit from Behind - Example 11.1 |

Anna was in a car accident while it was raining where she was hit from behind. She experienced whiplash in her neck and her glasses broke when they flew off her face. Afterwards, she was reluctant to drive, and her family complained that she had become the worst "backseat driver" ever, making everyone uncomfortable with her severe criticism of their driving habits.

When she thought of the accident, her anxiety was a SUDS intensity of 10! She experienced physical discomfort, but it was not where she was injured. Rather, the following physical spots bothered her.

Churning stomach	SUDS 6
Pounding heart	SUDS 8
Pressure in her temples	SUDS 4

All reminder phrases are in *italics*. Intentionally select the worst discomfort, because the others may collapse with it anyway.

Where felt in the body? *Pounding heart*

C 1) **C**hief complaint: "I am a horrible passenger, anxious and overreacting."

A 2) **A**spect: My heart pounds from within. SUDS = 8

R 3) **R**eminder phrase: *Pounding heart*

E 4) **E**FT: Apply light touch or tap on the 11 acupoints (using the Mind-Body Sweep Worksheet at the end of Chapter 6) while repeating the Reminder Phrase for 3 or more rounds, until calm, and the SUDS on this aspect is as low as possible.

-- Cycle back through steps 2 through 4, finding and desensitizing new aspects and defining moments.

S 5) **S**pontaneous insight: "I'm better, I did survive. Accidents are rare and I am ok."

After calming the *pounding heat,* the *pressure in her temples* and the *churning stomach* had SUDS = 0 also. It often happens, when the worst symptoms resolves, the lesser symptoms fall too.

We now proceed with more detective work and continue to look for more aspects associated with car accidents.

Peeling the onion: is there more about this?

Afraid to drive when it rains SUDS = 4

C 1) **C**hief complaint "I am now afraid to drive whenever it rains."

Where felt in the body? *Churning stomach again*

A 2) **A**spect: My body is acting up again. I feel it in my stomach with a SUDS or 4.

R 3) **R**eminder phrase: *Churning stomach again*

E 4) **E**FT: Apply light touch or tap on the 11 acupoints (using the Mind-Body Sweep Worksheet at the end of Chapter 6) while repeating the Reminder Phrase for 3 or more rounds, until calm, and the SUDS on this aspect is as low as possible. SUDS 4 -> 0 using the Mind Body Sweep

-- Cycle back through steps 2 through 4, finding and desensitizing new aspects and defining moments.

S 5) **S**pontaneous insight: "I have driven in the rain for years, I can do it."

When asked about driving in the rain now, there was no more body sensation. Here are some other typical reminder phrases gathered from people who have been in car accidents. See if one speaks to your issue. If so, decide whether you want to desensitize the issue and plug it into the Emotions Worksheet found at the end of Chapter 3. If you want to lessen the physical sensations first, you can begin with the Mind-Body Sweep Worksheet found at the end of Chapter 6. If your issue is not on this list, then create your own *reminder phrases.*

Hate about lane changing

Worried about others who may not stop

Upset about being hit from behind

Fretting about checking my rear view mirror too much

Worried about not being able to stop

Pissed off about being cut off

Freaked out about driving alone again

Unhappy about having to merge onto a highway

Furious about my driver going too fast

Worried about my driver being too close to the car in front of us

Nervous about my children or parents driving in the rain

Outraged about him honking when I was cautiously turning

Besides myself about the turn off being closed.

Terrified about that truck that approached me

Worried about no place to escape

Freaked out about others that were injured

Worried about my child in the back seat

Dislike about being beside a truck

Terrified about merging

Too scared about driving on the street where it happened

Worried about not able to escape getting hit

Not sure about the baby's car seat holding

Wondering about if I can get out of the car

Angry about the other person who was in my lane

Upset about my car that was my new dream car

> *Unhappy about the rescue workers*
>
> *Worried about my insurance rates going up*

My experience is that once 1-5 of these aspects are desensitized, the driving issue resolves. Remember that each aspect may be 1-10 minutes.

What one aspect of your car accident upsets you now?

_____

_____

Frequently, the most poignant part is the moment just before impact. It is that *"OH NO"* point when you know that it is about to happen. If you can dissipate this part, much will clear up.

Be warned that this poignant part of the accident can be overwhelming. Thus, you may want to desensitize other parts of the accident before going to the moment just before impact. You can also switch it quickly to the physical discomfort and desensitize that first with the Mind-Body Sweep Worksheet. Remember you only need to think about the upset for a mere 5 seconds for it to be activated.

Once desensitized, you often will have a spontaneous insight, a liberating moment.

> "It's over, I am okay."
>
> "Glad it was not worse."
>
> "I am okay with this new normal me."
>
> "I feel silly this bothered me for so long (but grateful it does not bother me after EFT)

Below is a technique to quell the *future* worries. This example is of a driver who focuses excessively on the rearview mirror, after being hit from behind. Please note turning to future worries is addressed <u>AFTER</u> desensitizing every single past and present aspect you can imagine.

The Future Performance Enhancement works to get your confidence concerning this behavior up as high as possible. It is when people say they are fine now, but worried about how they will be in the situation sometime in the future

Technique 54: **Future Performance Enhancement**

Sometimes people worry if the benefit found in the home or office will work later in a real life situation. After desensitizing and collapsing every single aspect of a particular problem you can try to firm up this benefit for the future. The technique comes from sports psychology, where the goal is to alleviate residual anxiety and keep a positive focus to improve an athlete's future performance. It can be applied to any situation where future performance is of concern.

Future Performance Enhancement is a way to reinforce the positive and cement the gains you have made once an old issue has been desensitized. Many of my clients feel fine in the office but worry whether it will hold later - when they need it. We are addressing their future performance and comfort. Issues might be public speaking, confronting someone, driving, and performance of any type. It can be especially helpful when a new behavior is to be attempted. I first heard of this technique from psychologist Dr. John Diepold, Jr. (heartassistedtherapy.net.) The acupoints used are under the eye and under the arm. (If you are unsure about where these acupoints are, they are pictures in Chapter 3, figure 3.3 acupoints 5 and 9; shown on page 228. Apply bilaterally to both the right and left eyes and then, under both arms.)

Future Driving

This example is *after* calming down fears developed from a car accident. The person was excessively looking out his rearview mirror, common after being hit from behind.

Tune into feeling very comfortable while driving with your eyes on the road ahead. Nothing interests you except the cars in front of you. With 100% representing total confidence while doing this, what percentage of confidence do you have that you can do this comfortably?

Possible Answer 70%.

While thinking positive and feeling confident that you can drive comfortably paying attention to only the cars in front of you:

Hold the under-eye acupoints under <u>both</u> eyes for 5 breaths;

Then - Hold the under-arm acupoints under <u>both</u> arms for 5 breaths.

What percentage of you is confident now?

 Probable Answer 85%

(repeat)

While thinking positive and feeling confident that you can drive comfortably paying attention to only the cars in front of you:

Hold the under-eye acupoints <u>bilaterally</u> for 5 breaths and then;

Hold the under-arm acupoints on <u>both</u> sides for 5 breaths.

What percentage of you is confident now?

Probable Answer: 99%

(repeat)

While thinking positive and feeling confident that you can drive comfortably paying attention to only the cars in front of you:

Hold the under-eye acupoints <u>bilaterally</u> for 5 breaths and then:

Hold the under-arm acupoints <u>bilaterally</u> for 5 breaths.

What percentage of you is confident now?

Final Expected Answer 100%

Spontaneous insight: (Laughing) "This was so easy and I really need to be able to drive. I have my personal freedom back."

Figure 11.1. Future Performance Enhancement

Remember you are focusing on the positive desired outcome while using the two acupoints holds explained above. The future doubt is quieted allowing confidence to emerge!

Another potentially stressed-out situation is seeking medical treatment due to the personal implication of ill-health and possible painful procedures. This is discussed next.

Medical Worries, Tests, and Medical Trauma

Unfortunately, the very nature of being ill is an affront to your physical integrity and sense of competence. Depending on the degree of medical problem, life as you know it can stop until the medical issue is resolved. Further, procedures can be difficult, painful, and scary. Who is totally calm about the enclosed cylinder of a MRI, painless though it may be? To varying degrees, most medical treatment is difficult. Add to the often serious worry and a possibility of a chaotic arrival or long wait at the hospital Emergency Room.

Upsetting experiences from the past may add to worries about upcoming procedures.

Below are some typical worries and *reminder phrases*. Pick which applies to you or create ones more relevant. Remember to put them into the 5-step EFT CARES model to defuse their intensity and to reach a spontaneous insight.

Worried about my breathing

Worried about myself

Freaked-out about that diagnosis

Terrified about the enclosed MRI

Freak-out about when they take blood

Annoyed about the wait at the Emergency Room

Scared about anesthesia

Nervous about my ability to function

Embarrassed about being naked and examined

Upset about remembering the pain I felt from that procedure

Confused about my medical options

Struggling about this brace

Afraid about pain

Worried about still being in remission

> *Worried about my family*
>
> *Scared about my future*
>
> *Worried about how serious this is*
>
> *Scared about being able to work*
>
> *Concerned about being a burden to my family*

Next a look at sleep and some ways to get more of it.

Technique 55: **Sleep Tips**

Sleep

Sleep is a crucial component of healthy living. Seven to nine hours for adults and ten hours for children is the norm. A typical sleep cycle is ninety minutes and adults need five of them a night. Once sleep gets disrupted, people begin to worry about sleeping and that makes them sleep even less! Worry is an enemy of sleep so remember to calm down those worries with EFT.

After a sleep-deprived night or two, most people are fine and will allow time to make up sleep. However, when it gets more chronic, all sorts of issues begin to show. Exhaustion and fatigue are not good bedfellows to productivity and competence. Furthermore, the anxiety of not sleeping becomes an enemy, itself! Check with your doctor whether sleep medication may be helpful. See other tips at the end of this section.

Here are tips on ways to get to sleep. Remember to use EFT and 3 Times 3 to calm you down too.

Worries interfere with sleep. You can certainly use the CARES steps explained in the beginning of Chapter 3 to figure out what your specific worry about at night. Insert your sleep stressors into that, in order to desensitize your issues.

Caffeine Experiment

Reduce caffeine or stop it altogether. Cut one cup (8 ounces) of your usual intake every 3-4 days until you are off caffeine. Remember, caffeine is an inexpensive, legal stimulant. Buy the best decaffeinated substitute you can find, so you do not feel deprived. Stay off caffeine for two weeks to determine if your sleep, anxiety, or stress is improved. If so, enjoy a cup now and then but not on a regular basis, in order to avoid a caffeine build-up in your body. Caffeine stays in your body for 20 hours, so even early use can hurt sleep.

Your Thoughts

Some people cannot stop thinking and even worry in their dreams and awaken with those upsetting thoughts. Dreams can be pretty crazy. Our reasoning goes to sleep and we dream in symbols, like red roses for love or snakes if agitated. We dream about things we feel intensely about, both good and bad and we process them in our dreams.

Try thinking of a few peaceful places you can imagine. Write them down on a piece of paper next to your bed. When you wake, focus your mind on these pleasant thoughts. Some of these may include: the ocean, beach; mountains, a lazy vacation spot, a church scene, a quiet story, a pleasant event, a season, or a favorite room.

With your eyes closed, try to picture 5 items in your bedroom (bed, dresser); hear 5 sounds (the heater, your head on the pillow); and feel 5 sensations on your body (blankets, softness of mattress). If still awake, repeat and decrease the count of thing to 4, then 3, 2 and 1. It is doubtful you will still be awake as this technique focuses the mind away from worries and is boring – the formula for sleep.

Your Body

Embrace the joy of your bedding and lying down on a comfortable mattress. Slide into your favorite sleeping position. Your body remembers this position means sleep. Make sure the room is a comfortable temperature for you. Count your breaths and try to breathe deeply and slowly. Using the open palm of your hand, lightly touch your arms, legs, and torso. and hold each spot for a count of three. A light massage is probably beneficial too.

Look at Chapter 15, Techniques 59, page 292, for several physical calming tools including self-massage.

Use the acupoints of EFT repeatedly until you yawn and relax. Good night, sleep well!

Couples

> "Men marry women with the hope they will never change.
> Women marry men with the hope they will change.
> Invariably, they are both disappointed." - Albert Einstein

We are attracted and tend to marry our opposites (in characteristics), because they balance out our shortcomings and make us grow in the areas of our deficient. A typical situation is an anxious woman marrying a very laid-back man. She likes his calm nature and he admires her being on top of every issue. One year later they will argue about the very qualities that brought them together. She will say, "Don't you take care of anything?" He will say, "Get off my back and let that go, relax on some things."

Ahhh, the battle between the sexes. There is too much fraternizing with the enemy. *Men are from Mars and Women are from Venus.* Do read John Gray's wonderful series of books. Also see a play out there called *Defending the Caveman.* (Rob Becker) (www.defendingthecaveman.com). This play is hilarious and scary in its accurate look at the differences between men and women. It is worth five sessions of couple counseling! We are attracted to each other. However, as we get closer, like the same poles of magnets, we repel and favor different directions.

Perhaps we are God's sitcom. Try to laugh at the differences or at least use some calming tool to take the edge off of every issue.

> Here is the use of EFT with couples, to take the excessive annoyance off frustrations.

CASE   Couple Frustration –Typical, Normal and Annoying – Example 11.2

Karen and Carl were opposites in style. He was ambitious, placing work before anything else, but she got anxious being alone night after night. By the time they got to couples therapy, both felt it was too late. I explained that both of them had issues that had spilled over into their relationship.

I began by doing EFT with them individually, so that they could calm themselves before they interfaced with exaggerated emotions. Here is what happened when the couple did EFT together.

233

C 1) Chief complaint: He overreacts by scolding her that she needed to leave him alone at work. His tone of voice made her angry.

A 2)	**A**spect: He was angry because she harped on him to come home (SUDS = 6) and she was angry he prioritized work over her (SUDS = 9).
R 3)	**R**eminder phrase: (used with both simultaneously) *Mad at the other.*
E 4)	**E**FT: Apply light touch or tap on the 11 acupoints (using the Emotion Worksheet at the end of Chapter 3) while repeating the Reminder Phrase for 3 or more rounds, until calm.
	-- Cycle from steps 2 through 4, finding and desensitizing new aspects and defining moments.
S 5)	**S**pontaneous insight: "We should use EFT to calm ourselves before we address each other when we are overly upset. Let's talk about this when calmer."
	He said: I am stuck with my boss's demands but I can understand how it hurts you. She said: I can use EFT if I am anxious at night. I still miss you.

Here are a few other nagging differences between couples that I helped calm by using these CARES steps where the joint RP still was, *Mad at the other:*

- A woman who took a long time getting ready and her husband's annoying efforts to get her to move faster.

- One parent who was overly permissive and the other way too stern.

- One woman who spent money casually and her accountant husband that tracked every dime.

- One man's obsessive cleanliness and his sloppy, haphazard wife.

Usually in all of these, the spontaneous insight ended up being, "I can live with the difference and let's continue talking to reach an acceptable agreement when calmer."

So how are you different from your spouse/partner and what do you need to calm down?

_____

_____

Remember to forgive you spouse for not being what you want him or her to be as explained in Technique 37 on Forgiveness on page 125.

- The opposite sex – Cannot live with them, cannot live without them!

REVIEW

Certain issues take a toll on you

Motor Vehicle Accidents:

Cars. We love them and we don't. Small accidents are common, but the bigger ones throw us off balance. Mobility is important. You can review the section in this chapter on auto accidents to enhance driving again after an accident. Has driving become a problem?

Medical Worries:

Medical worries and medical tests are part of everyone's experience. However, they unnerve us. We discussed in this chapter about ways to prepare and recover from this fright. What part of medical worries is bothering you?

Sleep: And lastly sleep, crucially important sleep. Shoot for 8 hours to nurture your body and mind. Sleep is a math problem, count back 8 hours from when you need to get up to know what time you must go to bed. What part of sleeping has you concerned?

Couples Conflicts

Couples marry people with opposite characteristics. It is predictable that couples will argue and hold grudges over the "small stuff," that often reoccur. Clear out these resentments with EFT!

You have learned to desensitize many events that throw you off-balance. The next chapter addresses work issues, which are associated with the place we spend 8 or more long hours of our day!

CHAPTER 12:

WORK STRESS ISSUES

Work

Job Loss

Technostress

Burn-out and Compassion Fatigue

Work Relationships

> *What we resist persists.*
>
> *–Dr. Carl Jung*

Here is a summary of the steps to use EFT to desensitize issues. It's time to apply them for work situations.

- Begin with one issue and then go deeper looking for its roots.

- Usually, the removal of 1 to 5 of the aspects collapses the entire issue.

- Take any similar situation and change the wording to meet your needs

- The abundant possible reminder phrases are *italicized* for easy reference.

- Chapter 3 reminds of the 11 acupoints used for emotions and thoughts

- Chapter 6, The Mind-Body Sweep, is useful for overwhelming issues felt physically

- The 5 steps mnemonic CARES (Chief Complaint, Aspects, Reminder Phrase, EFT, Spontaneous insight) is used to review cases.

Work has rewards and challenges.   Your work identity, emotional and financial health are involved. Often issues with co-workers and customers need attention. This chapter discusses several of these concerns.

CASE | Work and Loss of Job Issues –Example 12.1

My client, Mary, was laid off from her job and had been collecting unemployment for a year. She was about to start another job and was panicked. Her customer interaction would be recorded; thus, there would be comments about her job performance. She needed the job, and yet she was visibly shaking telling me this. Her chief complaint was her fear of being criticized.   This fear was a trigger for her. She was one among thousands getting laid off during the height of the 2008-2009 recession; however, she internalized that it was her fault. Her entire department was laid off, but the company told her it was due to customers' complaints. (Ironically, the company had a policy that encouraged complaints, because service was free if they were unhappy with it.)

Mary was embarrassed and ashamed that she was laid off. Below are some reminder phrases we worked with:

I feel flawed about myself

Angry about not holding onto my job

> *Upset about blaming myself*
>
> *Upset about being a failure*
>
> *Worried about failing again*
>
> *Embarrassed about having to tell my children*
>
> *Worried about unemployment covering my bills*
>
> *Fretting about my mother always said I was too much trouble*
>
> *Frightened about being criticized in this new job*
>
> *Worried about listening to my recorded customer interaction will show too many faults*

Here is one EFT set-up that was used on a stubborn issue – Mary's fear of being criticized. Who knew that it was this deep-seated until we got there? This type of deep insight happens a lot!

C 1) **C**hief Complaint: fear of being criticized.

A 2) **A**spect: (or defining moment) "frightened of being criticized at my new job"

R 3) **R**eminder Phrase: *Frightened of being criticized* SUDS = 8

E 4) **E**FT: Apply light touch to the 11 acupoints (using the Emotion Worksheet at the end of Chapter 3) while repeating the Reminder Phrase, for 3 or more rounds.

-- Cycle from Step 2 through 4 looking for more aspects

S 5) **S**pontaneous insight:

A smile came over Mary's face when she calmed down. This is what she remembered.

"After my mother criticized me for things I did, she also spanked me. No wonder I am panicked by criticism; it actually was dangerous to me in my childhood! I am about to be a new employee, and they will not be spanking me. It's not dangerous. It is new information that I don't know and I will

> grow and learn from it. I am OK with this now, and it may
> even be informative and fun! I can learn from their
> comments."

The basic CARES formula is the same - that of calming the upset by lightly touching or tapping the 11 acupoints while repeating the negative reminder phrase to desensitize its influence. What is remarkable is when the client's reaction is suddenly revealed by a change in her demeanor— her tense frown transformed into a tranquil, appreciative smile. She breathes easily and becomes relaxed. She has experienced a sudden "aha" moment and her fears have evaporated.

This clarity was hidden from Mary before EFT. She was stuck in panic and unable to make the connections. It is certainly possible that she could have figured this out in talk therapy as well. However, EFT quelled her stress, allowing her thinking brain to make the connection between being criticized and spanked.

What about your work or unemployment situation bothers you?

_____

_____

Try going through the CARES steps to settle your upsets.

Work Behaviors

Past issues triggered at work could be the subject matter for an entire book. What if your emotional clutter issues manifest themselves at work? Interestingly, work may actually be the very place you feel most effective. This may explain why many people become workaholics or overly identify with work. It is in this milieu that they feel the competence they didn't feel growing up or don't feel in their current family situation.

People who have minimal success at effective communication bring this into the workplace too. They might have an edgy "attitude", because this is what protected them in their difficult homes or neighborhoods. They might argue aggressively over a minor detail, as if a family crisis has occurred. Conversely, they might shy away from confrontation altogether, to the frustration of the team's need for their involvement.

They need to develop "professionalism," a public face which can be a calm tone of voice, a gracious way to ask for thing or to say "no". Related tools are discussed in Chapter 2.

Here are some typical work issues and their corresponding EFT reminder phrases in italics to plug into the Emotions Worksheet located at the end of Chapter 3.

> You've just been yelled at –
> *so pissed off about him yelling at me.*
>
> You lost an important document –
> *exasperated about losing that.*
>
> An important client said no to your proposal –
> *feel so foolish about failing on that proposal.*
>
> A co-worker seems to work less than you do –
> *aggravated about I can't finish all I have to do while he plays on his computer.*

Remember to create your reminder phrase like these above and repeat it while lightly touching the 11 acupoints discussed throughout this book.

Once all the aspects of a problem are desensitized, you are likely to have a spontaneous insight, or a find new way of looking at an old insult. You may even feel silly about the intensity you felt before EFT desensitized your issue. Silly feelings regarding the past are a huge sign that it no longer has a hold on you.

Next we move onto another pet peeve of the 21st century.

Technostress

What did you say? Technostress? We are in the Information age. Computers, smart phones, and social media rule. At a 2009 Energy Psychology conference, accomplished author and United Nations Development Group leader, Jean Houston, Ph.D., explained that the quantity of information doubles every four years.

There are so many positives to technology. Smart phones really are smart. They connect us to the internet and all that implies. Records and information are easily shared. But are all technology advances good? Is there stress involved and is there a downside? Technology is smart but there is another meaning to smart: it smarts (hurts) when it doesn't run efficiently.

Here is my favorite use of technology.

Technique 56: Video Conferencing - Magic for Long Distance Communication

These digital wonders close the world in business dealings, human relationships and news gathering.

As a communicator and someone who values relationships, I am very pleased with digital video communication - Skype, Facetime, Zoom and other similar products. Families are spread out all over the world for a variety of reasons. When your family member tells you they are moving far from home, don't despair. *Think* instead of shifting your relationship toward one of these digital video media. It is everything - but touch.

Here are some examples from my world. A picture is indeed worth 1000 words. I *saw* 50 mopeds outside my daughter's hotel room in Barcelona as she complained about excessive noise. I *took a walk* with her 3000 miles away as she turned the camera outward while narrating a tour of the adorable village of Mountain View, CA.

My husband and son *together watched* a Syracuse basketball game. They were screaming with excitement - my husband in our living room and a grey computer sitting on the couch which televised to my son on his computer in Armenia. We *attended* the opening of this son's project there. He carried us on his computer screen. We have *played* cards and even just *chatted* while I cooked dinner. My brother and his grandsons live 6 hours away but we *sing* songs and they know who I am. Weddings, holidays and parties can be *attended* even if out of state! Plus the work uses are too many to mention. I offer my thanks to the geniuses who created these up – close-and-personal ways to maintain intimate connections. They have saved my sanity with my very mobile family!

More about technostress. The hospital where I work wins awards for being the most computer and electronically wired. I am dragged across the cyber finish line! My last job barely had any typewriters. Imagine my chagrin and anxiety when I realized all clinically necessary forms were on the computer, and not in any filing cabinet! Now I am showing my age, but even the young get frustrated with slow computers, applications that do not work, and being suspended in teleprompt hell.

Cell phones didn't exist during the first forty years of my life. My daughter wanted one in high school, and we told her the common belief at the time - that only drug dealers carried them. She obtained her first cell phone when she became a new driver. I think growing up without a cell phone made her more independent, because she had to solve her issues without my instant opinion.

People of this present era are walking connections: we have phone, text, mail and internet access in our pockets and bags. We count on this, but there is a down side. We are always on-call – vulnerable to interruption and preoccupied with the happenings of our smart phones. Maybe it is not so smart to always be so preoccupied and available. Technology addiction is real and rampart.

I believe that texting is addictive, and has an opium-like addictive power. Computer gaming has a similar power for many. Once addicted, our youth, young adults and older ages too become fixated on this to the exclusion of actual human contact. They even risk their lives doing this impossible task while driving or crossing streets. Smart phones used excessively are making us dumb.

Facebook is another venue for technology addiction. A college student told me that while her classmates were taking notes on their computers during class, they were also checking their Facebook updates. I work with college students at risk of failing due to this addiction to technology. What happened to setting time limits on phone, television, computer and gaming usage?

If technology is stressing you out, plug these possible reminder phrases into the EFT CARES formula.

> ### *Addicted to texting* (Chief complaint)
>
> ASPECTS:
>
> *Urge about checking my Facebook account*
>
> *Desire to check my text messages*

Upset about my phone is with my parents and I cannot text

Curious about if I have any text responses on my phone

Furious about my child being more interested in texting than in me or school work

Annoyed about my colleagues are texting during staff meetings

Worried about knowing that I am addicted

Urge to text or check my texts while driving

Upset about my inability to navigate that application

Not studying because gaming is more exciting

Feel incompetent about being in real social situations

Fretting about if my Power Point presentation won't run

Worries about missing something when offline

Frustrated about need to reboot my computer

Angry about wasting time with personal cyber fun

Concerned about failing college due to technology obsession

Feel bad about stealing time at work with my phone

Frustrated about waiting for their computer to advance screens

Annoyed about being always "on call" by carrying my cell phone

Worried about my children not developing independence

Angry about him talking now to that person

Remember to select or create a *reminder phrase* and couple it with lightly touching the 11 acupoints to defuse its hold on you,

Another example of technostress is the dreaded automated phone teleprompts. It can take me over five minutes to get a real person, (and it's often the wrong person who then sends me back for another five minutes of additional teleprompt hell). I once timed 80 minutes lost in teleprompt limbo to get a simple insurance clarification. Sometimes it feels intentional. Automated messages do not recognize all issues and will often not transfer you to a live person.

(Spoiler Alert) Spiderman, the now closed NYC musical, contained a hysterical rendition of this torturous teleprompt hell! The villain bellows his doomsday, destruction threat into the phone and is told by the automated voice "Sorry, I do not recognize that request! Please press 1 if you want ..., press 2 if you want..."

If teleprompt torture causes you stress too, consider these reminder phrases:

> *Upset about not getting to a real person*
>
> *Upset about not finding this function*
>
> *Upset about my computer is frozen again*
>
> *Frustrated about my computer is running so slowly*
>
> *Upset about no one will take responsibility for my issue*
>
> *Furious about being stuck in teleprompt nowhere land*
>
> *Upset that I cannot remember my own password*
>
> *Upset about being transferred again and will have to repeat all my data*
>
> *Upset about losing significant insurance reimbursements because no one person owns my problem.*
>
> *Upset about their computer not working so we cannot finish our business transaction.*
>
> *Upset about being recorded – "for training purposes"*

Remember to use one of these or your own created reminder phrase and couple them with light touch or tapping on the 11 acupoints to lower your frustration level. Use as many rounds as needed.

Here are even more reminder phrases associated with technostress:

> *Upset about new and changing applications*
>
> *Irritated about not finding this folder*
>
> *Frustrated about creating a shortcut icon*
>
> *Upset about the help desk requesting info I have no clue about*
>
> *Annoyed about the computer being much slower than paper*
>
> *Worried about switching to a different computer system*
>
> *Anxious about being so dependent on colleagues that are frustrated with me*

Relationship, too, have changed too with technology. People expect instant, but superficial contact and are annoyed if someone chooses not to be wired in every minute.

Here are some technostress reminder phrases with relationships.

Almost every marriage session discusses some technology problem.

> *Irked about him not calling and only sending text messages*
>
> *Miffed about waiting for a text from my girlfriend, spouse, etc.*
>
> *Angry about him not carrying his cell phone*
>
> *Concerned about a co-worker who texts my husband all the time.*
>
> *Angry about her preference to be on the computer than snuggle with me*
>
> *Worried about her having an emotional affair with a co-worker by text*
>
> *Annoyed about him not answering immediately when I call*
>
> *Frustrated with overly long text messages.*
>
> *Upset about what my girlfriend posts on Facebook*
>
> *In trouble about my parents reading my text messages*

> Cyberbullying – *upset about what people post about me on Facebook*
>
> *Disgusted about people posting too much information (TMI) on Facebook*
>
> *Mad about her wasting company time doing personal stuff on the internet, or Facebook (also called "stealing time" from work).*

Another technostress issue is *time*. Computers have given us a central registry, but this comes at a cost. I just returned from a doctor's visit where my poor physician was typing away long after we were done. This is associated with his need to generate a new Electronic Medical Record. I remember the days he simply dictated information for a typist or via a voice recognition system. What a waste of time it is for this talented physician to do secretarial work. Teleprompts mentioned above also waste time. And waiting a long time for a computer screen to post material is beyond frustrating when compared to old fashioned handwriting.

By the way, I think my lack of computer savvy was equally painful for my younger colleagues, who can find their way around the computer in their sleep. They learned it in elementary school. Like any foreign language, the older you learn computer language, the more arduous is mastery. To repeatedly have to show me how to navigate was an effort in fortitude for my co-workers. Thank you via this public forum for dragging me along into the 21st century! (Thank Goodness I have clinical skills to offer!)

Here are some possible reminder phrases for my colleagues and others as you teach the technologically-challenged.

> *This is so darn simple*
>
> *Frustrated about her being slow to learn this*
>
> *Upset about her forgetting what I showed her last week*
>
> *Frustrated about we reviewing this again*
>
> *Annoyed about this is taking more patience than I have*
>
> *Hard about keeping doing this despite her appreciation*

Technostress is real. Staying current is a challenge. Avoiding addiction to text messaging, games and Facebook is a challenge, which many people are losing. Remember to laugh about technostress too. Throwing my computer out the window is an enjoyable fantasy. Imagining the power to zap and destroy teleprompts permanently also delights me!

More Technostress

- Cyberbullying is a new problem of technology

- A false sense of anonymity is experienced via cyber connections

- Technology is developing faster than norm and morality can evolve and legislate. Teen sexting is an example; of where the first few cases were criminalized under the child pornography laws.

These issues are definitely technostress that carry deeply hurtful outcomes! Sadly terrorists, the ultimate definition of bullies, are able to deliver their sick messages through various social media too. The Supreme Court is trying to weigh hostile online rants and freedom of speech.

What about technology stresses you?

_____

_____

Take one aspect off the lists above and plug it into the EFT CARES 5-step formula to lessen your frustration. You will probably arrive at some interesting Spontaneous Insights when complete.

Work can be a mine field of stresses. Another stressful work situation is where the workload is too large and stressful.

Burn-Out, Compassion Fatigue, and Overextended

In this time of reduced resources at work, many people are overstretched and doing more than one job function. Employers used to focus on "retention" of employees with efforts to make the work place a genuinely balanced environment. With recession, a shift seems to happen where increased productivity and focus on customer service dominates. Evaluations are requested for everything, even of a 5-minute phone call.

Thus, work-related stress seems to be on the climb. Even some hospital reimbursements are altered based on these patient evaluations. Lifework balance is off balance!

Burn-out and Compassion Fatigue are sometimes used interchangeably. Technically, burn-out is when you do too much and are just sick of it. Being overextended is being expected to complete important work in too short of a time period. Housekeeping is an area where I am burned-out. I am tired of doing it, but I do not have nightmares about it as in compassion fatigue.

Compassion Fatigue, a term coined by Dr. Charles Figley of Florida State University, is a form of vicarious trauma. It occurs when a helping professional has empathized to the degree that he or she also begins to experience symptoms. People in the helping fields including First Responders are prime candidates for Compassion Fatigue.

Trauma involves a horrific event that happened to you. Secondary trauma is when you witnessed the event or listened to its retelling. Compassion Fatigue is a form of secondary trauma.

A key factor of developing Post-Traumatic Stress Reaction (PTSD) is feeling *helpless* in these horrific events. Doing something considered useful in a catastrophe may mitigate against long-standing PTSD.

Many therapists and first responders in the trauma field experience secondary trauma. According to Professor Charles Figley, MS Ph.D., traumatologist, in an article on Medscape, sleep may be interrupted in secondary trauma. People lose their sense of humor, and they withdraw. The very characteristics that made them good first-responders or therapists--compassion and empathy--became overwhelming and detrimental to the helper. EFT can mutually benefit the client and the helper.

A typical caseload for a busy psychotherapist ranges from twenty-three to twenty-six sessions per week. During the seven years my children were in expensive colleges, I fulfilled this caseload at a mental health center by converting a full-time job into four days of work. I then worked another two days in my private practice. Some days I saw as many as eleven clients. My colleagues could not believe I was seeing so many clients!

I never experienced either secondary trauma or Compassion Fatigue during those seven years, despite seeing numerous psychologically distressed clients. Tired? Yes, of course, but not tearful, whiney, and fretful about seeing another client. EFT desensitized both my client and me to extreme and horrific situations that we worked on. Consider being the therapist working with a client using the following reminder *phrase* with EFT.

Upset my father beat my mother

My client is upset that it happened and so am I. It violates my values and tears at my heart. Fortunately, while treating this horrific memory in a "Simon Says copy the therapist" manner, we both get desensitized at the same time. We parallel each other's emotional upset and both have "aha" spontaneous insight moments. The client is able to let it go saying,

"It was a long time ago."

My therapeutic "aha" moment is a healing reframe:

"Your father taught you how NOT to behave."

Sometimes with trauma reminder phrases, there is no need to mention the emotions as they are inherent to the situation. Here are some examples.

Arrived on the scene and the entire family was shot dead

Overwhelmed about the Twin Towers collapsing completely

Triggered about hearing the chirping of the fireman's equipment that signified a firemen was down

Ran out of the burning building

Beaten until I was bloody

Left for dead

Robbed at gunpoint

EFT is a tool that can help the military and police notify family members of deaths. For example, the military person delivering the bad news could say that this tragic event is hard for both of us. He could also ask if the notified person is willing to use some simple acupressure to help face this terrible news. Possibly just holding the heart from 3 Times 3 could benefit too. EFT could be used during talk show interviews and news reporters (on or off camera) covering tragedies and their interviewees. Perhaps, the instinctive hug accomplishes a calming influence on the victimized person, since it hits so many meridians throughout the body.

A young psychotherapist supervisee told me that when she was tired and burned-out for the day, she added EFT to her session to perk her up too. I hope someday school systems will begin the day with EFT. An executive decided to begin all meetings with EFT to bring down the frustration brought into the room. Some business and personal coaches are insisting their clients use EFT daily.

In today's business climate with cost-cutting layoffs, many people are overextended and trying to do a job too big for one person. Working parents find themselves wishing they could be cut in half—one side for work, the other to be there for their children. EFT can calm this agitation too.

| CASE | **Working Mother – Example 12.2**

Olivia was a working mother with three small children. Frequently, she was asked to travel to exciting conferences for her job, but she could not participate because she wasn't able to arrange the childcare. She felt split in two, wanting to be with her children, but missing out on important educational training.

1) **C**hief Complaint:	Wanting to be in two places at the same time.
2) **A**spect:	Frustrated with parental responsibilities SUDS rating = 6
3) **R**eminder Phrase:	*Frustrated about not having enough help with my children*
4) **E**FT:	Do 3 or more EFT rounds of the 11 acupoints (using the Emotion Worksheet at the end of Chapter 3)

	while repeating the Reminder Phrase until calm.
	-- Cycle from steps 2 through 4, finding and desensitizing new aspects and defining moments.
5) **S**pontaneous Insight:	"I could go to one conference every year and enjoy it without feeling guilty. Let me trade some overnight childcare with a family member."

What are you overextended or burned out in your job? Are you suffering from compassion fatigue?

_____

_____

See if any of the reminder phrases in this chapter strike a chord with you. Try going through the CARES 5-steps to settle your upsets.

CASE	**Relationship Problems at Work –Example 12.3**

Wendy does the same job as Nancy, but Nancy is always looking over Wendy's shoulder and telling her better ways to do it. Wendy is flustered, and her speed at work is slowing down. Her boss wants to know what the problem is.

1) **C**hief Complaint:	My boss thinks I am working too slowly.
2) **A**spect:	I am flustered by Nancy commenting on my every move.
3) **R**eminder phrase:	_Upset that Nancy unnerves me_ SUDS rating = 7
4) **E**FT:	Do 3 or more EFT rounds of the 11 acupoints (using the Emotion Worksheet at the end of Chapter 3) while repeating the Reminder Phrase until calm.

	-- Cycle from steps 2 through 4, finding and desensitizing new aspects and defining moments.
5) **S**pontaneous Insight:	"Nancy is not my supervisor, but she does remind me of my older sister who dominated me. She is not my sister. I will tell her politely to hold her opinions to herself, and I will ask that my desk be moved so I can work uninterrupted."

**Wendy may want to go through this technique with whatever way her sister was bossy to her, in order to desensitize this thoroughly.

What is not going well at your job?

_____

_____

Consider taking another look at Example 5.2, on page 120, a difficult colleague on two levels - current and triggered from the past.

In the next chapter we are look at what happens when ongoing stress and anxiety become a style. This is true for 20% of the population. If it applies to you, remember you are not alone. Read it to understand those close to you who struggle chronically with anxiety issues.

CHAPTER 13

ANXIETY PROBLEMS

Anxiety and Stress

Generalized Anxiety

Panic

Social Anxiety and EFT and Initiating Conversation

Brides and Grooms, the Ultimate Social Anxiety Situation

Unwanted Habits

Acute Stress Reactions (Oh No!) and Longer Lasting PTSD

> "Every time you are tempted to react in the same way, ask if you want to be a prisoner of the past or a pioneer of the future."
>
> Deepak Chopra

Introduction

This chapter is going to look my specialty – stress and the anxiety spectrum. The effects of long-standing stress can shape your style of reacting to new things. If you have experienced a lot of stress in the past, you may anticipate that new situations will be stressful. That anticipation is anxiety. When anxiety is triggered, the body and mind enter into a frenetic overdrive. The body charges up and the mind may race from one catastrophic thought to another. This is called "what if" thinking, or doomsday thinking. Most of this is an overreaction, yet difficult to modulate.

We will look at anxiety in an example using a work issue. We also discuss brides, who often experience the ultimate social anxiety story. Unwanted behaviors like thumb sucking is discussed too. Later, in Chapter 14, we will look at some common phobias: test-taking, flying, mice and public speaking.

We will use our familiar format explained in Chapter 3. Here is a quick review.

- We begin with one issue and then go deeper, looking for its roots

- Usually, the removal of 1 to 5 of the aspects collapses the entire issue.

- Take any similar situation and change the wording to meet your needs.

- Possible reminder phrases are *italicized* for easy reference.

- Chapter 3 demonstrates the 11 acupoints, if you need a review.

- Chapter 6, The Mind-Body Sweep, is useful for overwhelming issues.

- Steps 1 through 5 spell CARES to remind you of how to proceed.

Most of the following are composite cases with the same issue. Do you recognize aspects of yourself in these cases?

Stress, Anxiety, Generalized Anxiety, and Panic

We have already learned about some very specific thoughts that stress you. Now we are going to look at anxiety itself, which is another label for stress. In generalized anxiety, there is a tendency when facing new situations to leap to worrisome conclusions. Using EFT regularly diminishes this tendency: you will see a cumulative benefit. In fact, the very nature of knowing how to manage stress can tame what might have become an out-of-control monster!

Due to my social anxiety and my fear of being judged, I did not raise my hand in a staff meeting until I was forty years old. (I think a few of my current supervisors wish I could revert back to that state!) I lived with a full-blown generalized anxiety disorder. My brother said he never worried, because growing up he had a sister that did enough worrying for the whole family. I worry about everything—time, money, people, events, etc. I worried about worry. EFT liberated me quickly and also made me a brief therapy expert!

EFT quells anxiety faster than anything I have ever encountered, and in the field of stress I've experienced a lot. Recently, a client with a driving phobia cleared it in one session. The reminder phrase was "fear of driving in the rain." Later during a phone call she said "I did not even know that was possible." Managed health care should embrace EFT because of its efficiency.

Anxiety is experienced as a profound emotional and often physical reaction. Some professionals are starting to call anxious people "highly sensitive." We are. Issues that irk other people, perhaps on a SUDS rating of 3, send us soaring to a SUDS of 8. It is not a comfortable place to be. No one chooses to be this reactive. Sometimes that acute awareness over-stimulates us. This state of constant vigilance can turn into hypervigilance and exhaustion from overload and over-stimulation. On the flip side, such awareness can foster intuition and being tuned into our environment.

All of us can be stressed out, depending on circumstances. One in five people has a tendency to fall somewhere on the anxiety spectrum. The anxiety spectrum includes:

- Phobias – Specific things that agitate you, i.e. heights, elevators, testing, creatures, public speaking (discussed later in Chapter 14)

- Generalized Anxiety – Quickly gearing-up over even small things

- Social Anxiety Disorder – Nervous or shy in social settings, including public speaking fear

- Panic Disorder – Sudden emotional and physical agitation, with or without a noticeable cause; people report rapid heartbeat, shortness of breath, and sweating. Sometimes they feel as if the room is closing in on them, or that they might faint, go crazy or even die- which they do not.

- Obsessive-Compulsive Disorder (OCD) – Intrusive irrational thoughts and/or excessive, repetitive behavior. These can't be resisted or controlled even though the person knows they are excessive. Obsessive thoughts are intrusive, upsetting about yourself or a feared issue that occur over and over. Examples are fears of germs or contamination; fear of fires from appliances left on or plugged in, fear of break-ins; or fear of causing harm. Compulsions are repeated behaviors that are often responses to obsessive thoughts such as hand washing with germ obsessions, checking the front door for obsessions about break ins, excessive cleaning for contamination fear. If you check something once, twice or even three times a day, that is not OCD. Some bad habits go here too, like thumb sucking, discussed later.

- Acute Stress Reactions to Traumatic Events – This is an overwhelming reaction to a horrific event; such as attacks, serious accidents, natural disasters, fires and war.

Acute Stress Reactions are normal reactions to extreme events and last about one month or so. Longer lasting reactions may become Post-Traumatic Stress Disorder.

- Post-Traumatic Stress Disorder (PTSD) is when the acute stress reaction does not go away. There are very specific criteria for this, in addition to exposure to a severe event, including re-experiencing the event through flashbacks or nightmares, some type of numbing or dissociation, exaggerated startle response, hypervigilance, and avoidance of reminders of the event. Helpless feeling was also present. PTSD can be crippling in specific situations, or may extend to almost every aspect of life. I suggest you find a therapist and ask if they know how to treat PTSD as it is beyond the scope of this book, but not beyond the scope of these meridian techniques. Dr. Fred Gallo's book called *Energy Tapping for Trauma* is an excellent resource.

So let's look at a typical upset a person with Generalized Anxiety might experience.

| CASE | **Worrying About Time, a Constant State of Urgency –** **Example 13.1**

Jan was on her way to a new location to give a lecture and it started to rain. Despite allowing fifteen extra minutes, her stomach tightened into knots as the traffic flowed more and more slowly. Her catastrophic thinking kicked in, she began to imagine worst case scenarios; she felt nauseous. These are symptoms that a person with generalized anxiety disorder might feel.

<u>**CARES** Steps</u>

TIP: Remember that to find the A (aspects): keep asking - what is it that bothers me about this?

> **C** 1) **C**hief Complaint: I don't want to be late, as I have to set up for the lecture.
>
> Optional Mind-body Sweep - not needed here
>
> **A** 2) **A**spect: The rain has slowed traffic down, SUDS = 7

> **R** 3) **R**eminder Phrase: *Upset traffic is moving too slow and might be late*
>
> **E** 4) **E**FT: Do 3 or more EFT rounds of the 11 acupoints (using the Emotion Worksheet at the end of Chapter 3) while repeating the Reminder Phrase until calm.
>
> -- Cycle again steps 2-4 working on more aspects.
>
> **S**. 5) **S**pontaneous Insight: "I feel calm. I gave myself extra time and if I happen to be late everyone can see it is raining."

Anxiety comes from fear and frequently accompanies issues that are uncomfortable but not dangerous, i.e., making a phone call, public speaking, new social events. Remind yourself that this issue is just annoying, not dangerous and treat it with EFT!

A more extreme variety of anxiety is called ***panic***.

Panic: a physical form of anxiety

The panicky client may say:

> "I can't catch my breath, my heart is beating through my chest, and my palms are too sweaty to shake anyone's hand! Do you think I am going to be okay? Should we call for help?"

These symptoms are alarming enough to be checked by a medical doctor, but very often are caused by panic. This is anxiety out-of-control. The body's reaction is so intense. It is so physical that you worry you're going to die, faint, or go crazy. You will not do any of these with panic.

Your heart may race, but, there isn't an aerobics instructor alive who would not tell you the benefit to getting your heart rate up. Regarding the fear of fainting, you may feel weak and have to gently sit down, but you will not lose consciousness from panic. And anxious people are too controlled to allow themselves to go crazy! Once you know the situation wasn't caused by too much stimulating caffeine or a medical problem, treat it with EFT.

Here is a reminder of the four dreaded F's of adrenaline-driven panic and anxiety are:

- **F**ight - desire to protect oneself by fighting the enemy
- **F**light - desire to run away from perceived danger
- **F**reeze – playing dead so the enemy loses interest
- **F**ogged brain – clouded and unclear thoughts

These reactions are understandable and even desirable if you are in real danger, because they are truly protective. In danger we use our reptilian brain, which like a reptile is ready to pounce!

The problems occur when anxiety overrides logic in the situations that are actually not dangerous. For example, panic in anticipation of giving a public speech, anger misdirected at a loved one, or the anxiety experienced in a group setting for someone suffering with Social Anxiety Disorder. None of these situations is dangerous. However, your body and mind are overreacting, responding as if there is a real threat to your life. EFT will calm all four F's.

To treat panic, you can focus on the physical manifestations or the issue. My suggestion is that you calm serious body discomfort first using the Mind-Body Sweep of Chapter 6. Next, look for aspects and be pleasantly surprised that the SUDS intensity is lower than expected, because the body was calmed first.

We now discuss *Social Anxiety*, which is a pervasive stress reaction in social situations. These folks are not introverts and want to be social, but their stress level rises around people.

The following is my article printed on the EFT online newsletter. It originally appeared on emofree.com (Gary Craig) and is also on the web site of EFTuniverse.com. (Dr. Dawson Church). A Spanish translation can be found on the internet, too.

Using EFT for Social Anxiety Disorder

Note: This article assumes you have a working knowledge of EFT.

Preface by EFT Founder Gary Craig (www.emofree.com):

Hi Everyone,

Long time EFT'er Robin Bilazarian uses EFT for many sophisticated issues. Here she outlines her approach for Social Anxiety Disorder.

Hugs, Gary

By Robin Bilazarian, LCSW

Social Anxiety Disorder is a crippling disease. Those afflicted have debilitating panic attacks, racing heart, disorganized thoughts, fear of dying, losing control or fainting, embarrassing tremors and feel frantic in social situations.

They fear being scrutinized and judged harshly, seeing others as a social threat. They do not trust their bodies to be calm in these events. It limits casual, spontaneous interactions and prohibits them from attending social gatherings. They fear any performance situation. Even riding the bus, eating in a restaurant or attending a movie can be feared.

The anxiety can be specific as in public speaking or pervasive--severely limiting most social interaction. They approach benign social interaction with the same trepidation as facing a firing squad. Limited social interactions have a cumulative effect that they do not develop competent social skills, are keenly aware of this and thus feel even more vulnerable and defenseless.

I am working with two clients currently and several in the past using EFT. Initially, I explore their first or worst memory of when they felt this early in their life. I remember working with a delightful young woman who was too shy to date and did not see herself for the beauty she was. Said with many tears, she had accepted she would always be alone. She remembered being rejected by a boy she liked in middle school. After quickly discussing how a young boy may not be the most stable person to obtain a lifetime opinion of one's self, we used EFT to defuse this. Her laughing demeanor after EFT highlighted a definite and liberating shift had occurred.

After clearing any *past* hurts and active memories, I use EFT on any and all remaining fears they have of social interactions in the *future*. This includes anxiety of walking into a party, (tune into your fear of walking into the party...); of smiling and saying hello to others, and of initiating small talk. With four petrified brides, I used EFT to clear and calm every aspect of their wedding, i.e. walking down the aisle with EVERYONE staring at them, saying their vows aloud, the father-daughter dance, etc. They had wonderful times at their weddings and continue to use EFT in their lives.

Since they cut off social interactions years ago, I believe good therapy removes the blocks using EFT, removes the fears of future interactions using EFT and then, gives them the new social skills to try.

I ask them to do homework daily to always be ready to initiate small talk (weather, sports, current events, ambiance in the room, movies, television) as a conversation starter. I teach them how to interject them into conversation "so...can you believe the beautiful weather we had, or the horrible weather they have had in Florida, etc."*

With many, I add the Future Performance Enhancement Protocol (Technique 54, page 237) of having them picture themselves calmly interacting while holding "under the eye" for 5 breaths and the "under the arm" for 5 breaths and repeating these two points until fully confident.

Using this formula, my recent client was another young woman stuck in a going nowhere 7 year relationship and too fearful of being alone to move on. She has now broken up with him, used internet dating safely and is dating seriously the fourth person she met – all within 3 months of ending her unhealthy relationship. I use EFT in both a private practice setting and as an EAP counselor with all types of staff in a regional trauma hospital.

Robin Bilazarian

Note: You can translate this article in 57 languages at: https://www.eftuniverse.com/anxiety-stress/using-eft-for-social-anxiety-disorder.

Technique 57: **Layers of Communication**

Words and talk are how we humans connect. Clients with social anxiety have often missed out on learning ways to interact. They universally tell me they don't know what to say to others privately, in a gathering, or at home. I teach layers of communication.

The outside layer is small talk, ice breakers or just gabbing, and the purpose is to initiate a connection. Humans connect by words and are uncomfortable with silence. Topics in small talk are:

- The weather – universal topic of interest

- Anything in the room – a picture, an attractive scarf someone is wearing

- Current events – the elections, daily news items, fires, car accidents

- Sports – know what sport season it is and ask about what is their favorite team and why

- Any television shows, movies, music or hobbies

- What you did today or what they did today

These can all be made into questions or brought up in conversation with the word "so…. (examples) – can you believe how rainy it has been?

So what movies have you seen? or I love watching *The Voice*.

What happens are the conversations starts moving toward more personal. Here is an example.

If I ask someone if they are watching the Phillies baseball in Philadelphia, the discussion eventually wind up that I am a Red Sox fan, having grown up in Boston. After the banter of which team is better, the topic will go in to discussing things of interest in Boston and voila! We now have conversation!

The inner core layer, noted in figure 13.1, is very personal; such as our sex life, how much money we make or rubs we have with family members. The middle is everything else and it is up to both people how much of the core you are comfortable exposing.

Also, small talk will save the day if someone intrudes too closely into your core issues. If the person asks about your sex life, you can give a quick brush off answer and then go to small talk.

"My sex life is fine and how did you make out with all this rain?"

The person will know you changed the subject and understand that topic (of sex) is off limits. If not, you may need to switch the subject a few times. Thus, I ask all my clients to be prepared with 4 topics of small talk daily. With weather as one stable, that leaves only 3 topics to have on hand. I promise it gets easier with time and practice.

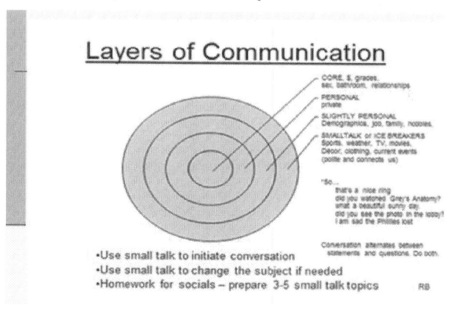

Figure 13.1 Layers of Conversation

Good small talk or icebreaker questions or comments: So… That is a nice ring? Are you watching American Idol? What a beautiful sunny day! Did you see that photo in the lobby? I am sad the Red Sox lost. What team do you route for?

Brides and Their Grooms - extreme example of social anxiety

So you are getting married. Your wedding day is the biggest day of your life and you are thrilled. This has been a goal and a lifetime dream since childhood. It is probably the most expensive day of your life too. However, you are happy about committing your life to a great person. You are having fun looking at banquet facilities and checking out potential bands. You even don't mind your mother's and future mother-in-law's input, because your happiness is overflowing. There is a growing nagging sensation that you try to suppress and usually this works. However, it's getting harder and harder. What is the issue?

You will be the CENTER of attention.

You will be EXAMINED by all.

How about satisfying those future in-laws?

You feel as if you are being SCRUTINIZED on every detail.

You will walk down the aisle with everyone watching you. All EYES will be on YOU.

Your father really does not want to do the father-daughter dance, as he does not like the attention either.

You are the center of attention but you hate people staring at you.

What if you are a perfectionist?

Perhaps a private Las Vegas wedding alone is a viable option! All weddings have some controversies, because two families with different values and ideas partake in the wedding.

EFT can come to the rescue. I have treated many brides and they report that they also treated their grooms. Perhaps this stress-relieving technique belongs in community education classes everywhere.

| CASE | **Wedding Jitters –Example 13.2**

This case uses the Mind-Body Sweep first and then standard EFT.

Beverly was so excited about getting married. She planned the wedding for one year, and it looked great until it was three months away. At this point, she began to dread the whole idea of a big wedding. Her sweet, future mother-in-law was upset with the wedding official, and her fiancé kept asking for an account of every dime she spent.

Further, she was nervous about walking down the aisle with her also nervous father. One of her bridesmaids was slow to pay for the dress, and the bridal boutique nagged her about this.

The decision was made to calm her down first using the mind-body sweep. I asked her to think of *all* her worries and problems and to bundle everything about the wedding for 5 seconds. Where did she feel them in her body? Here is what she reported with the accompanying SUDS rating of the intensity.

Gagging and tight throat	SUDS ___6___
Pressure on my chest	SUDS __10__
Weak legs	SUDS ___4___

CARES steps

C 1) **C**hief complaint: Freaking out about tons of things about my wedding

A 2) **A**spect: where do you feel the most physical discomfort? Pressure in my chest

R 3) **R**eminder Phrase: *Pressure in my chest* SUDS= 10

E 4) **E**FT: Apply light pressure on the 11 acupoints (using the Mind-Body Sweep-Ch. 6) SUDS 10→0

-- Cycle from steps 2 through 4, finding and desensitizing new aspects and defining moments. (Note – here we used these physical descriptions until all were calm.)

S 5) **S**pontaneous insight: "Ok, I can survive this day. I am just worried about the details. (SUDS =5) But I know this day will be full of happiness."

Go back through this protocol on "worried about the details"

We proceeded to peel the onion, looking for more and deeper aspects by asking: "Is there more about this that's bothering you?" Ah, the awful center of attention!

C 1) **C**hief complaint: I hate to be the CENTER of attention (and have some social anxiety)

A 2) **A**spect: What specifically are you worried about? I hate that everyone will stare at me when I walk down   the aisle. SUDS = 7

R 3) **R**eminder Phrase: *hate that everyone will stare at me walking down the aisle.* SUDS = 7

E 4) **E**FT: Apply light pressure on the 11 acupoints (using the Emotion Worksheet at the end of Chapter 3) while repeating the Reminder Phrase for 3 or more rounds, until calm.

-- Cycle from steps 2 through 4, finding and desensitizing new aspects and defining moments.

S 5) **S**pontaneous Insight: "I actually am excited about this wonderful day. I will have my hair and make-up done, and I love the dress; so no wonder everyone will stare."

People always ask – what should I say when using EFT? Below are several issues, to put into the *reminder phrase* format if they apply to you. Plug whatever fits into the CARES steps. Often desensitizing 1 to 5 of these collapses the whole issue. Do as many of them, one at a time, as it takes for you to be calm about your wedding.

Upset about being called bridezilla

Worried about my groom being on time

Upset about a relative who will not be there

Unhappy about one of my bridesmaid's attitude

Worried about everyone staring at me

Hurt about my in-laws not helping

Angry about these details are all stuck on me

Angry about my family not taking this seriously

Worried about Uncle John embarrassing me

Nervous about walking down the aisle and not falling

Concerned about my father or mother on that day

Sweating about the father-daughter dance

Apprehensive about it being too much for my grandmother

Worried about my in-laws being upset with my choices

Upset about the weather, the flowers, the meal

Troubled about the staff mix-up of what I ordered

Frustrated about my bridesmaid not paying for her dress

Exasperated about my fiancé not trusting how I spend money

Upset about my future mother-in-law's unhappiness with the clergy we selected

Worried about the flowers, music, tuxedo, etc.

Worried about being too young to make an ENTIRE life commitment

Worried about he will change (some of his good qualities)
Worried he won't change (some of his bad qualities)

Worried about HIM being a wrong decision

Don't let this long list scare you. It is here to offer variety of issues. Most people settle down completely after 1 to 5 aspects have been cleared.

What are you worried about in relation to your wedding?

_____

_____

Use the Emotion Worksheet in Chapter 3 or the Mind-Body Sweep in Chapter 6 to calm down and desensitize with the CARES steps.

Be prepared for a great wedding, but let go of believing you will have a perfect wedding. Perfection is a myth. In fact, if you just expect something to go wrong, you may relax and find the humor in whatever that error turns out to be. Everyone is admiring you that day with lots of love, too.

But there's always a level of nervousness on the big day. My head was saying that this is the greatest guy. My gut was screaming, "This is FOREVER. I'm too young (age twenty-six) to make any lifetime commitment, get me out of here!" (I am still married to him, guess it worked out!)

Unwanted Habits – Hand Biting, Thumb Sucking and Compulsions

Two young women in their 20's suffered from ongoing hand biting or thumb sucking. Both were embarrassed about it. The first dreaded handshakes or having others near here when she was writing, as her hand was red and raw. She bit the inside of her pointer finger 8 times a day for about 10 minutes each time. One session of EFT collapsed this issue, with only 1 slip all week. The key is to ask her to tune to her

URGE to bite her hand for 5 seconds, rate it and use that word "urge to bite my hand" as the reminder statement. Successive sessions did the same for her new URGES to bite her fingertips and later her cuticles.

The thumb sucker's embarrassment stopped her from ever sleeping at a friend's house or going away to college. The similar single session treatment for the adult thumb sucker had her tune into her URGE to suck her thumb for 5 seconds. This also works focusing on the URGE of other compulsive behaviors.

Acute Stress Reactions and Post Traumatic Stress Reactions

Long lasting PTSD is out of the scope of this self-help book, but it is nicely treated with a skilled EFT or Energy Psychology clinician. However, Acute Stress Reactions to recent traumatic events are within the range of this book. Examples of Acute Stress Reactions are reactions to recent accidents, shocking news, attacks, unforeseen life events like lay-offs, or new serious problems. Stuff happens, sometimes awful stuff. Review and use the Mind-Body Sweep of Chapter 6, page 133-147, to take down the dramatic reaction; then use EFT to calm the residual.

In the next chapter, major life inhibiting phobias are discussed. If you have a phobia, you know how it limits you. Read about gaining some rapid relief in the next chapter.

CHAPTER 14:

PHOBIAS & LIMITATIONS

Public Speaking

Rodent and Creature Phobias

Fear of Flying

Test Anxiety

> "The only thing we have to fear is fear itself –"
>
> ---- Franklin Delano Roosevelt, - First Inaugural Address,
> March 4, 1933

Introduction

Phobias are a specific form of stress. If you don't have a phobia, consider yourself extremely lucky. Anyone with a phobia will tell you how it limits one's freedom. Inability to speak in public, fear of flying or mentally freezing during exams greatly inhibits life. The good news is that phobias collapse pretty quickly with EFT.

This chapter covers several common phobias and actual cases where EFT calmed them. I often do a live demonstration on a phobia during workshops. The subjects volunteer anonymously from the audience. Here is a true story from a workshop that I led.

Public Speaking Phobias

CASE	**Public Speaking Phobia: A Workshop Demonstration Example 14.1**

Her wide eyes scanned right to left and back again. She could not find it. It was gone. Paradoxically, she was not sad. In fact, she felt immense relief. It had only been a brief fifteen minutes since she had anonymously been selected from the rear of a packed Atlantic City hotel auditorium. Perplexed, yet clearly laughing, she enjoyed the profound physiological release of her body's tension.

Incredibly, this relief correlated with the odd, innocuous light touch of facial, upper body, and hand acupoints, called EFT. Within minutes, this 2005 New Jersey Social Worker of the Year's lifetime terror of public speaking effortlessly dissolved. Further, 170 equally baffled workshop participants stood witness to this rapid change. This happens all the time with EFT.

That same evening, notes cast aside; her acceptance speech flowed passionately, as she articulated her efforts about working with international atrocities. "There wasn't a dry eye in the place", she reported of the 800 people in the audience. They felt privileged to celebrate her deserved honor and new found confidence in expressing herself. In an email in 2013, she said her public speaking fear continues to be gone! At an EFT workshop in 2014, she told colleagues that EFT and I changed her life! I am humbled!

Coincidentally, this astonishing experience was duplicated with the 2008 New Jersey Social Worker of the Year in another EFT workshop. After letting go of her fear of her acceptance speech, her spontaneous insight was, "This speech is not about me, but about the children of Camden struggling in poverty."

> Comedian Jerry Seinfeld remarked that people would rather be dead then give the eulogy. He said: "According to most studies, people's number one fear is public speaking. Death is number two. Does that sound right? This means to the average person, if you go to a funeral, you're better off in the casket than doing the eulogy."

Below are various aspects of public speaking that may apply to you too. Sometimes simply clearing the feared aspect is sufficient. Other times you need to locate the defining moment - that is the *first* or *worst* time you experienced this type of upset.

Use one reminder phrase at a time, while lightly touching the 11 acupoints for 3 or more rounds until the issue has no upset and is a SUDS rating of 3 or less. Pick the one from the list that applies, and then circle back to others if they exist for you. Remember, the removal of 1 to 5 aspects usually desensitizes the entire issue.

> The reminder phases for aspects of a public speaking phobia may include:
>
> *Fearful about being so nervous that I run out of the room*
>
> *Fearful about forgetting my speech*
>
> *Fearful about being judged as stupid*
>
> *Fearful about that people are staring at me*
>
> *Fearful about omitting an important point*
>
> *Fearful about panic attacks while speaking*
>
> *Fearful about losing my place in my speech*
>
> *Fearful about that people knowing how nervous I am*
>
> *Fearful about speaking to strangers*
>
> *Worried about embarrassing myself again*

Fearful about speaking to colleagues

Fearful about speaking to small groups

Fearful about speaking to men's groups

Fearful about speaking to college students

Nervous about speaking to those who I perceive as smarter

Upset about the possibility that my PowerPoint may not run

Every time one of these clears, my clients say, "That wasn't so bad; maybe I can do another speech." Sometimes I teach them to use EFT in camouflage (explained in Technique 31 on page 88), while being introduced. This means move your hands slowly to touch the acupoints while mimicking common body language. It helps!

CASE | Public Speaking Terror – Example 14.2

Here is an example of the CARES steps used to curtail a public speaking phobia.

C 1)   **C**hief complaint: Too frightened to do public speaking

A 2)   **A**spect: I cannot speak in public without blushing and forgetting my speech

R 3)   **R**eminder phrase: *Terrified my nerves will affect my memory* SUDS = 7

E 4)   **E**FT: Apply light pressure on the 11 acupoints (using the Emotion Worksheet at the end of Chapter 3) while repeating the Reminder Phrase, for 3 or more rounds, until calm.

    -- Cycle from steps 2 through 4, finding and desensitizing new aspects and defining moments.

S 5)   **S**pontaneous Insight: "This isn't so bad, maybe I can speak to this group."

> TIP - Toastmasters
>
> Recovering from my own public speaking phobia, I supplemented my EFT treatment with Toastmasters; an inexpensive public speech club. This experience helped smooth out the rough edges of my public speaking. Toastmasters (toastmasters.org) provided a place to practice and also to learn specific speaking skills. Who knew in public speaking one should articulate more slowly, with more body movement, more vocal variety, and a compelling opening? I recommend Toastmasters highly. EFT gave me the courage to speak publicly and Toastmasters gave me the skills!

I now lecture about twice a month. I love speaking. I am addicted to the very issue that used to paralyze me. I actually feel delightfully energized and full of excitement after speaking. Go figure…

Phobias - Explanation

I believe there are two types of phobic conditions. One is when the issue at hand does not make sense to our primitive animal instincts. For instance, flying, heights, bridges, elevators, and turbulence do not make sense to our animal survival instincts, and therefore we feel unsafe. To be calm about these experiences is counter- intuitive.

For example, I know that I cannot keep a single sheet of paper in the air because gravity will pull it to the ground. Therefore, my brain does not grasp the ability to keep a multi-ton aircraft in flight. Successful experiences with these issues are one route to integrating them as acceptable. If we fly several times and nothing bad happens, we learn that flying is safe. However, if we're still afraid of flying, we can desensitize this fear with EFT.

> TIP: I suggest you find one of the abundant www.YouTube.com flying videos and use EFT while watching them. I even suggest you watch the same video 3 times or so, to desensitize even more.

A common phobia is elevators. Riding in an elevator can seem like nothing more than an enclosed box that rumbles like an earthquake. It is one of those places we may instinctively fear. This was clearly demonstrated when I was a college student living in a Boston high rise. My family's suburban St. Bernard dog, Siegfried, visited for a weekend. He was terrified of the elevator. Truly, my father and I dragged and pushed him inside several times. He trembled in sync with the shaking of the elevator walls and floor.

Comically, one day on our sojourn to my eighth floor apartment, some unsuspected person stopped the elevator on level four. Siegfried bolted out of that elevator, dragging us two adults. It was also a possible trauma for that poor soul. We may have also created a new fear for that person after having a 150 pound dog charge unexpectedly out of an elevator- she may be skittish whenever elevator doors open. (I hope she knows EFT.)

I believe the other type of phobic conditions is connected to an upsetting event from our past (perhaps like the woman opening the elevator door above). Small "t" traumas, the little emotional punches we endure, leave a mark and a consequent apprehension under similar circumstances.

Additionally, the traumatic event does not actually have to happen to you. It can be something you heard from your parents or saw in a movie or television. Who does not have some trepidation of swimming in the ocean after seeing Steven Spielberg's movie Jaws?

Rodent and Creepy Creature Phobias

I actually believe my severe snake phobia has to do with an event that happened to my older brother and my mother before I was born. A snake appeared in his playpen when he was a baby, and fortunately nothing happened to my brother. While I have no memory of this, I am sure my mother must have repeated this story often, instilling in my unconscious the danger of snakes. I know she insisted they relocate to another state after this event. Through her fear and the retelling of this story, my instinctive predisposition was transformed into a full blow phobia.

An older woman told me her fear of mice probably started on a camping trip. Already somewhat anxious in the woods, she heard scratching in the cabins walls all night long. By calming down that memory with EFT, she calmed down her phobia. It does not mean that she is fine with mice; it means she does not obsess about mice unduly. In this case, the woman knew when the fear began.

In the following desensitization of a rodent phobia, this workshop participant had no recollection of any specific time or event that caused this fear. Yet, she too did significantly better after EFT treatment.

CASE   **Mice Phobia and Other Creepy Creatures – Example 14.3**

About ten years ago in an EFT level 1 training session, Maria volunteered to discuss her lifelong fear of rodents. She told us how on one occasion a field mouse had snuck into her house, and she was so afraid that she actually considered selling her home. She could not remember when the phobia began, but she had it her entire life. At the mere mention of mice, she shuddered.

When I asked how afraid of rodents she was on a scale from 0 to 10, she said with wide, terrified eyes, "15!" The audience of eighteen social workers in this Continuing Education Credited EFT workshop witnessed her accompanying quivering body and the disgust shown by her wrinkled nose.

This woman, a grandmother, became frustrated because she was unable to even see any animated rodent movies with her grandchildren. She could not watch *Stuart Little*, *Ratatouille* (an adorable cartoon about a rat becoming a chef), or *Enchanted*, a New York City Cinderella remake with animated rats helping to transform the princess.

We used the Emotion Worksheet for her EFT session. Her reminder phrases were as follows:

fearful about rodents

> *terrified about seeing any mice*
>
> *disgusted about rodents' appearance*
>
> *scared about rodents*

Here she picks one aspect of rodent behavior that freaks her out a lot!

C 1)   **C**hief Complaint: Terrified of any rodent images, even in the movies

A 2)   **A**spect: Cannot stand the way they look

R 3)   **R**eminder phrase: *Creped out by the way they look.* SUDS = 15! (on a scale only to 10)

E 4)   **E**FT: Apply light pressure on the 11 acupoints (using the Emotion Worksheet at the end of Chapter3), while repeating the Reminder Phrase, for 3 or more rounds, until calm.

-- Cycle from steps 2 through 4, finding and desensitizing new aspects and defining moments.

S 5)   **S**pontaneous Insight: " I feel silly, especially of images in the movies."

In 15 minutes, her fear SUDS went from 15 →2. A member of the workshop brought up a picture of mice on his cell phone. She shivered when she saw it, and we discussed that it was another aspect of her fear. The first was her imagination, and the next was a photo. However, her fear was not a 15, but a SUDS of 5. With a few rounds of EFT while looking at the picture, her fear went from 5→ 0.

I spoke to Maria five years later, and she said she had no longer has issues with rodents. She comfortably watches any movies and commercials with rats, and she even saw *Ratatouille* and *Enchanted* without any distress. She said "You'd be surprised how many commercials have rats in them."

Furthermore, when she visited a neighbor a few years ago, the daughter came into the room with a pet rat crawling on her shoulder. She thought it was disgusting and had no interest in touching it, but she was not terrified or panicked about it at all, much to the intense surprise of her husband. Her words, "I am clearly cured of this phobia."

An additional Facebook update from Maria, now 10 years later. She is babysitting for her grand dog and two rodents without any concern!

When desensitizing a phobia of any creepy creature (animals, reptiles, and insects), also consider the proximity the creature is to the person. A snake on television is different from a snake being held in front of you. Therefore, you may want to add a round of EFT on physical distance tolerated from the creature.

Do any of these reminder phrases apply to you? If so, desensitize using the EFT and the CARES steps.

> *Worried about the creature if seen on television*
>
> *More scared about the creature if it is my house*
>
> *More terrified about the creature if it is in my room*
>
> *Petrified about the creature if it is moving*
>
> *Scared stiff about the creature if it is above my head*
>
> *Upset about possibly being bitten by this creature*

What animals, insects, or creatures unnerve you?

_____

_____

Try going through the CARES steps to settle your upset.

Fear of Flying is next.

FEAR of FLYING

Here are some of the possible aspects to desensitize with EFT.

> Fear about turbulence
>
> Fear about not being in control
>
> Fear about enclosed spaces (claustrophobia)
>
> Fear about heights
>
> Fear about the unfamiliar
>
> Thinking about 9/11 plane crashes

So you are invited to a wonderful trip in the Caribbean, and you want to go. You are excited to get onto a warm sunny beach with tropical breezes and handsome staff catering to your every need. You only have to stretch out on the sand and let your mind totally drift. You are excited and readily agreed.

However, there is an issue bubbling up. You cannot drive to the Caribbean. You are not interested in a cruise, although you may consider this when it finally dawns on you that your trip to paradise is an airplane trip away. "AIRPLANE TRIP away," you think. Ugh!

Now, you begin to ruminate, fret, and worry about whether or not you can handle it all. There are so many aspects to flying that you just don't want to engage in. You don't like turbulence at all, even though you have been on plenty of bumpy roads in your car. You have been told repeatedly that turbulence is normal in flying and planes are built for it. You are okay if a flag dances in the wind, but a bumpy plane ride heightens your alarm system telling you it's going to crash.

You recall a trip that was windier than others, but you forget that by the mere act of remembering it, you survived. You probably even got your food on that flight, although they may have held off serving beverages. You do not like the G-force of take-off, but it's no different than rapid acceleration entering the highway or that flume log ride you actually pay to go on!

Plane crashes are so rare that when one happens, the broadcast news covers it for weeks. You hear they found the black box and are assembling the fuselage to figure out what happened. They are sending in divers, etc. etc. So much news time is spent on the *one* accident that your system erroneously registers planes crashes as common and flying as unsafe. Remember, news reports cover rare events and dramatize it.

| CASE | **Fear of Flying in Two Co-workers - Example 14.4**

I used EFT with two co-workers who shared an office. I became aware of their flying fears unexpectedly as I overheard their conversation while waiting for my next client. One had never flown in her life, and the other was about to fly alone for the first time. Both verbalized fright and despair. I spent 15 minutes with each, explaining EFT and using EFT on their stated fear. (I sometimes think the explanation takes longer than the EFT application!)

Both their SUDS levels of upset were very high—one a 9, the other a 10—and both upsets came down nicely.

PERSON 1

C 1) **C**hief Complaint: frightened because have never flown *SUDS* =10

A 2) **A**spect: I don't know what to expect.

R 3) **R**eminder phrase: *Frightened because I don't know what to expect*

E 4) **E**FT: Apply light pressure on the 11 acupoints (using the Emotion Worksheet at the end of Chapter 3) while repeating the Reminder Phrase, for 3 or more rounds until calm.

-- Cycle from steps 2 through 4, finding and desensitizing new aspects and defining moments.

S 5) **S**pontaneous insight: "This will be an adventure and I will be proud of myself."

PERSON 2

C 1) **C**hief Complaint: Don't want to fly alone

A 2) **A**spect: I am worried about getting lost and end up on the wrong plane

R 3) **R**eminder Phrase: *Worried I will end up at the wrong gate*

E 4) **E**FT: Apply light pressure on the 11 acupoints (using the Emotion Worksheet at the end of Chapter 3), while repeating the Reminder Phrase, for 3 or more rounds until calm.

-- Cycle from steps 2 through 4, finding and desensitizing new aspects and defining moments.

S 5) **S**pontaneous Insight: "I can read and I can ask the staff if I am not sure where to be. A good magazine will keep me company. I will be fine."

The funniest part was that, for the rest of the day, these colleagues kept checking in with each other and asking incredulously, "Are you sure you're not worried anymore???"

"No, not at all worried," was the surprised reply.

"'Me neither," responded the other, amazed.

EFT happens so fast that the two people recited this perplexing conversation often - not believing their anxiety was so low. I wish I could capture the look on their faces. It is one of the joys of doing EFT. People look like they have just seen a magic trick with that wide eyed, confused look begging the question, "How did you do that so painlessly and rapidly?" Some just laugh.

So if you have a fear of flying, start treating it by dissecting the various aspects. Here is a potential list of reminder phrases. Pick one or create your own and combine it with the EFT 11 acupoints on the Emotions sheet at the end of Chapter 3; and following the CARES steps described in Chapter. 3.

Fear about turbulence

Hate the security check

Worried about being squeamish during take-offs

Fear about take-offs or not liking the motion of take-offs

Claustrophobic about the inside seat

Nervous about an actual scary flying event from the past

Afraid about the plane will crash

Scared about a plane crashes on television

Still scared about a terrible landing

Nervous about the fear my mother shared about flying

Upset about seeing too many 9/11 tapes of planes crashing into the Twin Towers

What upsets *you* about flying?

_____

_____

Try using the CARES steps to calm your upset so you too can have a spontaneous, freeing insight. Your liberating insights might be:

"I can fly to Bermuda now. I heard it is beautiful."

"I will go to Hawaii."

"I can visit my cousins in Spain."

"What happened? Flying is no longer a worry."

Now to a mean kind of anxiety, test anxiety. You know the material but…. the brain is frozen and foggy!

Test Anxiety

So you study for hours for your science class test, but you wonder why you waste your time. You have done this exact thing so many times, only to find that you mentally freeze and your mind goes blank in class when the test is in front of you.

You try to walk in with confidence that you can do this, because you are well prepared and answered every question your parent or friend asked you before the test. You sit down, and slowly you hear your own heart thump. You practice distraction and thinking positively, and this helps.

However, now that the teacher is giving you the instructions, you hear your heartbeat becomes much louder. You bite your lip and are angry and scared, thinking to yourself:

"NO! Not again, please brain, do not freeze on me. I need you."

You now feel this stress in the pit of your stomach and in your chest too. You even note a hand tremor and think this is just unfair. You truly did know the material, but currently, you do not, because your brain feels like it's lost in a fog bank.

Test anxiety. You've got it, and you do not know how to get rid of it. When there is no quiz, you could recite the material backwards. But even the word "quiz" kicks up your stress level.

Your self-talk is flawless. "I can do this, I am smart and I can handle it."

The little devil on your shoulder hints that maybe you cannot. This tiny frustrating self-doubt begins to magnify, and is growing exponentially.

Calm the body first. Below are possible reminder phrases for you to plug into the Mind-Body Sweep Worksheet at the end of Chapter 6; as you think about tests. Remember to think about your issue for 5 seconds and then note where you feel that tension in your body.

Nausea

Hand tremor

Brain freeze

Stomach churning

Heart pumping loudly in my chest

Pressure in my temple, shoulders and/or back

And after your body is calm, finish the test anxiety desensitization using the reminder phrases from the issues, such as those below.

> *Hate about taking tests*
>
> *Worry about cannot think*
>
> *Pissed off about my brain freezing*
>
> *Panicked about quizzes*
>
> *Doubt about this getting better*
>
> *Drowning in self-doubt about failure*
>
> *Upset about my mind going blank*
>
> *Frustrated about studying and getting nowhere*

You say the awful thought as the reminder phrase, because you are desensitizing it and calming down while thinking it.

By the way, no one feels all these things. This list is a composite of what many clients have told me. They are discouraged, yet hard working and frustrated, and they are seeking where to turn. They want to do well, because they have ambition and care about their education and classes. Remember to stay hydrated too. EFT and your body perform better with enough fluids.

Some lucky students are able to use EFT on the current issue and watch the anxiety and terror melt. *Most* have to do *earlier work* and look for a defining moment. So let's begin.

What is the first or worst time that you froze on a test or did poorly despite studying?

_____

_____

Here is an example. You were in third grade, and you were working on the multiplication table of 8's. You remember you got to 8 times 3 and you froze. When you think about it now, you remember that your stomach was aching as if it was on fire and your cheeks began to burn. Even today, the SUDS on this physical discomfort is a SUDS intensity of 7. First, take the edge off by using the Mind–Body Sweep on the upset stomach that kicks up with the memory with the Reminder Phrase of:

Upset about my stomach is aching

You remember even as a third grader, you were embarrassed and angry. You knew the answers the night before. Your teacher stared at you with contempt, as if you were cheating by looking at someone else's test. Ask yourself, what is the worst part of this? Here are a few possible Reminder Phrases. Desensitize one at a time using the EFT Emotion Worksheet from Chapter 3, until the childhood incident has no charging upset at all.

Upset about that I studied and got nowhere

Upset about the teacher thought I was cheating in third grade

Upset about my teacher stared at me

Upset about my teacher may have thought I was stupid

Embarrassed about I could not remember

| CASE | Test Anxiety - Several Levels –Example 14.5 |

C 1) **C**hief complaint: Afraid I will freeze taking a test. SUDS =8

A 2) **A**spect/defining moment: I froze during a test on multiplication tables in 3rd grade.

R 3) **R**eminder phrase (worst part): *Embarrassed about the teacher thought I was cheating and looking at another student's work.*

E 4) **E**FT: Apply light pressure on the 11 acupoints (using the Emotion Worksheet at the end of Chapter 3) while repeating the Reminder Phrase, for 3 or more rounds, until calm.

-- Cycle from steps 2 through 4, finding and desensitizing new aspects and defining moments.

> **S** 5) **S**pontaneous insight: "Gee it was a long time ago; I feel as if I am now over that."

But is there more? Now go find other childhood or early memories of test anxiety and begin the process over until you cannot find anymore. Keep searching for more old stuff, or for old hooks holding onto this fear. Once you have completed this, come back into the present. For example, you are worried about your science test this week.

What test do you have in front of you and what are your worries about it?

_____

_____

> **Future Performance Enhancement** – Revisited this from
> **Technique 54, page 227**

Plug your test issues into the CARES steps discussed above. To be thorough, dig to find as many as you can and as early in your life as you can.

After every single issue is desensitized, you can consider applying the Future Performance Enhancement, Technique 54 found on page 227 to desensitize any *future* worries you have about test taking. You use this after clearing out all the past worrisome memories on this issue. Remember, this is where you focus on the positive and use two acupoints – under the eyes for 5 breaths and under the arms for 5 breaths - to increase your confidence.

An example is you would be saying – "I am confident, comfortable and well prepared to take this test" while you hold the under eyes acupoints for 5 breaths and then under the arms acupoints for 5 breaths until very confident, take it to 100% confident.

Test Day

On the day of your test, go through the acupoints again on any remaining or new worry. Do this in private at home, in the car, or inconspicuously in class, camouflaging it as an itch as you *slowly* touch the acupoints. Perhaps someday your class will do this together to calm everyone.

Good luck!

("Luck is what happens when preparation meets opportunity."- Seneca, Roman Philosopher 1st Century AD)

Read the next chapter for three more mind-body techniques, including non-medication pain management. Then, I offer some suggestion for therapists and coaches in the EFT, Meridian Therapy and Energy Psychology world. You are welcome to join in. This next chapter also has several untested observations that I offer as possibilities for future research and exploration.

CHAPTER 15:

THE BODY AND PAIN

"The intuitive mind is a sacred gift and the rational mind is a faithful servant. We have created a society that honors the servant and has forgotten the gift."

--Albert Einstein

Technique 58: Energy Too Low? Try Energy Medicine

Most of this book is about calming down and desensitizing the residual of the bumps in life. However, there are times when your energy falls too low. Depression is one of these times. So is night shift work in a hospital or factory, or patrolling the streets. Other low energy times are the end of the day or for me, the middle of the day.

Take a look at Donna Eden's 5-minute routine at her site www.innersource.net. Also, watch her on YouTube.com. I suggest you learn her 5-minute routine and implement it daily. Her well-written and important books include *Energy Medicine* and *Energy Medicine for Women.* Her work is a "must do daily" for depression and other maladies.

Try this experiment. Measure your energy right now on a scale of 0% (ready to sleep) to 100% (ready to climb a mountain.) Write that number down or note it. Now try this beginning exercise of her 5-minute routine.

As a short-cut to the entire 5-minute routine, I often use her four "thumps" – tapping with some mild to moderate pressure for about 7-10 thumps on:

1) Under the eyes;

2) On both sides of the collarbone;

3) Deep center on the sternum about 5 inches above the heart on the thymus gland; and

4) Under the breasts area - all around the side and front on the body.

I may repeat 2-4 rounds until I feel my energy climbing. What is your energy now on that scale to 0% to 100%?_____.This is faster than caffeine!

Her 5-minute routine is an excellent maneuver to *immediately* lessen the melancholy of depression, bring up energy and rebalance!

Technique 59: Massage and Self-Massage

The practice of "massage" is now credentialed by state licensing. But how about performing "self-massage" or massage among family members? With no pressure at all, about the strength it take to hold a light book, move your hand slowly around your arms, shoulders, and torso. Move slowly and rest your open hand on each spot for a count of 3. This is even a sort of self-applied Reiki.

Furthermore, if you have a partner, demonstrate on that person to lightly go down their spine with the palm of the hand - neck to waist; pausing every inch or two for 5 seconds. Use light touch and remember to provide very little pressure. It is more like a light hold, moving in increments down the spine. Check in with person to make sure your touch is not too heavy or too light, but just right, as it is felt as a loving hold. Now ask them to do the same to you. You can even do your pets just tap lightly down the spine, head to tail.

You can also do this to yourself down the front of your body. This activity is called a "chest glide" named by Dr. Fred Gallo in his book *Energy Tapping for Trauma*. The hands are simply placed one after the other. Start at the neck and place one hand, then the next, down the front of you to the belly button area. Repeat 3 times or so. The chest glide is like a self-hug.

We know that a 20-second hug releases the bonding hormone and neurotransmitter oxytocin, which is a natural antidepressant and produces an antianxiety effect. In fact, how about performing a hug with someone else every so often? Several of my widowed or divorced clients express gratitude for this chest glide technique. I think it may be because they miss the touch that stopped when they lost their partner.

Technique 60: **Physical Pain and EFT** (aka Tapping)

While the focus of many of my workshops is stress management, people with physical pain often benefit from EFT. This is an inadvertent benefit of EFT, without any focus on pain. On one occasion, I ran an EFT training for stress management with 40 nurse managers. By a show of hands, 11 had physical pain at the beginning of the workshop. At the end of that workshop 8 participants reported no pain. It often happens that pain dissolves using EFT. A woman in this workshop initially rated the pain in her knees at a SUDS of 5; she rated the pain at a SUDS of 0 at the end of the workshop. This makes some sense, because acupuncture is used for pain and EFT is a sister of acupuncture. Several of my EFT colleagues specialize in pain relief with these methods. Do a computer search on "EFT and pain" to find a specialist. Also you can read authors Nick Ortner's *The Tapping Solution for Pain Relief,* Maggie Phillips, PhD book *Reversing Chronic Pain* or Daniel Benor, MD, *Seven Minutes to Natural Pain Release.* Focus on the pain or on the event when the pain was first noticed while using EFT. Besides the pain-reducing side effect of using EFT, pain can actually be the direct focus of our efforts.

Check with your medical doctor first to determine if it is safe to quiet your pain. Your pain may be needed diagnostically, meaning pain can help to determine the nature of the physical problem. Pain can be a warning to slow down, take care and get medical care.

The Gamut Point

The Gamut point, shown here and on page 170, is an acupoint that frequently diminishes pain. Begin by thinking about your pain for 5 seconds. Rate that pain using SUDS (Subjective Unit of Distress Scale), an intensity scale of 0 to 10, where 10 is the worst pain ever. Very lightly touch the gamut point at least 15 normal breaths or more; re-rate the SUDS and if the intensity dropped, repeat until the pain is as low as possible.

I have used this gamut point for the past 18 years for all types of dental procedures. I know he is in my mouth, but I do not feel pain, even with extensive drilling.

Recently, this gamut point helped a client with a visible hand deformity resulting from an accident. It calmed the intense throbbing pain SUDS 8→2. Pain measuring a SUDS of 2 is a slight annoyance while a SUDS of 8 preoccupies all thought and is debilitating. A sinus headache went 7→0 in a Nashville workshop. A group of 8 in unison, at Cooper University Hospital's Women's Center, all had their pain diminish, average of 4.5→1.

A neighbor frustrated with all medical and pain management attempts used this gamut point to unlock a frozen shoulder. When doing this, slowly move enough to bring the pain intensity to a SUDS of only a 3. Treat that pain by holding the gamut point until that level 3 pain is quiet. You can then progressively increase the movement, bringing that pain intensity to another SUDS of 3 and treat that.

If the gamut point does not provide enough relief, move to using all the EFT acupoints for 3 rounds. Lastly, you can add the metaphors explained next.

Interesting Pain Phenomena

There are 2 phenomena about pain to note in order to avoid worry. First, pain may move. Gary Craig, founder of EFT, called it "chasing the pain". Stay with the new pain and that gamut point hold. My experience is that pain usually moves once. A dental student during a presentation at The University of Pennsylvania Dental School had pain in his shoulder. While quietly holding the gamut point, he shouted "ouch" as he grabbed his lower side, the new site of his pain. Staying with the gamut point hold, both sites of his pain resolved.

Second, the SUDS intensity of pain may go up when focusing on pain. This is because pain patients usually mentally block pain and, now, you are intentionally focusing is on it.

Remember, pain has important purposes—to warn you to slow you down, to rest what hurts and/or to call attention to a medical problem. Unfortunately, pain may linger after that problem heals, sometimes called chronic pain. *In this book, the focus is on healing the pain, but you still need to get treatment for the injury or medical problem.*

EFT, Tapping, Metaphors, Emotions and Pain

Pain is not imagined in your head. It is processed in your head, so let's change that processing by using metaphors that go to both sides of your brain and are somewhere between conscious and unconscious. David Grove, *Healing through Metaphor*, brilliantly demonstrated that a person's descriptive metaphor of a knot in their stomach imaginatively could be untied and even used to tie up someone who used to hit them, resolving their upset. Metaphors create a "picture", such as "pain pounding like a jack hammer." Metaphors may feel silly, but they probably are intervening in the emotional and pain responding limbic system.

Let's work on chronic pain, that pain which lingers even if the injury may have healed. This pain often sends you to the Pain Management doctors.

Notice if the metaphors and emotions change going from step to step.

Here is my adaptation of a workshop presented by CJ Puotinen, (TapTheWorldeft.com) at the Spring Energy Event Conference in New York, April 2017.

Three Questions to find the Metaphors and the Emotions.

1. What is your pain like? Part of pain is in your brain. We are looking for a metaphor, a picture of what it looks like. An example might be leg pain feels like "an inserted rod that is shooting out sparks." Back pain may feel like "a drill

grinding or a throbbing hammer."
What picture is your pain like?_____

2. What emotion is your pain expressing? The number one answer is anger. However, other emotions might be fear, sadness, overwhelm, or others.
What emotion is your pain expressing? _____

3. If your pain could talk to you, what would it say to you? Some examples have said "help me;" "you were dumb to lift that box;" "why did I ever exercise that hard?" or "Is this ever going to be better?"
What is your pain saying to you? _____

Step 1 Example

This example is from an overzealous day of swimming, where the pain woke the person with throbbing SUDS of 7.   Here are her answers to the above three questions and these answers will now be used as the wording for three rounds of tapping on the side of your hand (pictured on page 67, picture 1) and two rounds of EFT.

Even though my leg hurts, it feels like

1) a rod with shooting electric sparks;

2) it is angry; and

3) You are to blame for this; I am okay and accept myself.

> (Repeat 3 times tapping on the side of my hand, pictured on page 65, picture 1, Chapter 3)

****

ADD two rounds of the 11 acupoints of EFT (pictured page 65-67), while saying the same answers here, taken from questions 1, 2 and 3. (See website RobinEFT.net for a demo or my YouTube video on Pain, Tapping & EFT)

Lightly touch or tap these 11 acupoints. Do two rounds of this.

Side of Hand   Saying   *My leg hurts*

Top of Head	Saying	*Feels like a rod, shooting sparks*
Inner Eye	Saying	*It is Angry*
Outer Eye	Saying	*You are to blame for this*
Under the Eye	Saying	*My leg hurts*
Under Nose	Saying	*Feels like a rod, shooting sparks*
Under Lip	Saying	*It is Angry*
Collarbone	Saying	*You are to blame for this*
Under Arm	Saying	*My Leg hurts*
Gamut Point	Saying	*Feels like a rod shooting sparks*
Heart Hold	Saying	*It is Angry*

Step 2 Example

Focus back on the actual pain (leg) for 5 seconds and ask what the pain level is NOW? _____

Return to the three questions above but this time ask if the answers are the same, or if they have changed. Record those new answers to 1, 2 and 3.

The pain, metaphor, emotion and message often shift, move, change and diminish. Example of how those answers may have now changed.

Even though I still have pain in my leg but now it feels

1)*Still a rod, but without any sparks.*

2)*Just frustrated now.*

3)*Swim with less vigor, I am okay and I accept myself.*

(Do three rounds tapping on the side of my hand, pictured on page 65, picture 1) while saying those changed words. Conclude with the statement: "I am okay and I accept myself," as noted above.

****

ADD two rounds of the 11 acupoints of EFT (pictured page 65-67), while saying the words from Round 2. This is the same set-up of Step 1 but with the new words inserted.

Focus back on the actual pain (leg) and what is the pain level now?_____ Her pain dropped to a SUDS of 3 and she did do the next step and brought her pain to a SUDS of 0. The pain returned and she repeated it again and it did not come back.

You may need to do another a Step 3 or Step 4, and the procedure is the same as Step 2.

Your turn now. You fill in your answers.

Step 1

Focus on your actual pain_____ for 5 seconds, and what is the pain level SUDS intensity now, 0 to 10, where 10 is the worst pain ever? _____

Three Questions to find the Metaphors and the Emotions.

Answer and record your answers to the three questions found on page 304.

Even though I have pain in my _____, that feels like

1) (the metaphor)_____

2 (the emotion) _____

3) (pain saying...)_____

I am okay and I accept myself.

(Do three rounds tapping on the side of my hand,- pictured on page 65, picture 1- while saying those changed words. Conclude with "I am okay and I accept myself" as noted above.

****

ADD 2 rounds of the 11 acupoints of EFT (pictured page 65-67), while saying the same answers here, taken from questions 1, 2, and 3.

Lightly touch or tap these 11 acupoints. Do two rounds of this.		
Side of Hand	Saying	*Pain in my* _____
Top of Head	Saying	*Answer # 1*
Inner Eye	Saying	*Answer #2*
Outer Eye	Saying	*Answer #3*
Under the Eye	Saying	*Pain in my* _____
Under Nose	Saying	*Answer #1*
Under Lip	Saying	*Answer #2*
Collarbone	Saying	*Answer #3*
Under Arm	Saying	*Pain in my*_____
Gamut Point	Saying	*Answer #1*
Heart Hold	Saying	*Answer #2*

Focus on your actual pain for 5 seconds, and what is the pain level SUDS intensity <u>now</u>, 0 to 10, where 10 is the worst pain ever? _____ Hopefully, the number is lower than before Step 1.

Step 2

Return to the **Three Questions to find the Metaphors and the Emotions** found on page 298 but now ask if the answers are the same, or if they have changed. Record those <u>new </u>answers to 1, 2 and 3. The metaphors and emotions often diminish in intensity.

Even though I still have some pain in my _____, that now feels like
<u>1) *(new metaphor*_____</u>
<u>2)*(new emotion)*_____</u>
<u>3)*(new pain saying...)*_____</u>
I am okay and I accept myself.

Do three rounds tapping on the side of my hand, pictured on page 65, picture 1- while saying those changed answers. Conclude with "I am okay and I accept myself" as noted above.

****

ADD two rounds of the 11 acupoints of EFT (pictured page 65-67), while saying the new answers here, taken from these questions 1, 2 and 3.

Lightly touch or tap these 11 acupoints. Do two rounds of this.

Side of Hand	Saying	*Pain in my _____*
Top of Head	Saying	*New Answer # 1*
Inner Eye	Saying	*New Answer #2*
Outer Eye	Saying	*New Answer #3*
Under the Eye	Saying	*Pain in my _____*
Under Nose	Saying	*New Answer #1*
Under Lip	Saying	*New Answer #2*
Collarbone	Saying	*New Answer #3*
Under Arm	Saying	*Pain in my _____*
Gamut Point	Saying	*New Answer #1*
Heart Hold	Saying	*New Answer #2*

Step 3

Return to the three questions found on page 298, but ask if the answers are the same or if they have changed again. Record those new answers to 1, 2 and 3. You can continue adding a Step 3 or Step 4 by following the same outlined procedure as Step 2. The tapping is the same but the pain metaphor, emotion and pain statement probably have changed.

Repeat until your pain is gone or you are not getting any more relief. Most people say the pain is now gone permanently, or it returns but at a much lower level. Some people may have to reapply this in the future, but this is only a 10-minute procedure that usually gives relief for hours, days and often permanently. Most pain medicines only last 4-6 hours and only covers the pain temporarily, so don't despair if this needs repeating too.

Another way to address pain is via the 3 Times 3 method found in Chapter 3. Referring back to the 3 questions, use the answer to question 1 for a complete 3 Times 3 round. (Ex. "I am okay even though I have pain in my leg that feels like a rod, shooting sparks.") Next, use the answer to question 2 for a complete 3 Times 3 round. Repeat 3 Times 3 round for the answer to question 3. Now see if those answers have modified and repeat the process.

Pain may be tied to old issues as well. It may be why pain often diminishes, even without a pain focus, when using EFT or 3 Times 3 for upsetting issues. Or, it might just be the acupressure involved.

Now Some Word to Therapists, Coaches and Healers -
but everyone is welcome to read on.

This book is a hybrid between the self-help genre and clinician education. It is the culmination of my 35 plus years as a therapist. My belief is that anything a clinician knows should be taught to the general population. I suggest that clinicians also learn the tools within this book to teach their stressed-out and anxious clients. Clinicians should also share the communication tips with everyone.

Introducing these Meridian Therapies (EFT) to the Client

Your biggest challenge is *your* comfort incorporating EFT and tapping, meridian based acupressure modalities, into your standard treatment of clients. Spend some time preparing a transition statement that you are comfortable with. Here are some examples of what I often say to clients,

> "I'd like to show you something that is 2000 to 5000 years old and from China. It is a sister to acupuncture and may seem fun, funny, and weird to you and me, because we grew up with Western medicine. Western medicine has us accustomed to medication, bandages, and surgery. In China and the East, they rely on acupuncture and acupressure. They rely on meridian-based theories, which are more mind-body connected. Many things from the East

are becoming part of our culture, such as yoga, reiki, and the martial arts. This is another one, want to try?"

Or:

"I'd like to show you some acupressure, a sister to acupuncture but without the needles. In this country we call this alternative, complementary, or integrative, medicine.

Most hospitals have a department offering complementary treatments as well as standard ones. Truly, they should call these therapies what they are, Chinese and Eastern medicine, which are 2000 to 5000 years old."

Most of my clients appreciate that I continue to train in better ways to help them. Another approach is to say: "I am back from a workshop or just read a book, and I think those techniques may be helpful. Do you want to try?"

Slow It Down and Gain Rapport

Unless EFT is requested by your client, I suggest that you wait until the second session to introduce EFT. Rapport is not a necessary ingredient for EFT to be helpful, however, new clients also are checking out the therapist to determine whether they are competent and EFT can seem too gimmicky. Also, *the client needs to have their story heard respectfully first,* by active listening, Technique 1, page 15.

In the first session—which is a full clinical assessment—I frequently guide a person away from telling me all the gruesome details of the main reason they are seeking counseling. I want to list all their stressors. I do ask about what has changed for them since the event, in order to be aware of the residual effects of the issue; such as not sleeping, can't go by a certain area, poor concentration at work, etc.

I want clients to have some comfort level, and I want EFT aboard in the second session when they dive into the gruesome details. The essence of being an EFT therapist is to listen to a client with your therapeutic radar to pick up anything that might be possible to *desensitize*; even past arguments

302

and relationships problems. Try to find those uncomfortable thoughts, emotions and even physical complaints that agitate your client. These become the focus of EFT treatment.

Teach EFT via a Demonstration on a Non-Serious Issue

When I teach EFT, I always tell them it is weird and unusual looking to Americans or others, who are typically familiar with Western medicine. It is Chinese and Eastern. As I mentioned earlier, we are familiar with bandages, surgeries, and medicines, while Eastern medicine is meridian-based. After explaining the 2 parts (acupoints and wording) I always use a demonstration from their life—something annoying, but not serious.

On a SUDS rating from 0 to 10, where 10 is the worst, I use something no higher than a SUDS of 4 or occasionally a 5. Examples of these might be a billing error, a chore, a missed phone call, and one argument with a child over something specific, a report coming due, an auto repair miscalculated, even what happened in their day prior to our session.

The rationale is that I'm showing them something novel, that may seem weird or funny. I want them to be comfortable and experience the gentle, relaxing power of EFT, before we address their serious issues. I do not want them worrying about what I am doing as they go into their darkest places.

Warning

Please do not go where you don't belong. Don't ask about trauma unless you know how to safely address it. Be gentle. If the trauma is awful but you do feel comfortable going there, sneak up on it carefully and slowly by asking "what about the trauma bothers you today?" You may hear them discuss triggers, like the place it happened, a certain time of day, or a date. You may hear them discuss their current malfunctioning emotional or thinking or their physical discomfort, and the Mind-Body Sweep (Chapter 6) can be very helpful for that.

If the trauma involves a death, asking them to tune into missing the deceased person is too strong, particularly for the earliest interventions. On the internet, find Gary Craig's "tearless trauma technique". Here is my version. You wonder with the client *"if* you were to think about this." The word *"if"* puts one gentle layer of distance between the client and their intense pain. Stay with the tentative *"If* you thought about it" until their SUDS rating is very low. Later, you can ask them to think about the actual issue directly and continue on with more EFT. *The Mind-Body Sweep* taught in Chapter 6 is an excellent first choice to calm down the physical symptoms associated with trauma by 50% or more.

Therapy Groups and Meetings

I've heard of an administer who began all her meetings with EFT. This is quite clever. EFT might also be a great way to start the school day, right after the pledge of allegiance. It could defuse whatever family nonsense the children endured before school. After 9/11, mental health staff assisting victims and their loved ones would occasionally defuse themselves using EFT, even if it were done comically. Work groups, conferences, military member events, sports and performance endeavors, and other gathering might also benefit from using EFT.

EFT could be a used to start a therapy group, but it could also be done during the group session as issues arise. I extensively used EFT in an anxiety therapy group, and I even stopped a few panic attacks mid-stream during the group.

At a busy hospital benefits fair located in the main noisy hospital cafeteria, I once asked thirteen passing staff members to describe stress felt anywhere in their body. In a 1 ½ minute demonstration (meaning 3 rounds of EFT), ten of them felt significant release and a drop in SUDS of 3 points or more. Hospital staff is generally a medically skeptical audience. Stress was felt throughout their bodies: their neck, pressure on their chest, churning stomach, tight shoulders, etc. The other three staff felt no change, but no harm. This event produced an EFT success rate of "77% helpful" in a noisy, less than optimal public situation. I demonstrate EFT often at health fairs.

In the next two sections are some observations that may be on the EFT horizon.

New Ideas and My Observations regarding EFT

Movies often have sequels. Here are some possible sequels that come from my observations of EFT. Performing approximately 15,000 EFT interventions over 22 years, one notices trends. These are solely my observations, and I take full responsibility for them as such.

Yawning

Clients do often yawn and sigh during EFT. So do I. Perhaps it is an energy release, and it means EFT is working. Here is the science behind this yawning observation.

According to Dr. Amy G. Love, a brilliant psychiatrist from southern New Jersey.

> "Yawning and sighing are signs that sympathetic nervous system "fight or flight" physiology is yielding to its counterpart, the "rest and digest" parasympathetic system. It is a sign of relaxation. When we're in danger (or think we are) "fight or flight" is in command. But life's other needs, - sleeping, eating, digesting, take over when we are safe again. Our stress level is a reflection of where the balance of these opposing systems is set. In modern times we are rarely in danger requiring us to fight or flee; anxiety and emotional pain activate the sympathetic nervous system but we can choose to calm it and give over to its relaxing counterpart."

If given the choice of yawning and sighing versus agitation and despair, I choose the yawn. My all day workshop participants often struggle to stay awake because we repeat EFT all day long. I often will add Donna Eden's "Five Minute" routine, when I want to bring back their energy. (Technique 58, page 291.)

My first client with whom I used EFT was a brilliant professor stuck in a family dilemma of being angry at his son-in-law. He yawned and sighed throughout the intervention. Since I was simply playing "Simon Says copy me", showing him the placement of the acupoints, my mind was free to worry if I was now boring him. Our previous sessions had been dynamic and challenging. I worried that I was just dull during the current session.

However, his anger dissolved that day, and he was no longer agitated by his son-in-law. (He still considered him a fool; it just did not upset him.)

Eye Movement

Neuro-Linguistic Programming (NLP) therapists believe that while thinking, people unconsciously move their eyes, such as up or down to the right or left depending on what they are thinking or feeling. They call it "eye accessing", because they believe the direction of eye movement helps people access specific types of mental processes. To date, I have not heard EFT people discuss eye accessing, so this is going out on a limb. However, sitting across a multitude of clients, unencumbered by lots of thinking, I notice things. So here is my observation, offered in the vein of possibility.

It seems that when a person is very upset, with a SUDS of 9 or 10, the person's eye gaze goes upwards when you ask them to "tune into their upset." When the person is midway to recovery, at a SUDS of 5 or so, and asked to tune into the upset again, his/her eyes will look horizontally to the right or left (or straight ahead, dead center in the eye socket.) It is sometimes observable while doing the EFT steps.

When the emotional issue is resolved, the client's eyes look down or may even scan *downward* side-to-side as if they are looking for the upset and can't find it. Again this is at the moment when you ask the client to "tune into their upset."

This eye movement is split second. I use it only as a gauge. Clients will often tell me after 3 rounds of EFT that they feel wonderful and at this moment their eyes are horizontal. I make a guess with myself about their new SUDS is (and even secretly hold 4 or 5 fingers), and I am usually close. I then tell them that we can go lower if they like, or ask them if it is OK to go lower. Often, they have just had so much relief that they would be OK if I stopped at this point; I often can and do go lower with their permission. I tell them I am greedy with this technique. They laugh, and with EFT I can do what have offered. This is really a miracle for them! Only research will prove if this is true and if so, it may be another marker that EFT has neurological effects.

Group Benefits of EFT

EFT, Tapping and their sister techniques of Meridian therapies and Energy Psychology are not limited to one client and one therapist in comparing to another hot new kid on the block, EMDR (Eye Movement Desensitization and Reprocessing). EFT far surpasses the group possibilities of EMDR. EMDR is strictly a one-on-one application with a skilled therapist. EFT is more flexible with comparable results.

EFT is effective in groups. Because of this, EFT has far-reaching implications for disasters, the military, school, work, and critical stress management debriefings. You can debrief an entire group to an issue. A second group approach for EFT is called "borrowing benefits' is done working on one person, but the others in the group are thinking or writing down their different issues, and frequently benefit too. In the future I envision EFT being projected via television in disaster areas, in order to calm down the population.

Imagine debriefing soldiers with EFT at the end of a raid, and while on their journey home. Imagine playing EFT "Simon Says" by copying a person demonstrating the acupoints on television after 9/11, Hurricane Katrina, a tsunami, or for the Haiti earthquake relief workers and community. Consider starting every school day with the pledge of allegiance and then EFT to calm whatever irritation or crisis the child faced at home. EFT is not a cure-all, but has tremendous capacity to desensitize, rebalance and relax. Coupled with the words of what agitates you, it mellows you and the issue. Thus, the group can now think rationally again. Holding hands across the heart in the Heart Assisted 3 Times 3 pose is soothing too.

EFT is superior in self-application to its sister acupuncture, because it is self-applied and is thus available all the time. No appointment necessary; as its application lies literally at your fingertips

My Hope

I want everyone to know how to use EFT aka Tapping, the same way everyone knows any home remedy. Life is an endurance race, and EFT serves a basic need –helping one to get over the hills. Picture a child who comes home from school crying. First the mother invites the child to tell her what happened, then helps the child use EFT to take the edge off her wounded feelings. Then they brain-storm and problem-solve how to correct it. A slight smile emerges, and she goes out to play. Complete! My hope and dream is for EFT to be in every household, every hospital, every school, and every workplace for any upset or tragedy!

I hope this book opens up lots of solutions that enhance your life. I want everyone to know counseling techniques as all they are is good ideas and good communication.

Wishing you the best,

Robin

Robin Bilazarian, LCSW, DCSW, DCEP

AAMET International Certified Master EFT Trainer

ACEP Diplomat in Clinical Energy Psychology

Web. RobinEFT.net

YouTube.com demos: EFT-AAA Instructional

YouTube.com: Heart Assisted 2 Minute Stress Relief

YouTube.com: Pain, Tapping & EFT

YouTube.com: Robin Bilazarian– (more YouTube videos to come to compliment this book)

Pesi National Training DVD. Bilazarian, R. (2017). Emotional Freedom Techniques & Tapping: Evidence-Based, Mind-Body Treatment Approach to the Anxiety Spectrum Disorders 6 hour training DVD with CEU's. https://www.pesi.com/store/detail/21530/emotional-freedom-techniques-eft-and-tapping (pain demo included in video),

Online Audio Relief Workshop: Social Work Online CE Institute with CEU's Bilazarian, R. Clinical Application of the Emotional Freedom Techniques: Desensitizing Undesirable Emotional and Mind-Body Reactions

RECOMMENDED BIBLIOGRAPHY

YouTube Demonstrations by Robin Bilazarian on www.YouTube.com **type in:**

EFT-AAA instructional (follow along changing the words to your issue.)

Heart Assisted 2 Minute Stress Relief

Pain, Tapping & EFT

(Note you can also type my name to get to these and future demonstrations: Robin Bilazarian)

Web Sites and Online Training

RobinEFT.net (me);

-Association for the Advancement of Meridian Energy Techniques. AAMETInternational.org.

- Association of Energy Psychology (ACEP). Energypsych.org,

Bilazarian, R (2017) Pesi National Training DVD. *Emotional Freedom Techniques & Tapping: Evidence-Based, Mind-Body Treatment Approach to the Anxiety Spectrum Disorders* 6 hour training DVD with CEU's. https://www.pesi.com/store/detail/21530/emotional-freedom-techniques-eft-and-tapping   (pain demo included in video)

Bilazarian, R. Online Audio Relief Workshop: Social Work Online CE Institute with CEU's *Clinical Application of the Emotional Freedom*

Techniques: Desensitizing Undesirable Emotional and Mind-Body Reactions

-EFTuniverse.com (Dr. Dawson Church-cortisol stress hormone → drop 24% and veteran research), also many articles can be translated to 57 languages.

**Stressproject.org (Dr. Dawson Church -access EFT for Wartime vets movies)

-Emofree.com (Gary Craig's site)

-Innersource.net/ep (Dr. David Feinstein – newly accepted published research)

TaptheWorldEFT.com (CJ Puotinen, EFT Coach, Trainer & Writer, Emotion Code.I attended her multiple weekends & pain workshop)

Recommended Books and Published Articles

Bender, S., & Sise, M. (2008) *The Energy of Belief.* Santa Rosa, CA: Energy Psychology Press.

Benor, Daniel J. (2008).*Seven Minutes to Natural Pain Release (WHEE Tapping).* Santa Rosa, CA: Energy Psychology Press.

Bilazarian, Robin (2008) Using EFT for Social Anxiety Disorder, at https://www.eftuniverse.com/anxiety-stress/using-eft-for-social-anxiety-disorder. (Able to translating into 57 languages)

Callahan, Roger (2001). *Tapping the Healer Within: Using Thought Field Therapy to Instantly Conquer Your Fears, Anxieties, and Emotional Distress.* Chicago: Contemporary Books

Church, D. (2010). The treatment of combat trauma in veterans using EFT (Emotional Freedom Techniques): A pilot protocol. *Traumatology,* 16(1), 55–65. doi:10.1177/1534765609347549

Church, D., & Feinstein, D. (2012). Energy psychology in the treatment of PTSD: Psychobiology and clinical principles. *Psychology of Trauma,* edited by Thijs Van Leeuwen & Marieke Brouwer (Hauppauge, NY: Nova Science).

Church, D., Yount, G., & Brooks, A. J. (2012). The effect of Emotional Freedom Techniques (EFT) on stress biochemistry: A randomized controlled trial. *Journal of Nervous and Mental Disease.* 200(10), 891-896. doi: 10.1097/NMD.0b013e31826b9fc1.

Church, D., Hawk, C., Brooks, A., Toukolehto, O., Wren, M., Dinter, I., & Stein, P. (2013). Psychological trauma in veterans using EFT (Emotional Freedom Techniques): A randomized controlled trial. Journal of Nervous and Mental Disease, 201, 153-160. doi: 10.1097/ NMD.0b013e31827f6351

Craig, Gary. (Puotinen, CJ-editor). (2008). *EFT for PTSD.* Fulton, CA: Bang Printing.

Diamond, John. Life Energy: (1990). *Using the Meridians to Unlock the Hidden Power of Your Emotions.* New York: Paragon House.

Diepold, John H., Brett, V and Bender, S. (2004). *Evolving Thought Field Therapy: the Clinician's Handbook of Diagnoses, Treatment, and Theory.* New York: W.W. Norton & Company.

Eden, D, (with Feinstein, D.). (1999). *Energy Medicine.* New York: Tarcher/Penguin Putnam. Also see www.innersource.net

Feinstein, David. (2004). *Energy Psychology Interactive.* Ashland, OR: Innersource. Also see: www.innersource.net/ep.

Feinstein, D. (2012). Acupoint stimulation in treating psychological disorders: Evidence of efficacy. *Review of General Psychology.* doi:10.1037/ a0028602.

Feinstein, David. Eden, Donna and Craig, Gary. (2005). *The Promise of Energy Psychology.* New York: Penguin Group.

Fone, Helena. (2008). *Emotional Freedom Techniques for Dummies.* West Sussex, England.: John Wiley & Sons, Ltd.

Freedom, John. (2013) *Heal Yourself with Emotional Freedom Techniques.* London: Hodder & & Stoughton Ltd. Also The McGraw-Hill Companies, Inc.

Gallo, Fred P. (2000). *Energy Diagnostic and Treatment Methods.* New York, NY: W.W. Norton & Company.

Gallo, Fred. P. (2002) *Energy Psychology Psychotherapy,* New York, NY: W.W. Norton & Company.

Gallo, Fred. P, (2007) *Energy Tapping for Trauma,* Oakland, CA: New Harbinger Publications.

Gach, Michael R., & Henning, Beth A. (2004) *Acupressure for Emotional Healing.* New York: Bantam Dell.

Lambrou, Peter and Pratt, George. (2000). *Instant Emotional Healing: Acupressure for the Emotions.* New York: Broadway Books-a Division of Random House.

Miller, Deborah, Ph.D, (2014) *The Dragon with Flames of Love – Tapping for Kids with Serious Illness.* Deborah Miller (Amazon)

Mountrose, Phillip & Jane. (2000). *Getting Thru to Your Emotions with EFT.* Sacramento, CA: Holistic Communications.

312

Ortner, Nick. (2013) *The Tapping Solution: A Revolutionary System for Stress-Free Living.* New York: Hay House, Inc.

Ortner, Nick.(2015) *The Tapping Solution for Pain Relief.* New York: Hay House, Inc.

Phillips, Maggie. (2007). *Reversing Chronic Pain.* Berkley, CA: North Atlantic Books.

Rowe, J. E. (2005). The effects of EFT on long-term psychological symptoms. *Counseling and Clinical Psychology,* 2(3), 104-111.

Stapleton., P., Chatwin., H., Shepperd, L., & McSwan, J. (2016). The Lived Experience of Chronic Pain and the Impact of Brief Emotional Freedom Techniques (EFT) Group Therapy on Coping. Energy Psychology: Theory, Research, and Treatment, 8(2), 18-28.

Van Der Kolk, B.(2014)*The Body Keeps the Score--Brain, Mind, and Body in the Healing of Trauma,* New York: Penguin Books.

INDEX

INDEX